The Life and Legacy of
FRED NEWTON SCOTT

PITTSBURGH

SERIES IN COMPOSITION,

LITERACY, AND CULTURE

David Bartholomae

and

Jean Ferguson Carr,

Editors

The Life and Legacy of

FRED NEWTON
SCOTT

DONALD C. STEWART

and

PATRICIA L. STEWART

University of Pittsburgh Press

Published by the University of Pittsburgh Press,
Pittsburgh, Pa. 15261
Copyright © 1997, University of Pittsburgh Press
Manufactured in the United States of America
Printed on acid-free paper

10 9 8 7 6 5 4 3 2 1

Library of Congress Cataloging-in-Publication Data
Stewart, Donald C.
  The life and legacy of Fred Newton Scott / Donald C. Stewart and
Patricia L. Stewart.
        p. cm.—(Pittsburgh series in composition, literacy, and culture)
    Includes bibliographical references and index.
    ISBN 0-8229-3992-4 (alk. paper)
    1. Scott, Fred Newton, 1860–1931. 2. English teachers—United
States—Biography. 3. English philology—Study and teaching
(Higher)—United States. 4. English language—Rhetoric—Study and
teaching—United States—History. 5. Critics—United States
—Biography. I. Stewart, Patricia L. II. Title. III. Series.
PE64.S39S74   1997
428'.0092—dc21
    [B]   97-21006

A CIP catalog record for this book is available from the
British Library.

To
the Scott and Stewart families,
in whose lives riches and adversity
have been dispensed
without distinction.

CONTENTS

ABBREVIATIONS

CLSA   College of Literature, Science, and the Arts,
        Bentley Historical Library, University of Michigan

DEP   Department of English papers,
        Bentley Historical Library, University of Michigan

FNSD   Fred Newton Scott daybook, Fred Newton Scott papers,
        Bentley Historical Library, University of Michigan

FNSP   Fred Newton Scott papers, Michigan Historical Collection,
        Bentley Historical Library, University of Michigan

LWP   Lee White papers,
        Bentley Historical Library, University of Michigan

MG   Letters supplied by Marilyn Guenther

PFM   Papers of Frank Manny,
        Bentley Historical Library, University of Michigan

PMFNS   Papers of Mrs. Fred Newton Scott, in Fred Newton Scott
        Papers, Bentley Historical Library, University of Michigan

PMP   Papers of Maude Perry,
        Bentley Historical Library, University of Michigan

RP   Regents Proceedings, 1901–1906, Bentley Historical
        Library, University of Michigan

SSP   Shirley Smith papers,
        Bentley Historical Library, University of Michigan

UCALB   University of California, Berkeley, University Archives,
        The Bancroft Library

UCALC   University of California calendar

UMBR   University of Michigan Board of Regents,
        Bentley Historical Library

UMC   University of Michigan catalogs

PREFACE

❖ This book was a long time in the making. Don's first interest in Fred Newton Scott was embodied in an essay, "The Barnyard Goose, History, and Fred Newton Scott," published in 1978. Inspired by Albert R. Kitzhaber's observations about Scott in *Rhetoric in American Colleges: 1875–1900,* and prodded into action by Richard Young's call, in the mid-1970s, for historical studies in rhetoric, Don applied in 1979 for funding to travel to the University of Michigan's Bentley Historical Library, home of the Scott papers. The following year he visited Scott's daughter Marion in New Hampshire and began a decade of correspondence with Scott's family, especially Marion's daughter, Marilyn Guenther. He taped numerous conversations—with Scott's son Richard and some of Scott's former colleagues, students, and friends. Initially, in his funding proposals Don projected 1981 as the completion date for the book, but he got sidetracked by professional commitments and other interests. In the long run, it was a blessing that he still had the bulk of the work ahead of him in 1986, for it served as a respite from pain and the inevitability of his prognosis.

There were some curious, almost eerie, aspects to Don's preoccupation with Scott. As he got into the study, Don discovered a direct academic link with Scott. One of Scott's students was Sterling Leonard, who found a career at the University of Wisconsin in the 1920s. There, one of Leonard's students was Robert Pooley. In 1955, when Don and I applied to the University of Wisconsin as a married couple, we were allowed joint teaching assistantships for only one year, after which time one of us would have to find other employment. Fortuitously, Don was hired by the Department of Integrated Liberal Studies headed by Bob Pooley. Pooley served as Don's mentor as well as his boss for six years.

Another unusual aspect was Don's comfortable affinity with Scott's rhetorical theories. Don was Scott reincarnated—in his reformist zeal and his pragmatic attitudes toward composition and rhetoric. Scott's character, his high ideals and purist positions, his energetic, disciplined work ethic, and his uncompromising ethical standards—all were traits Don shared. In fact, had Scott died one year earlier, I would believe in transmutation, so uncanny are the similarities, both personal and professional.

An additional act of fate which led to the production of this book was the direct association of both Don and myself with Albert Kitzhaber. Don had been strongly influenced in his years at the University of Kansas by what he considered a sane approach to the teaching of composition while Kitzhaber served as director of freshman composition. Kitzhaber's dissertation later renewed the link. During the one year I attended the University of Kansas, where I acquired Don as a lifetime partner, I also worked under Kitzhaber's direction. During the late period of Don's affliction with cancer, Kitzhaber kindly supplied him with slides, a map, and correlated taped commentary from his numerous trips to New Zealand, a place Don had hoped to visit. Upon Don's death, I assumed the correspondence with Kitzhaber, who not only supported my work and generously offered advice, but who has proved to be an entertaining and valued friend.

And, finally, my own part in the production of this book seemed foreordained. I had unwittingly been groomed to undertake its completion through my involvement with Don on various publications and through my teaching at Wisconsin, Illinois, and Kansas State. As a result, upon Don's death in 1992, I was ready to shape the mass of materials and partial manuscript into Don's vision. The work was a gratifying diversion that got me through the difficult reality of Don's death, but it was not without its hazards. At one point, upon reading the foreword to Frances Blanshard's biography of Frank Aydelotte, I began to imagine myself, like her, slumped lifeless over the keyboard. The enormous task is now complete. I hope Don would have applauded the result.

There are a number of persons whose generous efforts in the research must be acknowledged: Mary Jo Pugh, Nancy Bartlett, and Kenneth P. Scheffel of the Bentley Historical Library, and William B. Stegath of the Alumni Association of the University of Michigan; Nancy Sherrill, genealogy librarian at Vigo County Public Library, Indiana; Herbert J. Rissler, chair of the Department of History and J. Thomas Brown, university archivist, Indiana State University; Eric L. Mundell, head of Reference Services, Indiana Historical Society; William M. Roberts, university archivist and Marie Myers, Alumni Records, University of California, Berkeley; Susan Coffman, archivist, Pasadena Historical Society; Linda L. Long, public services manager, Department of Special Collections and University Archives, Stanford University Libraries; Harold

L. Miller, archivist, State Historical Society of Wisconsin; Jennifer McGill, executive director, Association for Education in Journalism and Mass Communication, University of South Carolina; Nancy Sprehe, reference librarian, Tony Crawford, archivist, and Kathy Coleman, Interlibrary Loan of Farrell Library, Kansas State University; Carlton Wells, professor emeritus in English, University of Michigan; the children and grandchildren of Fred N. Scott—Marion Scott Goodrich, Richard Scott, Marilyn Guenther, and Janet Gallup; my daughter and son-in-law, Mary and Jim Lathrop, for computer assistance; David Bartholomae, for initial acceptance of the project and Jean Ferguson Carr, for invaluable editorial advice, University of Pittsburgh; Catherine Marshall, University of Pittsburgh Press, for her superb assistance in refining the manuscript; Kathy McLaughlin, managing editor at the Press; Gary Gore, the book and cover designer; and any and all others who helped Don before I took over.

Appreciation is extended to those agencies which provided grants for the research for over a decade: Kansas State University's Bureau of General Research, and the College of Arts and Sciences Faculty Summer Fellowship program; the Research Foundation of NCTE; the American Council of Learned Societies; and the National Endowment for the Humanities.

PATRICIA L. STEWART

The Life and Legacy of Fred Newton Scott

Introduction

THIS IS the story of a man whose vision of education extended beyond the confines of his own professional career in rhetoric. He saw a world that integrated all areas of human knowledge, each supplementing and complementing another. In his own research he crossed the boundary from the humanities to the sciences, grounding all in a rich, conceptual understanding of cognitive psychology. He used empirical methods to expand the parameters of rhetoric, aesthetics, and linguistics. Most of all, out of his dynamic energy and fertile imagination, he fashioned an impressive array of works: essays, speeches, and books—a generous legacy indeed.

Until Don's own exhumation of Fred Newton Scott's professional career and contributions in the late 1970s, his work lay fallow, his importance acknowledged only in the then unpublished dissertation of Albert R. Kitzhaber. Kitzhaber identified four men as significantly influencing the course of rhetoric in the period from 1850 to 1900—Adams Sherman Hill, John Franklin Genung, Barrett Wendell, and Fred Newton Scott; of them, Scott alone, he said, could be considered "an original theorist" (*Rhetoric* 59).

What was it about Scott that was unique? Stimulated by Kitzhaber's portrait of Scott, Don began this study to find out. Kitzhaber had clearly outlined Scott's primary efforts, which identified Scott as a man too prescient for his time. He looked beyond current practice to discover the tradition within which he worked—where was it going, where had it been, what was his role? A reformer, Scott was not anxious to break with the past, but rather wished to build on it. He had an organic view of education, and it led him in the field of composition to look to the fundamental function of rhetoric. Where others were busy merely correcting grammar and spelling, he concluded that "the main purpose of training in composition is free speech, direct and sincere communion with our fellows, that swift and untrammeled exchange of opinion, feeling, and experience, which is the working instrument of the social instinct and the motive power of civilization" ("What the West Wants" [1909] 19). This definition was revolutionary at a time when it was unclear to others that rhetoric and its partner, composition, were even legitimate intellectual fields.

But Scott saw even larger vistas. Where others may have discovered innovative theories, they lacked Scott's overview. He alone owned a conceptual scheme that embraced the whole of rhetoric, giving meaning to all the bits and pieces upon which his contemporaries focused. For example, unlike A. S. Hill, who had a similar background in journalism, Scott perceived the relationship between journalism and rhetoric. Similarly, he asserted a connection between rhetoric and aesthetics. In this area, he produced a series of editions for use in rhetoric instruction: Spencer's *Philosophy of Style* (1891); Lewes's *The Principles of Success in Literature* (1891); DeQuincey's *Essays on Style, Rhetoric and Language* (1893). With Charles M. Gayley, he produced *A Guide to the Literature of Aesthetics* (1890) and the staggeringly complex *Introduction to the Methods and Materials of Literary Criticism* (1899).

Scott also insisted upon the necessary unity between high schools and colleges. For many years he served on the National Conference on Uniform Entrance Requirements, defining the responsibilities of both schools and colleges to their students and working for cooperation between the two levels. From this involvement came even more publications detailing his beliefs about the role of the teacher. "The teacher of composition who does not somehow make his pupils . . . feel that all of the verbal machinery is but for the purpose of fulfilling this great end (the use of speech to influence social action), is false to his trust" ("What the West Wants" 19). He defined the teacher's work: "The practice of composition, when it is well taught, arouses in the pupil feelings of health, power, sanity and hope—the invariable attendants of mental growth. Badly taught it arrests development, and the result is a feeling of abnormality, a feeling of exhaustion, a feeling of powerlessness and failure" (*Aphorisms* [1905] 3–4). And he answered the question of why someone would want to undertake such an awesome task: "It is the knowledge that from his teaching men and women have gained power—power to strike hard blows for truth, good government and right living" (4). No one else in Scott's time elevated rhetoric or its instruction to this level.

But Scott was even more active in seeking to make of rhetoric a legitimate field, insisting it was a science, not an art. His empirical approach to language issues was certainly unique in his time. When he wrote "The Genesis of Speech," for example, he turned to works in anthropology, biology, linguistics, physiology, and anatomy to support his theory. On another occasion, he examined what the parts of speech meant to young people, securing personal anecdotes to show that they meant less and more than their teachers had suspected, and that their teachers had, for the most part, wasted their time with meaningless nomenclature. He studied the physiology of the voice and throat and involuntary responses in order to write "The Colloquial Nasals" (1922). In essence, there were no "compartments" in his intellectual world; his was a boundless world of knowledge, the fences down, the gates open to his restive mind, his thirst for truth. Rhetoric was his interest, but not his field.

Scott was fortunate to be at the University of Michigan where, within the broad vision of its president, James B. Angell, he was able not only to create the first college course in newspaper writing in the country, but to establish a separate Department of Rhetoric in 1903. No one was more impressed with Michigan's progressive stance than Professor F. H. Hedge of Harvard who (calculating the university's founding date from its opening in Ann Arbor) wrote in the *Atlantic Monthly* for July 1866: "Look at the State University of Michigan. Here is an institution but twenty-five years old, already numbering thirty-two professors and over twelve hundred students, having public buildings equal in extent to those which two centuries have given to Cambridge, and all the apparatus of a well-established, thoroughly furnished university. All this within twenty-five years! The State itself which has generated this wonderful growth had no place in the Union until after Harvard had celebrated her two-hundredth birthday. In twenty-five years, in a country five hundred miles from the seaboard,—a country which fifty years ago was known only to the fur trade,—a university has sprung up, to which students flock from all parts of the land, and which offers to thousands, free of expense, the best education this continent affords" (qtd. in Peckham 57).

Even earlier, Scott had offered graduate courses, and a number of master's degrees and one Ph.D. had been earned under his direction before 1900.[1] By his retirement in 1927, close to one hundred fifty master's degrees and nearly twenty-five doctorates had been awarded in the field of rhetoric. No other college had such a record. Part of this prolific output was due to Scott's own integrity as a teacher. Early on, he had established a "seminary" in advanced writing that drew not only those interested in rhetoric, but a number of talented creative writers, such as Ray Stannard Baker and Avery Hopwood. His students later bore testimony to his teaching acumen and his charm and wit. As a teacher, they said, he tended to lead students to "discover" their subject. In his mind, even an untrained student lacking any special gift could write meaningful prose if properly encouraged and stimulated. He was original for his time in believing in what is now called prewriting techniques, for insisting on topics appropriate to the developmental level of the student, for emphasizing writing to an audience, and for following cognitive rather than faculty psychology.

In "Rhetoric Rediviva" (1909), he noted that "there is hardly a topic in subject-matter of formal rhetoric which does not require reinterpretation in light of psychological theory . . . internal speech . . . the nature of rhythm . . . the theory of expression, the mental images." These ideas were more fully explored by Scott's contemporary, the Russian psychologist Lev Vygotsky, and, later, by others in the rhetoric revival of the 1960s. The extent of Scott's influence in his lifetime can be appreciated when one checks the list of Scott's students, among them two presidents of the National Council of Teachers of English (NCTE), Sterling A. Leonard and Ruth Mary Weeks, and one president of the Modern Language Association (MLA), Marjorie Nicolson.

In his later years, Scott's rhetorical interests carried him further into the realm of philology and linguistics. He was one of the earliest to advance the idea that language changed, that usage was determined not by "rules," but by the popularity of words in the vernacular. He examined British-American vocabulary and speech patterns to support his hypotheses. He also gathered slang phrases, intending someday to complete a dictionary of slang. He studied speech rhythms and attempted a codification of prose rhythms.

Scott's achievements in language, journalism, aesthetics, philology, and linguistics can be easily seen in a perusal of his bibliography as well as in his professional affiliations. He served as MLA's twenty-fourth president, NCTE's first and only two-time president, as president of the North Central Association of Secondary Schools, and as president of the

American Association of Teachers of Journalism. In addition, he was a
member of the International Conference of Professors of English, the Society for Pure English, the English Association of Great Britain, British
and American Professors of English, the Modern Humanities Research
Association, the British Philological Association, the British Institute of
Philosophical Studies, the International English Council, and the Linguistic Society of America. As late as 1927, President Clarence C. Little
appointed him to represent the University of Michigan at the convention
of the Press Congress of the World in Geneva, Switzerland.

As Kitzhaber has written, "Scott was ahead of his time. The new
psychology, that offered so many opportunities for enriching rhetorical
theory, was not widely enough understood for its bearing on rhetoric to
be appreciated. The same may be said of linguistics. Therefore, when the
clamor aroused by the Harvard Reports reached its height, Scott's ideas
were smothered by the demand for correctness" (*Rhetoric* 223). According to James Berlin, "the narrowness of the composing process they [Hill
and Wendell] did recommend was in part due to its [the Committee of
Three] influence. Furthermore, the conspicuous position they occupied
insured their success in promulgating a view that, as we shall see, de-
feated its better" (*Writing Instruction* 62).

Obviously, Scott's influence in the larger context of language studies
is enormous. His reputation in his lifetime extended beyond the boundaries of the United States; he associated with scholars, writers, political
figures, and men of consequence both in the United States and abroad.
This biography intends, then, to reexamine the career and contributions of Fred Newton Scott, a remarkable Renaissance man, whose passions and interests ranged unrestricted within the vistas of intellectual
experience.

2

The Formative Years

FRED NEWTON SCOTT was born in Terre Haute, Indiana, August 20, 1860. He was the fifth of Harvey David Scott's and Mary Bannister's six children, only three of whom survived into maturity: Frances Electa, born in 1850; Harriet Maria, 1854; and himself. Members of Scott's family have no idea how his parents happened to give him the name Fred.[1] Newton, however, derived from Newton Booth, his father's law partner from 1856 to 1860, a man who eventually became governor of the state of California in 1871 and one of its senators in 1875.

Harvey Scott practiced law, serving as the prosecuting attorney of the sixth circuit court from 1852 to 1854. Many years later he assumed the bench as a judge for the fourteenth circuit, 1881–1882 and the forty-third circuit, 1883–1884, and in the interim was elected Vigo County representative to the Indiana state legislature from 1852 to 1854; Indiana representative to the U.S. Congress, 1855–1857; Vigo County treasurer, 1858–1862; commissioner to inspect the Pacific Railroad, 1859–1863; state senator, 1868–1876. The rigors of such an active professional life took its toll, of course. In his sketch of the young Fred Newton Scott, John Dewey mentions the fact that because of poor health, after the close of the Civil War, Scott's father bought a farm outside Terre Haute where the family lived for several years (4:119).[2]

Fred remembered the years on the farm with great nostalgia. It consisted of one hundred acres, "with great apple and peach orchards, a sugar camp, wide fields of corn and wheat, woods, pastures, greenhouses, and a flower garden in which one could get lost" ("Biography of Miss Harriet M. Scott"). Dewey observed years later that "Mr. Scott's tendency as a teacher to keep literature and aesthetics in connection with the concrete may have been favored somewhat by the concreteness of his early surroundings. At any rate, he has never forgotten in later life the lesson taught in early years—that real life is made of things like ploughs, and mud turtles and fields of growing grain. He has never allowed himself to be so caught in the machinery of science as to forget that the grist ground for life is, after all, the main thing" (4:119).

Scott's sisters—Fannie and Harriet—were both in the first class to matriculate at the Normal School (now Indiana State University) in 1870; both were among the school's first graduates in 1872; and both took the Advanced Course from 1876 to 1878, graduating from that program also (Lynch 44, 67). Fannie was an instructor in the Primary Model Training School at least from 1871 to 1874, and possibly from 1876 to 1887 (68). At the graduation exercises in June of 1872, the younger Harriet was commended for her work in the Intermediate Model Training School (45), a class which contained her younger brother, Fred. In 1883, after teaching in Crawfordsville and Terre Haute, she moved to Detroit to assist Amanda Funnelle, her former teacher and colleague, now principal of the Normal Training School in Detroit, an institution that was garnering significant attention for its creative and innovative ideas in both the education of students and the preparation of teachers. When Miss Funnelle resigned in 1886, Harriet was appointed principal of the school, a position she held until 1899 (FNSP).

Scott greatly admired his sister and may have been profoundly influenced in his thinking about the nature of education by her. Philosophically, the Normal School's curriculum exemplified the basic tenets of American Herbartianism, a movement which was for "at most fifteen years . . . a lively enterprise, probably reaching its peak about 1896," after which a rapid decline in the movement occurred (Dunkel 123). The essential features of Herbartianism were "concentration centers" and "culture epochs," concepts introduced by Tuiskon Ziller, the former a general topic on which the work of a whole school year focused, the latter assuming that "just as the embryo retraces the biological evolution of the species, so the child's education should move through the major stages of man's intellectual and moral development" (108).

Harriet's work in Detroit is important to any understanding of Scott's early growth and development. Her insistence on education being an organic process, developing naturally out of a child's interests, suggests the whole notion of organic conceptions which one finds in the mature work of Scott. In Harriet's school, lessons in science, for example, develop from curiosity about the plants the people ate, the animals they killed for food, and other related matters. Lessons in arithmetic develop from children's attempts to make representative clothing for the people of a given era (see Buck, "Another"). Harriet resigned her position in the midst of controversy over her principles of instruction; she chose to abide by her principles, a trait that appears to have been a staple of the Scott family.

It is difficult to say exactly when Scott's formal education began. The gifted younger brother (by ten and six years) of accomplished older sisters who were interested in education, it is quite probable that he received much basic early education from his sisters. The entry on Scott in the *Dictionary of American Biography,* written while he was still alive, says that "he began his education at the schools of his birthplace and in Indianapolis, but moved to Battle Creek, Mich., in 1878 and attended the high school there."

Information supplied in Dewey's sketch, inaccurate as it is, suggests another important educational influence in Scott's early life: Hermann Boisen. Noting Scott's early interest in things scientific and technological, Dewey says that "Mr. Scott was switched off from the opening career of electrical engineer by a German tutor, a Mr. Boyesen, afterwards an instructor in Boston University. He it is who persuaded the youth that salvation was found along the line of Greek, who awakened in him a desire for a University education, and who tutored him in his preparation" (4:119–20). In a eulogy, David Starr Jordan, eventual president of Stanford University, described Hermann Balthasar Boisen as "a teacher who inspired all with whom he came in contact, who touched everything with life, and made even the vagaries of the German article a thing of beauty and light. A linguist to whom all languages and all literatures came as a natural inheritance, who rejoiced alike in the misty dreams of the stormy Northmen, the homely life of the Platt Deutscher and the polished imagery of the Greeks" (qtd. in Woodburn 358).

Another of the important influences in Scott's early education was William A. Jones, first president of Indiana State University (Lynch 25). Scott's praise is unqualified, and he thanks Jones for introducing him to the science of psychology. The profound and enduring effects of Scott's schooling are immediately apparent in his life and work. Especially from Jones, he acquired a scientific approach to all issues (Lynch 54ff). For example, in "Verbal Taboos" (1912), Scott confronts a usage problem by questioning basic linguistic habits. Why do "authorities" like Adams Sherman Hill of Harvard vilify usages such as "to wash" as synonyms for "to launder," especially when they have been in the language for centuries? What is the nature of this phenomenon? What causes it? What are other manifestations of it?

Another individual who served on the Normal School faculty and who may well have played a decisive role in Scott's educational development was Josiah Scovill, the science teacher (Lynch 62). As an indefatigable collector of scientific data, he would have influenced the young Scott, for, as Dewey tells us, Scott had a closet full of apparatus he had designed. On one occasion, Scott made an electric battery of forty Leyden jars; the shock it generated was powerful enough to kill a cat.

According to his granddaughter, Marilyn Guenther, Scott went to Michigan because the family thought the Michigan schools were better than those in Indiana. Michigan was rapidly emerging as one of the outstanding universities west of the Appalachians. Two of its early presidents, Henry Philip Tappan and James Burrill Angell, were men of broad vision and superb administrative skills.

Dewey reports that Scott had mastered shorthand while doing some newspaper work in Cleveland (he had also acquired the skill of an expert telegrapher); that he became, at this time, private secretary to Dr. John Harvey Kellogg, the principal force behind the Battle Creek Sanitarium; and that he traveled rather extensively with Dr. Kellogg, to the Pacific Coast on one occasion, to Washington, D.C., on another (Dewey 4:120). The correspondence of Scott's later years is filled with letters from Dr. Kellogg who frequently invited him to Battle Creek. In Battle Creek, Scott accomplished several objectives: he qualified for entrance into the University of Michigan by attending and obtaining a high school diploma; he acquired a job which provided him with needed financial assistance; and he established an important lifelong friendship with a renowned innovator in the field of medicine.

In the fall of 1880, Scott matriculated at the University of Michigan. His transcript shows a preponderance of language study. Between 1880 and 1884 he took seventeen hours of Greek, sixteen of Latin, sixteen of French, twelve of German, four of Sanskrit, and four of Italian. The accumulation is sixty-nine hours of work in six different languages![3] In addition to all his language work, he took sixteen hours of math, eighteen of English, six each in history and philosophy, three in political economy, and two in music. More than anything else, this background may have been crucial in shaping his nondogmatic approach to English language study and his driving devotion to linguistics.

Scott very quickly immersed himself in his studies and in campus literary activities. Dewey says that he "made his record as a clever writer as well as a thorough student. He was managing editor of the *Oracle*. . . . He was also one of the founders of the *Argonaut,* and, as its exchange editor, created what may be termed a sensation in that usually perfunctory department, by the brightness and humor of his touch" (4:120). The campus newspaper of that time, the *Chronicle,* had been in existence since 1867 and had distinguished itself for the quality of its journalism. In 1882, a rival paper, the *University Argonaut,* appeared with Scott as one of the principal managers.

Aside from time given to the magazines with which he was involved, Scott the undergraduate also enjoyed, although briefly, some extracurricular dramatic and musical activity. Along with Charles Mills Gayley and Albert Stanley, Scott collaborated on *Songs of the Yellow and Blue,* published in 1889. With a very few exceptions, Scott and Gayley provided the lyrics, Stanley the music. A departure for Scott, the scholar and educator, these songs are a delightful and refreshing glimpse into his youth. The silliest song in the collection, an example of the student's occasional and necessary irreverence for the subject he is studying, is "Romeo and Juliet." A note at the bottom of the page on which this song is printed says: "As sung by the Club, the part of Romeo was taken by a phenomenally short and rotund tenor, the part of Juliet by an inordinately tall and slender basso." In a letter to "The Alumni Forum" of the *Michigan Alumnus,* John Jameson of the class of 1891 writes that "the song proved extraordinarily successful from the first and remained for many years a stock feature of Michigan Glee Club entertainments. It now appears in most collections of college songs, generally, it may be noted, without acknowledgment to Prof. Scott."

During these years, Scott formed important associations. He collaborated with Gayley on books on aesthetics, and when Gayley departed for the University of California, Scott filled the opening as instructor in English. Two other undergraduate associates were important to Scott for the duration of his life. One was Joseph Villiers Denney, with whom Scott collaborated on his most successful textbooks. Denney became head of the English Department and dean of the College of Arts and Sciences at Ohio State. The other was Isadore Thompson from Saginaw, Michigan, who matriculated at the University of Michigan in 1880. She was eighteen, Scott twenty, when they first met. It would be seven years before they married, but she proved to be an intelligent, capable, and stable companion for him for the rest of her life.

When he graduated in the spring of 1884, Scott had a superb preparation in languages, considerable experience as a writer and editor of campus publications, and a tremendous fund of energy. He stayed in Ann Arbor, taking some graduate classes in English and working as a library assistant. In a letter to Bert Miller, May 29, 1885, he reflects on his situation: "As regards the position which I now hold. . . . It has given me a most excellent chance to study and—experiment. And the latter exercise has fully repaid me. That is to say, I didn't have to plunge into some sort of work that I fancied would suit me, only to plunge out again when I found that it didn't" (FNSP).

In January 1885 Scott published his first piece of work not for a campus literary magazine. Titled "The Missing Pronoun," it appeared in the *Current,* January 17, 1885. With considerable wit Scott makes fun of linguists who are searching for a suitable pronoun of common gender. His candidate is *they,* the term both the educated and uneducated public is using quite consistently. He concludes: "To the fast-coming objections that the proposed use of the word [they] is ungrammatical, inconsistent, illogical, and impracticable, it may be replied, in general, that the English language is full of absurdities and inconsistencies, and with all its faults we love it still; while as for its impracticability, the word *they* is being used as a pronoun of the common gender every day by millions of persons who are not particular about their language, and every other day by several thousands who *are* particular, but who cannot be always watching their unruly member" (44).[4] This little essay reveals an already developed allegiance to descriptive, not prescriptive, attitudes toward usage which was to set Scott distinctly apart from most of his contemporaries and which would be reflected in the work of some of his most distinguished students.

Actually, the teaching of English was not Scott's first vocation. In the fall of 1885 he was ready to try newspapering, a career that lasted only two years. He was associate editor of Cleveland's *Sentinel* from 1886 to 1887 and editor of the *East End Signal* the following year. Although brief, Scott's newspaper experience was influential in his teaching career: he introduced a course called "Rapid Writing," deemed the first college course in newspaper writing offered in this country.

In the fall of 1887, Scott was back in Ann Arbor, again as a library assistant. On September 26, 1887, he married Isadore in East Saginaw at the Thompson family home, the family having settled there when Isadore's father, Bradley Thompson, joined the faculty of the Law Department as a lecturer that fall. One of the most touching documents in the Scott papers, because it was Scott's wedding present to Isadore, is a narrative entitled "Alicia. A Fancy." The tale itself combines elements of the plots of *The Prince and the Pauper* and *Romeo and Juliet*. The young count of Bordinaux, bored with his life, exchanges places with his minstrel and goes into the city. There he entertains and eventually falls in love with Alicia, whose father demands that she marry, not the minstrel of her choosing, but the count of Bordinaux. Obviously, the count looks forward to the moment when he will reveal himself to Alicia, but he makes the mistake of carrying the deception too far. In his role as the minstrel, he tells the girl that a true lover would die before she would marry anyone else. She takes him at his word and kills herself just before he reveals himself to her (FNSP).

In 1888, Scott was promoted to assistant librarian. The work was evidently enjoyable, and he was given some important tasks to perform. One of them, mentioned in an unpublished work, "Serendipity," was the cataloguing of the entire Parsons library, one of the university's important early acquisitions. Presented by Philo Parsons of Detroit, it consisted of books and pamphlets relating principally to the science of political economy from the library of Professor Karl H. Rau of Heidelberg. In 1898 the Parsons Collection, with subsequent acquisitions, contained 4,325 bound volumes and 5,000 pamphlets (Shaw, *Survey* 4:1371).

Scott moved rapidly ahead with his academic career. In 1888, he completed work for the M.A. and took his Ph.D. oral examination June 18, 1889. His handwritten doctoral dissertation, "Italian Critics of the Renaissance as Source for the Earliest English Criticism," reveals Scott's command of Renaissance English and Italian literatures, his knowledge of the literary criticism of the age and of principles of literary criticism in general, and his command of the emerging field of aesthetics. John Dewey had been scheduled to serve on Scott's examining committee, but he had left Ann Arbor, briefly, during 1888–1889 to assume the chair of mental and moral philosophy at the University of Minnesota. Then, when George Sylvester Morris, who had originally drawn Dewey to the University of Michigan, died unexpectedly in March 1889, Dewey returned to Michigan to fill his position. It was at that time that Dewey made arrangements "for Fred Newton Scott, newly appointed brilliant young instructor of English and Rhetoric at the university, to give a course in aesthetics in the department" (Dykuizen 64).

Statements which suggest that Dewey was a strong influence on Scott in these early years must be tempered. From what we know of

Scott's education before he ever met Dewey, and the fact that he was but one year Dewey's junior, it might be safer to conclude that Scott and Dewey were philosophically compatible, that they found in each other intelligence and ideas which mutually reinforced each other.[5]

On August 1, 1889, President Angell appointed Scott instructor in English. He was now ready to embark upon a professional career. But, superbly prepared as he was, he was not without misgivings. According to Jean Paul Slusser, artist and professor of art at Michigan, as Scott saw Gayley depart the Ann Arbor station for the University of California, he realized he had not asked Gayley for any advice in getting ready to meet his first class. He called to Gayley, "What should I do? I've never taught before. How do I conduct myself until I acquire some experience in teaching?" Gayley yelled back, as the train pulled out: "Don't let them make fun of you!" That was the only preparation for teaching that Scott ever received.

When Scott joined the Michigan English Department it was a very small enterprise, as compared to typical departments in modern universities. There were but four men responsible for the work of the department: Isaac Demmon, the head, who taught virtually all the choice literature courses; George Hempl, an assistant professor, who was essentially a linguist; Alexis Frederick Lange who was "shared" with the German Department—English needed him to teach courses in Anglo-Saxon; and Scott, whose specialty was rhetoric and composition.

Demmon was perceived by some of his colleagues as resistant to innovation and not particularly supportive of scholarly endeavor. In a department head, particularly of a department which contained two future MLA presidents, those were not particularly good qualities. Hempl, a man of many contradictions, was particularly restive. It is difficult, at this distance, to reconcile the obvious respect that Hempl commanded as a scholar with the ridicule to which he was subject because of his apparent hypochondria and eccentric behavior. As to Lange, although he served the English Department just the one year, 1889–1890, his association with Scott and with Denney was more than superficial. In the preface to their *Paragraph Writing* (1893), they express their indebtedness to him for developing an "ingenious and workable method of drill" in paragraph study. Lange had individual students write introductory, developmental, and concluding paragraphs for essays on particular subjects. After each student had written his or her paragraph, all were assembled to see how well they fit together.

From the start, Scott's allegiance was to rhetoric. Louis Strauss said, many years later, that Scott "had burned his boats and declared himself wholly and exclusively committed to rhetoric as his field of investigation and instruction—a daring venture at that time, when it was anything but a popular subject, and utterly without standing as a field of graduate study and research" (331).

Scott's teaching schedule that first year was a full one. The fall semester he had four classes of English 1, "Composition and Speeches," each of them two-hour courses. He was also offering Philosophy 11, "Aesthetics; or, The Philosophy of the Beautiful in Nature, and in the Products of Human Art." It, too, was a two-hour course. Thus, although Scott was in the classroom only ten hours per week, he was teaching five classes, four of them requiring considerable student writing and the grading of papers, the fifth, in-depth preparation for lectures.

The very next year, 1890–1891, there is a marked change in assignments. Given Demmon's personality and apparent fondness for the status quo, it is probably safe to surmise that these changes were initiated by Scott himself, with Demmon's concurrence. To begin with, Scott had been promoted, after only one year, from instructor to assistant professor. With Lange no longer teaching in the department, his place, but not his courses, had been taken by Joseph Villiers Denney, who graduated a year behind Scott. Denney taught the four sections of English 1, now described as "Practical Rhetoric and Composition."

Scott now offered two sections of English 2, "The *Science* of Rhetoric," and a new course called "Principles of Style. Inductive study of masterpieces of English prose, with a view to verifying rhetorical principles." The previous year English 2 had been called, simply, "Rhetoric." The addition of the term *science* was one of the early indications of Scott's perception of the subject, a perception which set him apart, particularly from his eastern contemporaries, in two significant ways. First, he was clearly not in sympathy with the position that the ability to express oneself was primarily a matter of inherited gifts and therefore unteachable, essentially a Romantic position. If one could systematically identify and describe rhetoric's effects, then it follows that one could learn, to some degree anyway, to produce them. Second, whereas the teaching of introductory composition courses appears to have been intellectually pretty arid work in the eastern schools, Scott was intent upon giving it some intellectual substance and dignity.

From the 1890–1891 catalogue description, it appears that course 15, "The Principles of Style," was arranged either tutorially or that students who enrolled conferred with Scott at a suitable meeting time.

Whatever the case, the course was obviously much more sophisticated than introductory freshman composition. Scott also continued to offer the course in aesthetics in the Philosophy Department.

One notices significant changes in the department's second semester offerings, also, and in the assignments given to the staff. Denney is teaching not only "Practical Rhetoric and Composition" but "Paragraph Writing." The latter may have been the genesis of his and Scott's most successful collaboration, *Paragraph Writing.* Scott taught the two sections of "Science of Rhetoric," and had developed some more new courses: a seminar entitled "Problems in Higher Rhetoric and Literary Criticism," and the course "Rapid Writing." The latter, open only to those who received special permission, is described as the first course in newspaper writing offered in American colleges.[6] Scott was also offering, with Dewey, a graduate course in philosophy entitled "Conferences in Aesthetics."

When one compares Scott's assignments for his first year with those of his second, one can appreciate what a quantum leap he had made. His first year was given, with the exception of the course in aesthetics, entirely to the most basic freshman writing course. However, in this second year he is teaching the department's sequel to the first course, "The Science of Rhetoric," advanced courses in rhetorical theory and rhetoric and literary criticism, a journalism course, and both undergraduate and graduate courses in aesthetics. Obviously, he had more time in the interim period to prepare materials for the second year. Also, it is crucial to note the interests that emerge. These are the areas that constitute his primary concern throughout his career, and their origins are easy to establish. His dissertation evidences his bent toward literary analysis and his ability to do close reading; his association with his friend and mentor, Charles Mills Gayley, would have promoted his involvement in aesthetics, as would have his relationship with John Dewey. His practical work as a journalist was obviously latent background for his journalism class; and the interest in rhetoric had now been given some philosophical base, no doubt deriving from his early education and his classroom work in the previous year. Scott was a quick study.

Scott appears always to have been a somewhat reserved and quiet man, but he had volcanic energies. These derived, in part, from his intense and wide-ranging intellectual curiosity, but now were encouraged by a very practical need. He had a wife and child (Harvey was born in 1888) for whom he had to provide on $900 a year. (In 1889, $900 was

roughly the equivalent of $14,000 in 1990.)[7] In his very first year of
work, he was already involved in a number of projects. By the spring of
1890 he had added five publications to his bibliography, all published in
that year: *Aesthetics: Its Problems and Literature; The Principles of Style: Topics and References; A Guide to the Literature of Aesthetics* (with Charles Mills
Gayley); "Simple, Sensuous, and Passionate"; and "Albert A. Stanley."
He was also engaged in writing poetry for campus magazines and was
collaborating with Charles Gayley and Albert Stanley on the *Songs of the
Yellow and Blue*.

The first three of these ventures obviously developed from his work
in Philosophy 11, "Aesthetics; of the Philosophy of the Beautiful in Nature" and "Products of Human Art." *Aesthetics: Its Problems and Literature*
is primarily an annotated bibliography, but it has significant philosophical, theoretical, and pedagogical dimensions. In the introduction, Scott
remarks that it is unfortunate that the study of works of art and the
study of art theory are looked upon as two distinct lines of research.
"Each of these two important branches of knowledge, when rightly considered, is seen to be essential to the well-being of the other" (iii). They
should be joined, and further, "such study has infinitely to gain in real
value and attractiveness by seeking for the relation of its subject-matter
to human experience in general" (iv). Scott acknowledges that this is not
the prevailing view. But, he asks, if one is reading Browning, wouldn't
it be wise to know something about lyric poetry, about the relations of
lyric to other kinds of poetry, and finally about general principles of
artistic expression?

He goes on to identify several problems in aesthetics: the physiological sources of aesthetic pleasure; the psychological sources of aesthetic pleasure; and the relations of aesthetics to human experience (he
calls these "speculative"). His questions about the physiological sources
of aesthetic pleasure reveal how thoroughly he could penetrate a particular problem and identify the lines of inquiry which needed to be pursued: "(1) What changes in the nervous system, resulting from the application of stimuli, produce the sensation of pleasure? (2) (a) What
classes of objects supply these stimuli? (b) What are the attributes of
these objects? (c) Do dissimilar qualities furnish the same result, or is
there some one quality, existing in different forms, in all objects that occasion pleasure? (3) Is the relation between the stimulus and the pleasurable feeling necessary and invariable, or accidental and mutable? (4)
How are pleasurable feelings related to the vital functions? (5) (a) What

quality in the stimulus, or (b) what modification of the neural process, occasions the aesthetic quality of the feeling? (6) What are the pre-eminently aesthetic senses?" (1–2).

The annotated bibliography itself is divided into two sections, one for those who wish to get some general ideas about aesthetics without putting out the effort to study original sources, a second for "those who wish to go to the bottom of the matter" (7). One finds, in the more demanding list, the titles one would expect: Plato's *Ion, Phaedo, Symposium, Gorgias, Philebus,* and *Republic;* Aristotle's *Poetics,* to be read, if possible, in the original; Kant's *Kritik der Aesthetischen Urtheilskraft* and *Critique of Judgment;* Schelling's *Philosophie der Kunst;* and Hegel's *Vorlesungen über die Aesthetik* to cite but a few. Other German writers, plus French and a few English (he thinks the English are nearly out of touch with significant work in this field) and American writers, most notable among them William James, are also cited. Scott, possibly at the instigation of John Dewey, sent a copy of this pamphlet to William Torrey Harris, then U.S. commissioner of education. Harris responded January 31, 1891: "Your paper is one of the most valuable for aesthetics that has come under my attention" (FNSP).

The Principles of Style was quite clearly conceived as a pedagogical document, the contents taken from the materials he developed for his class. He defines rhetoric as "in its broadest sense . . . the principles and practice of literary effect," but delineates three ways a student can study the subject profitably. In the first stage, rhetoric serves as a source of practical rules for preparing sermons, harangues, stories, sketches, letters, editorials, essays. A student who is at this level is not likely to profit from any explanation of the reasons behind the rules.

In the second stage, a student moves to rhetoric as a science. At some point, the student begins to "suspect" that some general principle organizes the rules. "The verification of this suspicion and the discovery that the larger principle is that annoying formula which the instructor has been harping on ever since the first lesson was assigned, mark a decided advance in intellectual development" (2–3). After having "torn his palms on division, definition, amplification and the like for months," Scott says this student may suddenly experience a moment of enlightenment, and the exhortation to let the subject dictate its organization comes to him. Likewise, he may at last begin to comprehend matters of sentential stress and rhythm in the internal structure of a paragraph. Rhetorical instruction, at this stage, has reached its limit as a science. Most textbooks, says Scott, if they want to be favorably reviewed by pro-

fessional journals, stop at this point, with their collections of rules and
some basic generalizations explaining the reasons behind the rules.[8] This
he characterizes as the Lower Rhetoric, not in a derogatory sense, but
simply to indicate a rhetoric that does not aspire to deal with matters
seemingly more vague and difficult to generalize about.

The Higher Rhetoric, the third stage of rhetorical study, attempts to
address apparently vague matters, to account for the "blooms and
charms" of literature. In order to give new meanings to old words and
phrases, a student "must come to feel the thing itself before he can feel
any value in the symbol of the thing" (7). In this, he refers to the cultivation of taste, of course, one aim of the Higher Rhetoric.

> If we say cultivation of taste, what should we mean but holding on stead-
> fastly and sincerely to what takes hold on us—satisfied, that is, what of person-
> ality we have achieved up to that point in our development—and striving to
> grow in grace and knowledge so that more things may take hold on us? Or if
> we say that a writer must obey the Laws of Composition, what should we mean
> but that he is to make these laws a part of his own personality and then utter
> himself? Or if finally we say that such and such compositions are masterpieces
> of style, what can or ought we to mean but that they are the perfect expression
> of personalities worth expressing? (7–8)

Scott's course, for which this book served, was designed to lead students to an understanding of the Higher Rhetoric. He characterizes the
rationale and methods of the course as lectures that relate the rules of the
Lower Rhetoric to logic, psychology, and aesthetics. At once, we see how
he perceives rhetoric in interdisciplinary terms, a position uncommon in
1890. His reading suggestions are worth noting, also. For example, for
"Relations of Thought and Language," he sends students to works on
psychology, specifically Max Mueller's *The Science of Thought,* John
Dewey's *Psychology,* William James's *Psychology.* For rhythm and meter,
he cites Herbert Spencer's *First Principles* (the chapter on rhythm),
Helmholtz's *Sensations of Tone* (he calls Helmholtz the great authority on
musical rhythm), and Hauptmann's *The Nature of Harmony and Metre.*
The table of contents alone suggests the richness, depth, and variety of
topics covered in the course and, by extension, the breadth and depth of
Scott's conception of rhetoric. The book deals with definition and classification of literature, relations of thought and language, poetry and
prose, rhythm and meter, tone color and harmony, figures, logical structure, and a definition of style.

A Guide to the Literature of Aesthetics was Scott's first collaboration with his old Latin teacher and friend, Charles Mills Gayley. The work is identified as "mainly a list of the books consulted, in two libraries, during the preparation of lectures on Aesthetics, and of a text-book on Literary Criticism." The table of contents has six major headings: Aesthetic Doctrines, Subject-Matter of Aesthetic Theory, The Fine Arts, Literature, Criticism, and Miscellaneous. Their individual citations include works in Greek, Latin, English, French, and German. Under the first heading alone, they list Aristotle's *Poetics, Nichomachean Ethics, Metaphysics, Politics,* and *Rhetoric;* Cicero's *Brutus* and *De Oratore;* Longinus, *On the Sublime;* Plato's *Ion, Phaedo, Symposium, Phaedrus,* and parts of the *Republic, Gorgias, Philebus,* and *Laws;* Quintilian's *Institutes of Oratory;* and works by Addison, Bacon, Bain, Blair, Carlyle, Coleridge, Dryden, Emerson, Gray, Hazlitt, Hobbes, Hume, Johnson, Kames, Lamb, Macaulay, Mill (James), Reynolds, Ruskin, Shaftesbury, and Spencer. Although the authors say the list is suggestive, not inclusive, its breadth and depth is still impressive.

In "Simple, Sensuous, and Passionate," Scott ventures into literary analysis.[9] He argues that Milton, in his "Tractate on Education," is commonly misquoted: because Milton saw poetry as appealing more directly to imagination and feeling, he wants young men to study what Scott calls the Higher Rhetoric of poetry—its aesthetics, its status as a fine art. Thus, even in these early publications, Scott is already making connections between aesthetics, literary forms, and rhetoric.

From the very beginning, Scott's published work reveals his deep and thorough scholarship; an ability to organize his material systematically, from large general concepts to the smallest of details; original and provocative insights; and a prose style that is lucid and unpretentious. A good many scholars possess one, or possibly two, of these attributes, but seldom does one find all four in a single individual.

3

Discovering a Career

B Y THE FALL of 1891, Scott was a securely established assistant professor and an apparently happy husband and father of two small children (his daughter Marion was born February 4, 1891). Considering the amount of time he had to give to teaching alone, his other achievements seem almost superhuman. According to the catalogues, from the fall of 1891 through the spring of 1901, he taught English 2, "Science of Rhetoric. Essays," every semester. Scott taught two sections which met two hours each week until the fall of 1893, when enrollment in this course jumped rapidly. Instead of two sections of the course, Scott now had five. In 1894 the number of sections dropped to four, but a companion course appeared in his schedule: English 2a, "intended for students who, having passed Course 2 in the second semester, desire to continue their work in composition. It is open only to those who receive special permission." From this time until 1901, Scott's schedule regularly shows four sections of English 2 and four sections of English 2a (in the fall) or 2b (in the spring) each semester. Those two courses represented only half of his teaching load. And by their very nature, they would have generated an horrendous number of papers to grade.[1]

Scott described the teaching of English at Michigan in an article which he wrote for the *Dial*. This article was among a number contributed by heads of departments. The *Dial*'s associate editor, Payne, collected them as a book in 1895 (see for comparison with other universities). In that year, the work in English was divided among the department head (Isaac Demmon), a junior professor (George Hempl), an assistant professor of rhetoric (himself), an instructor in English composition (Louis Strauss), and two graduate students. Scott notes that 1,198 students elected courses in English that fall. In addition, there were 110 who elected composition courses but could not get in them. Scott says the aims of this work are simple: "If we can get [students] first to think straightforwardly about subjects in which they are genuinely interested, and then, after such fashion as nature has fitted them for, to express themselves clearly and connectedly, we have done about all we can hope to do" (120–21). Scott's aims were markedly divergent from those of others of his time, who were more likely to search out errors in grammar and spelling, as can be verified in the Harvard Reports. These reports evolved when, in 1891, the Board of Overseers of Harvard appointed a committee of three laymen to study the Harvard rhetoric program. In 1892, the first of three reports to be published cited the inexcusable waste of time spent by professors in correcting student themes in English A. The committee sarcastically criticized the quality of sample themes and soundly condemned the preparatory schools for failing to teach writing skills adequately. In 1895 and 1897, two other reports further excoriated the lower schools and urged stiffer entrance requirements at Harvard. The consequence of the reports was that the importance of "correctness" was unduly emphasized for decades afterward.

To realize his goals, Scott directed his energies toward three essentials: "first, continuity and regularity of written exercises; second, much writing, much criticism, and much consultation; third, adaptation of method to the needs of the individual student. To secure the first, the student is made to write frequently and at regularly recurring periods, and is encouraged to write at set hours regardless of mood or inspiration. The second point I may be permitted to illustrate by saying that I have read and re-read this year something over 3,000 essays, most of them written by a class of 216 students. The third essential seems to me the most important of the three. That the instructor should somehow lay hold of the student as an individual is, for successful composition work, simply indispensable" (Payne 121). Scott asserts that individual instruction, Edward Channing's method at Harvard, was the reason Channing was so successful in stimulating a generation of fine writers. Scott says he looks enviously at his colleagues' chemistry lab with its ten instructors and annual expenditure of ten thousand dollars. If the teacher of composition had anything comparable, "on the whole he would be a happier man, and I am certain that in the end he would do a vast deal more of good in the world" (122–23).

Scott's involvement in Philosophy 11 lasted through the fall of
1891. In the spring of 1892 he offered, with Dewey, Philosophy 15,
"Conference in Aesthetics," a one-hour, possibly tutorial course. During
the academic year 1892–1893 he offered Philosophy 12, described simply as "Aesthetics"; students are informed that illustrative material that
year would be drawn from the works of Michelangelo and Leonardo da
Vinci. In the spring, course 22 concentrated on aesthetics and Renaissance art. Scott's association with the Philosophy Department ended in
the spring of 1893 for reasons about which one can only speculate. Although Dewey taught Course 12 in the fall of 1893 and remained as department head, he then departed for the University of Chicago. One
senses that a personal bond between English and Philosophy had been
severed, for Dewey's replacement, Alfred Henry Lloyd, appears to have
shown no interest in Scott.

Scott offered English 18, Rapid Writing, from 1891 to 1893. Then,
in 1894, English 18 becomes "Advanced Composition," a two-hour
course, "intended for those who are already proficient in writing but who
feel the need of practice and criticism. It is open only to those who receive special permission, and will be limited in number to six." Whether
he simply renamed Rapid Writing or significantly changed the nature of
the course is not clear. He taught it until 1900. English 10, the seminar
in rhetoric and literary criticism which he started in the spring of 1891,
appears until 1893. English 15, the Principles of Style which was begun
in the fall of 1890, appears every year through 1901. In the spring of
1896 he offered English 15a with a concentration on English prose of the
nineteenth century.

In the fall of 1895 he offered, one time only, a course in translation
for which proficiency in French and German was required. And he offered a course in the analysis of English prose in the summers of 1895,
1898, 1899, and 1900. More important, however, were two other
courses he developed during this decade. Scott first offered English 21,
"Development of Rhetorical Theory," in the fall of 1894. The course is
described as "a historical and comparative study of the growth of rhetorical theory from Aristotle to the present time." English 17 was a
two-hour teachers' course, first offered in the spring of 1898. It is described as "Methods of Teaching English Composition and Rhetoric"
and enrolled fifty students that semester.[2] Together, these courses provided teachers the pedagogy and theoretical background essential for effective conduct of the classroom and complete understanding of their
subject. Had such courses, as Scott taught them, become a significant

part of the undergraduate major's program at that time, the entire history of composition teaching in this country might have been very different.

In examining Scott's teaching assignments during the first decade of his career, one finds that he taught sixteen different courses in fields ranging from introductory composition and rhetoric to advanced rhetorical theory, aesthetics, stylistic analysis, and pedagogy. The other significant feature is a sudden and dramatic shift in the nature and size of his work load beginning in the fall of 1894. When he first began, he taught mostly writing courses whose paper-grading demands are time-consuming and exhausting, but his class load was apparently manageable. His assignments vary from a low of eight hours and one preparation in the spring of 1890 to fourteen hours and four preparations in the fall of 1893 and the spring of 1894.

Then, if the printed schedule is to be believed, Scott's teaching load in the fall of 1895 was twenty hours and five preparations. In addition to the course in translation and the courses he had developed in the principles of style and the development of rhetorical theory, he had four three-hour composition classes. However, he was getting some help from Willard Gore, one of his graduate students, and Gertrude Buck, who assisted him when she was working on her master's and doctoral degrees ("Tribute" [1923] 3). In the spring of 1896 the number is twenty-four hours, and in the fall of that year, thirty-six hours. By that fall, there were seven sections of English 1 and four each of English 2 and 2a. Louis Strauss and Mr. Gray assisted with English 1. From this point on, through the spring of 1901, Scott's teaching load, semester after semester, is twenty-four hours.

Impressive and exhausting as that teaching load looks, it does not tell us what is really important: what material he covered and his effectiveness with his students. Included among Scott's papers is an item labeled "Materials for the Study of Rhetoric and Composition," an apparent reading list for the "Development of Rhetorical Theory," which Scott first offered in the fall of 1894. There are 214 items representing rhetoric, grammar, logic, mental science, psychology, and the teaching of English. Included in the list are Aristotle's *Rhetoric* (in two translations, by Bohn and by Welldon); Cicero's *De Oratore* and *Brutus;* Quintilian's *Institutes of Oratory;* Hugh Blair's *Lectures on Rhetoric and Belles Lettres;* George Campbell's *Philosophy of Rhetoric;* Richard Whately's *Elements of Rhetoric;* nine works by Alexander Bain, including, of course, *English Composition and Rhetoric;* Edward Channing's *Lectures on Rhetoric;* De-

Quincey's *Essays on Style, Rhetoric and Language;* John Dewey's *Psychology;* J. F. Genung's *Practical Rhetoric;* and William James's *Principles of Psychology* (FNSP). Most writers of any stature at all in the history of rhetoric are represented here. The total list is so imposing that one cannot believe that Scott expected his students to read all these works in a single semester although the scope and depth of his own reading may have led him to forget that most students lacked his discipline and abilities.

Scott's general directions to students taking the course seem pedestrian to our times, but in the 1890s they were considerably enlightened. "Keep in mind the purpose of the essay and the requirements of the reader. Try to make what you write so clear and simple that your reader will have no excuse for misunderstanding you." He suggests an outline, but urges the student to alter it, or the subject, if it seems too long. In addition, Scott advises students to produce short but attention-getting, even nonconventional introductions (perhaps beginning with some feature of the subject), to reject ideas that do not fall naturally within the purview of the subject, to omit the conclusion unless it comes to one while writing and, more important, to omit the conventional summary conclusion. Opposing the Romantic notion of a muse, he suggests setting a time and a place to work and disciplining oneself to get there at regular times (FNSP). All this reflects an application of cognitive psychology to composing and an empirical understanding based on his own prolific output.

Scott's directions contain inventional aids which, while not systematic, are considerable, and he adds sane and useful advice about organization and style. For example, in an assignment intended to get students to examine their behaviors as writers, he asks thirty-five different questions under four general headings: "Previous Training and Influences," "Methods of Work," "Likes and Dislikes," and "Defects." The questions under the heading "Methods of Work," are most interesting to us today:

1. Do you compose rapidly or slowly? 2. Is your first draft generally the best you can do, or are you in the habit of making numerous changes and corrections? 3. What is the most difficult part of the task of composition? 4. Under what conditions do you produce your best work, as for example, when you are at leisure or hard-pressed, when you are alone or with others who are writing? 5. At what time of day can you do your best work? 6. Do you write better with or without an outline? 7. If you use an outline, at what stage of the work do you prepare it? (Give your natural inclination and actual method of work, in case these differ from what you have been taught or from what you believe to be the right method of work.) 8. What form does the outline, if you use one, naturally as-

sume when you are planning an essay? a. Do you see, in imagination, the heads and subheads in tabular form? or b. Do you hear the words or pronounce them to yourself? or c. Do you feel your ideas "move" in a certain direction? 9. Does an outline in tabular or bracketed form give you much idea of the contents of an essay or satisfy you in any way? 10. Do you, when writing, picture to yourself a hearer (or audience) or reader? If so, of what character, grade of intelligence, etc.? (Give details.) 11. Do whole sentences or paragraphs shape themselves in your mind before you write them? If so, what form do they take? Do you see them (visualize them) or hear them? 12. Do you read your sentences aloud in order to test the rhythm? or punctuation? 13. Are you apt to talk to yourself when composing? 14. Can you dictate readily? (FNSP)

Already, at this time, Scott was probing for the link between written and spoken discourse.

Several points about Scott's composition teaching emerge, even from this brief sample of his directions to students. First, we note his curiosity about the composing process itself. Second, we note the lack of dogmatism in these instructions. Third, the preponderance of the questions suggests that Scott placed high priority on the generation of subject matter, rather than on organization and style. Fourth, he consistently opposes flowery or decorative language and stresses the fact that good figurative language grows out of the subject. Finally, his instructions remind students that writing, to be effective, must have a context. In a simple assignment in which he asks them to describe something, a campus scene or building, he says that they should "determine (a) the purpose for which the description is written, (b) the reader, real or imaginary, to whom the description is to be adapted" (FNSP).

From the preface to his edition of Lewes's *Principles of Success in Literature,* published in 1891, we learn that Scott conducts his classes like seminars in which students are assumed to have assimilated the reading and are prepared to discuss as many of its salient points as possible with the instructor and other members of the class. "Advantage may be taken of the interest thus aroused to suggest other lines of reading. In this way the student will be led to undertake original research and ultimately, perhaps, to do a little independent thinking for himself" (3, 4). Scott may have been influenced here by his colleague C. K. Adams, who in 1869 introduced the German seminar method of teaching. One fact supporting this assumption is that Scott insisted on seating his students around a large circular table, a seating arrangement common to the German method—which is not to say that Scott could not have thought of this system on his own. The seminar caught on in America and was utilized in other universities (Peckham 56). This type of classroom will not seem so striking to modern teachers, but one must consider that this was the 1890s, an era in which recitation from a textbook was the standard method of teaching.

We learn still more about Scott the teacher from fragments of his correspondence with Maude Caldwell Perry.[3] He recognized genuine talent when he saw it and knew how to nourish it, with just the right amounts of encouragement and constructive but honest criticism. It is important to make this point because Allan Seager, in *The Glass-House: The Life of Theodore Roethke,* maligns Scott both directly and by implication, on this very point. Describing Roethke's freshman year at Michigan, Seager tells us what went wrong:

The teachers of writing or "Rhetoric" as it was then called, were protégés of Professor Fred N. Scott, who later achieved the left-handed dignity of a footnote making fun of him in Mencken's *American Language.* He was co-author of a textbook, Scott & Denney's *Paragraph Writing,* which was used in beginning Rhetoric classes. It was a dull, bad book and since Rhetoric was required of all freshmen, all had at least to own it. No courses were given in the short story or the novel as such; rather courses were given in Narration and Exposition as if the student, wishing to write fiction, and having learned how to narrate and expose, could hitch these together and come up with a short story or a novel. It was criticism played backward. The writing of poetry, not being susceptible to this facile analysis, was ignored altogether. (51)

Seager calls Scott's protégés very bad influences on the young Roethke "who had come to them seething with murky, inconcluded intensities in the hope of being straightened out" (51). By implication, he suggests that Roethke would have fared equally poorly had he been one of Scott's students.[4] The correspondence with Maude Perry suggests otherwise. While certainly not as gifted as Roethke, she had talent yet undeveloped because of her own "murky, inconcluded intensities," and she turned to the teacher best able, in her judgment, to assist her in working them out.

On April 24, 1891, Scott writes to Maude's father, William Caldwell, explaining his work with her:

I think I can hardly be mistaken in my judgment that your daughter has literary capabilities of an unusual kind, capabilities, not actualities, because her productions are as yet crude, uneven, and amateurish to a degree. Some of her work is very bad indeed; most of it is ordinary; but—and here is the hopeful sign—some of it is very fine indeed. If her writing were smoothly elegant and faultlessly tame, I should set her down as simply "clever" and not likely to amount to much; but that is not her way at all, and consequently I have hopes. (PMP)

After Perry left the university, she continued to send her work to Scott for comment and criticism. His remarks show a close reading and address specifics.

"I know not where His islands lift / Their fronded palms in air." What a wealth of suggestion in that verb *lift*! "Golden date's imperial crown" doesn't stir one nerve-cell. It's not the natural language of the starved soul pleading with its maker, but just scene-painting. And the next line is just as bad. . . .

The idea of the fantasy is good, but you have drawn it out to too great length. It should be treated with a little more reserve. . . . The examples of the effect of the Great Man's novels on his readers do not impress me as real. They seem to be made up for the occasion. . . . Try especially to put more individuality into the characters. (PMP)

His criticism in the letter of January 20, 1898, relates to one poem and provides an interesting insight into ways he perceives poetry is written.

I feel sure that you haven't imagined it all clearly to yourself. In part you have, but in part you have just given way to your emotions and let the words surge out anyway they would. Good poetry is not so written, at least not in its final form. What you have to do now is to keep it all up to the pitch of the 7th stanza. I don't know whether you can do that or not. It may not be your way of composing. Perhaps you can only strike things out at white heat. If so, then you must learn to hold yourself in when you write and let no word go down on the page which will not mean as much to others as it means to you. (PMP)

Scott's analysis admits to possible variables; he suggests options for improving the final version. It is truly constructive criticism.

In 1897, the university regents requested the faculty of the Literature, Science, and Arts Department "to report to the Board some general plan for getting University news before the people of the State" (Shaw, *Survey* 1:352–53). A committee was appointed to comply, one of whose members was Acting President Harry B. Hutchins. They recommended that a bureau of university news be organized with a member of the literary faculty in charge, to be known as the university editor. Scott took on this responsibility, which required the gathering and publishing of alumni news and the supervision of a university news report every two weeks. Under Scott's direction, the special news section in the *Michigan Alumnus* was reprinted in the form of a newsletter and distributed to the newspaper editors of the state. The first issue appeared January 6, 1898, followed by thirteen more in the late winter and spring. The next year they created a number of special editions. Scott continued in this job until the fall of 1900 when Shirley Smith became general secretary of the Alumni Association and took over. It is no wonder that Scott complains at this time that "my work as University Editor has taken the last remnant of my time" (letter to Frank Manny, March 16, 1898, PFM).

It is perhaps appropriate to mention exactly what Scott was getting paid for carrying this tremendous work load. In the fall of 1893, he was making $1,600. When he was promoted to junior or associate professor in 1896, his salary went to $2,000, where it remained for six years. In 1901, the regents promoted Scott to professor of rhetoric, and his salary was set at $2,500. These salary increases, although modest, were welcome. Richard, the third and last of the Scotts' children, was born in 1895.

Scott's professional associations, both at MLA and at Michigan, plus some knowledge of the quality of his work, possibly lay behind an offer he received from the Massachusetts Institute of Technology, April 21, 1893. At that time MIT's English Department had a staff of four persons: one associate professor, George Rice Carpenter, and three instructors. The school was seeking a replacement for Carpenter (one of Scott's professional friends), who was leaving them for Columbia. The offer was for an associate professorship at $2,500 a year. Since Scott was making only about $1,200 by the spring of 1893, the offer must have been tempting. (In modern terms it represented a jump in salary from about $19,000 annually to $39,000!) John Dewey's older brother, Davis Rich Dewey, who became a distinguished professor of economics, was on the MIT staff and may have been another source of endorsement for him. In the inquiry letter, MIT President Francis Amasa Walker explained that "there is no reason why, in case of an entire success achieved, the position should not soon be enlarged to a full professorship." Since this was such an attractive offer, it is puzzling that Scott turned it down (FNSP).

Although it is quite clear that Scott had plenty to do right in Ann Arbor, probably the most enjoyable and memorable experience for him in this decade was a trip to Germany in the summer of 1892. The purpose of this trip, which one can infer from a remark made in a letter to Isadore, was primarily to improve his command of German. But he was also anxious to hear lectures on aesthetics and art and to see a number of art works. From his letters we get a profile of Scott which shows him to be a very winning person, confident of his abilities but not overbearing, observing the human comedy with much wit and good humor.[5]

Crossing the Atlantic, Scott traveled with a number of people who were nationally visible in the English profession: Hiram Corson of Cornell, A. Marshall Elliott and James Bright of Johns Hopkins. Corson was the oldest, a man proficient in both mathematics and classical languages; Elliott was a philologist, a pioneer linguist, and one of the founders of MLA; Bright was also a scientific philologist, a specialist in Anglo-Saxon language and literature, and, like Elliott, one of the early leaders of MLA. Also among the travelers were Jim Angell, the son of James Angell, Sr., then president of the University of Michigan, and Roman Warner, who took his degree at Munich, taught in the United States for a few years, and was returning to Munich where he expected to become prince-docent at the university the second semester. Since Warner was a specialist in comparative literature, Scott had much in common with him. Warner offered to introduce Scott to various members of the Munich faculty and to assist him in general while he was there.[6]

One note in Scott's letters is positively chilling in light of what transpired twenty years after he took this voyage. On June 18, he says, "as icebergs have been reported, the Captain is taking a route far south of the usual one. The fog horn blows its melancholy note at intervals of fifty seconds and will keep the music up all night." As boredom set in, a certain amount of horseplay also started up. Scott said they would rise suddenly and look out a porthole in great astonishment, as if they saw a water spout or something else equally striking. Then 150 people would jump up and try to look out. Much laughter and talking followed. "But," he says, "the general tone is dismal. Dr. Bright got to the point when he turned suddenly to the young lady opposite and asked abruptly: 'By the way, talking of lunatics, how's your mother?' This was the last flicker. We filed solemnly out and fell to walking the decks. Samuel Johnson was right. A ship is a floating prison" (MG).

One of Scott's first communiques from Munich is a charming letter directed to his oldest son, Harvey, who would have been four that summer. "Your Papa writes this letter to you from away off here in Germany." He tells Harvey that his supper consisted of large cherries and a big piece of brown bread, so hard that "if somebody hit you on the head with it, it would knock you down." Then he tells him to take care of Mama and Marion, "and after awhile Papa will come home to play with you and tell you stories when he puts you to bed." Scott writes Isa of his encounter with a stuffy Ober-Pedell (a school supervisor) at the University. "I must bring, he said, a note from each professor whom I wished to hear. Otherwise he could not recognize me. Feeling that I was momentarily increasing my knowledge of German, I let him get as angry as he wanted to. He harangued me for as long as 10 minutes on his duties as Pedell" (MG, June 29, 1892).

Because he also wishes to pursue his interests in art, Scott looks up a man named John Pickard, a professor of classical archeology and the history of art at the University of Missouri, who was completing his Ph.D. in Munich that summer. He carries a letter of introduction from Walter Miller, his classmate and long-time friend, also a professor at the University of Missouri. He found Pickard at the old Pinakothek (a famous art museum in Munich) examining Italian pictures. "We had a discussion on Art and Archeology on the spot. He will help me in numerous ways. I am to attend lectures by Prof. Riehl given in the Pinakothek with demonstration from the pictures themselves. Pickard tells me to go right into all the lectures I wish to hear and say nothing to anybody."

By early July, Scott had found lodgings in Munich. His landlady, Frau Schopper, is very kind and quite useful to him. "For one who was anxious to study, she would be a little troublesome, for she is *sehr gesprachig*. She wants to tell me all the news and advise me about my meals and discuss the weather and the neighbors. In my case, however, that is exactly what I desire. I let her talk on, with a pleased consciousness that I am saving at least a mark an hour which I would otherwise pay to a teacher. I have no great difficulty in understanding her, and she has as little in understanding me. In fact she usually anticipates what I am about to say and shovels in the various infinitives and past participles which I am very apt to forget" (MG, July 3, 1892).

But learning German is not easy. "My trouble is mainly with the little words and chopped off colloquialisms. For example, I, like the other Americans whom I see and hear—and avoid at the restaurants, at first always said Wie viel? when I wanted to pay my bill. But no German ever said that. What they did say, I couldn't catch. Schwartz [a law student whose English is much less advanced than Scott's German; they agree to meet and talk English one day, German the next] explained that the proper formula was: was kostet es? or was macht es? but that everyone shortened it to kostet or macht?" He also tells of a German chemist he went to see, on behalf of a student who wanted to attend his lectures, and that he could understand the man's German quite well and the man dealt nicely with his [Scott's] German because he could anticipate what he was trying to say. "The rub comes when a stranger stops you on the street and asks a wholly unexpected and unexpectable question. Generally there is some colloquialism in it that takes all the wind out of your sails" (MG, July 3, 1892).

The whole journey provided Scott an introduction to European culture. On July 10 he tells Isa that one of his contacts, Professor Koeppel, is astonished to discover that he is the author of the article in *Modern Language Notes* on Sidney.[7] Koeppel plans to do some lectures on American authors next year, so Scott promises to send him a list of representative authors and some bibliography. Scott has also begun to meet other Germans who are assisting him in finding his way around the city and the university. One of these is Herr Fuchs, "the old music teacher of whom I wrote before and who is acting as a kind of Cicerone to me, to call on Dr. Muther, Priveldozene in the University and director of the Kupferstickkabinett of the Alte Pinakothek" (MG, July 10, 1892).

Muther gives Scott the name of an American artist named Ullrich who lives in Venice "but belongs to the Dresden Kunstverein and has recently been appointed on some committee connected with the World's Fair." Ullrich explains to Scott a developing conflict among artists in Germany:

The management of the World's Fair Exhibit has been put into the hands of the Art Societies in the city's principal art centers of Germany, — Munich, Dresden, Berlin, Karlsruhe, Dusseldorf and Stuttgart. In each of these centers a division has occurred between the old Academicians who are in power officially, and the young Secezionisten, as they are called, who have revolted against the methods of their elders. In most cases, as is natural, the most original work is that which is being done by the Secezionisten, but as all the juries will be composed largely or entirely of the Academicians, the younger men feel that they will not have a fair opportunity. (MG, July 10, 1892)

Ullrich proposes that Scott go with him to the Allotria, a famous artists' club in Munich and then to the studios of several artists of both schools. Scott reported the conflict between the artists in Munich and his concern that the entire scope of art in that city would not be represented at the World's Fair in an article entitled "Deutsche Kunst auf der Weltaustellung zu Chicago." Originally written in English, it was translated into German by the editors of *Münchner Neueste Nachrichten* for publication in the September 21, 1892, issue of the magazine. The editors identified Scott as "one of the most respected art connoisseurs and art critics in America."

At the same time, he was attending informal gatherings where there was drinking and joking. On one occasion, he joined a meeting of the Akademisch-Litteraturverein where there was singing from the Könners-Bücher. One person would start a jingling couplet and everyone had to add to it; Scott said he did his in English. Despite his pleasure, Scott was disheartened by his stay in Germany. "If I could only have a year, not exactly of that sort of thing, but a daily intercourse with these young Germans, I could soak up the language like a sponge. As it is, all that I shall be able to get is a taste of it." He is considering foregoing trips to London, Paris, or Italy in order to say in Munich, "grinding away at the language." It is the one thing for which he made the trip (MG, July 10, 1892).

Scott also reports on his visit to two libraries. Having worked in the University of Michigan Library, a much smaller collection in 1892, obviously, than is now there, he still had a pretty good idea of what a library's resources should be. The University of Munich's library, containing three hundred thousand volumes, he describes as a "small affair." The Royal Library is another matter. "Today one of the officials of the Library. . . took me through the monstrous file. There are over a million vols. and some 30,000 mss. But it is not the easiest thing to get at them." Scott writes Isa about this library:

I call it a tour because it seems to me now that we tramped for miles. At any rate we kept steadily on the go for over an hour. All I can remember now is an interminable series of great, desolate, lonesome rooms that looked as though no man might have been in them for a thousand years, connected by narrow winding corridors and rickety stairs. All was as barren as a wind-swept moor. The books stood close-packed on wooden shelves along the walls. Now and then we came upon one of the attendants prowling along a gallery, and once there was an old woman, sitting on a stairway, but for the rest the silence and the desolation were unbroken. (MG, July 17, 1892)

An incidental item in the July 14 letter to Isa gives a clue as to the way in which Scott was able to get so much work done. "If you happen to have the time I wish you would go to the library and get up a De-Quincey bibliography for me—send me a list of all the books in which DeQuincey is criticised or otherwise written about, as well as a list of editions." He published an edition of DeQuincey's *Essays on Style, Rhetoric and Language* the next year (MG).

The available letters from abroad during the summer of 1892 tell us a great deal about Scott's intellectual interests, about his own personal gifts and eccentricities, and about his family. When he returned to Ann Arbor in the fall of 1892, his German was obviously much improved, and his knowledge of European customs was more sophisticated.

It is impossible to do justice to the full range of Scott's professional activities and interests before the turn of the century, but some selected examples indicate the large issues which were increasingly to command his attention in the following decades. A good portion of Scott's off-campus time was given to MLA. Very likely because of Hempl, he became active in this fledgling enterprise in its first decade of existence, joining in 1890.[8] Some of the men who sustained it in the early years were those he met on the boat to Europe during the summer of 1892: Corson, Bright, and particularly Elliott.[9]

Scott began to take an active role in MLA in 1896. He was on the nominating committee, he functioned as discussant on a paper by Hempl, he was elected president of the Pedagogical Section, and he gave a paper: "Diseases of English Prose: A Study in Rhetorical Pathology" (unpub. ms., FNSP). The latter merits examination here because of the way in which it reveals the qualities of his mind and the effort he was making, early in his career, to raise the study of rhetoric to a genuine intellectual discipline. Necessary to its meaning is a medical analogy Scott develops:

He [the teacher] assumes a character. With solemn professional face he looks about over the rows of young patients who have been sent to him for treatment, and shakes his head dubiously as he recognizes the well-known symptoms of disorder, organic or functional. Some of his patients limp, some squint, some cough. Here is one who is clammy with chills, there is another who burns with fever. (i)

According to Scott, all are infected early in their schooling, but the teacher can only turn to "his instruments and his drugs." Eventually, some show improvement, but there are "rows and rows of incurables" (i).

When he comes to A. S. Hill's *The Foundations of Rhetoric,* a tone of suppressed irony pervades his description: "Symptoms of disordered expressions, collected from the essays of students rhetorically diseased, are in its pages scientifically classified and compared with symptoms of good health" (ii). Ultimately, Scott cites the Report of the Committee of Ten and the Harvard Reports of the 1890s, particularly the 1892 report.[10] Scott questions whether composition teachers have any respectable scientific rationale for the work they do, but finds that most serve only as error-hunters. His conviction is that teachers need to look to the cause of the student's "ailment." (Scott's association with Dr. John Harvey Kellogg may have colored the analogy drawn in this paper. See Kellogg.)

Most important in this paper, Scott develops as full a statement as one will find anywhere of his organic perception of the nature of discourse. He likens a discourse to a seed containing potentialities. It grows and develops like a plant. But it may "be deflected from its normal course, checked in its development, or become subject to a variety of disorders" (1). He suggests that bad English has its origins in the early development of the organism. He cites Charles Creighton, author of a piece on pathology in the *Encyclopedia Britannica,* as saying that "when the organism goes wrong, it retreats to broader ground, or reverts to modes of life which it had come through" (2). Scott reflects on his own experience: "the disorders of expression observed in the essays of my students might be examples of reversions to older forms of speech, the writer's mind in deviating from the normal mode of expression going back unconsciously to the primitive language-types preserved for us in the speech of children and of savages" (2).

He tested this hypothesis, comparing the undeveloped speech of infants and of savages and found that "certain typical examples taken from the essays of my students may properly be regarded as reversions to these early forms" (3). He found that primitive peoples lack the power to examine their own thought processes and have few if any abstract words. This tendency of the aboriginal mind produces several peculiarities in their speech: (1) the use of sentence-words or conglomerate-words—omnibus expressions; (2) use of gestures, grimaces, attitudes, tones, and emphasis as aids or substitutes for conventional speech symbols; (3) "undue explicitness of statement."

Scott anticipates the findings of developmental psychologists when he makes the correlation between primitive speech and that of children. Citing research current at the time, he notes particularly the work of Kathleen Carter Moore, John Dewey, and Frederick Tracy, and reaches this conclusion: "What is needed is in short that the student should gain habitual control of his feelings and imagination instead of being controlled by them. The acquisition of such power as this would in my opinion oppose an effectual barrier to a relapse of any student's language into a state of barbarism" (18–19). Scott's perception of writing is antiromantic insofar as it distrusts emotion not brought under control. In the 1890s his approach was much more original and advanced than that of anyone else working in this field.

4

In the Public Arena

IN THE DECADE from 1890 to 1900, Scott was inordinately productive. Shirley Smith wrote of him after his death: "In the hurly-burly of the dismissal of one class and assembly of another . . . he seemed detached as a Buddha. He was, I believe, one of the very few men I have ever known who could and did really think to a purpose during such brief and inauspicious intervals" (Smith n.p.). His writings related to his chief interests at this time: rhetoric, aesthetics, and journalism. He produced editions of G. H. Lewes's *The Principles of Success in Literature* (1891), Herbert Spencer's *The Philosophy of Style* (1891), Daniel Webster's *First Bunker Hill Oration Together with Other Essays Relating to the Revolution* (1895), Thomas DeQuincey's *Essays on Style, Rhetoric and Language* (1893), and Samuel Johnson's *Rasselas* (1891).

The Principles of Success began as a series of articles that Lewes wrote when he was editor of the *Fortnightly Review* during the first two years of the magazine's existence. The essays were first collected in pamphlet form in 1885 (as they had appeared in the magazine) by A. S. Cook. But Scott was the first and only true editor of them, correcting not only copy-reading mistakes in the original versions but also obvious inaccuracies which were intrinsic to the original essays. Given what we know about Scott at this period of his life, it is not difficult to see why he was drawn to Lewes's work. It had practical value, of course. The advice it contains for young writers is sound and unsentimental. But there are deeper philosophical and psychological reasons for its appeal. Clearly, Lewes's attraction to German philosophical idealism struck a responsive chord in

Scott. Its celebration of art as the highest truth of human endeavor appealed to his idealism. Its method, the persistent attempt to get beneath the surface manifestations of any phenomenon to determine the basic features of a subject, and that method's representation of the way the mind should work, mirror the values Scott had developed. Lewes, like others, not only attracted Scott, but became a primary influence in the shaping of his views and attitudes.

Scott's edition of Spencer's *Philosophy of Style* is the second in this series: "the object [of these books] is to bring helpful discussions of the principles of literary criticism within the reach of teachers of rhetoric" (iii). But for Scott personally, Spencer provided a congenial schemata. According to the preface: "From this year [1839] may be dated the beginning of Spencer's prolonged effort to interpret all the facts of nature in the light of the central principle of evolution" (viii, ix). (Three of Spencer's essays, "Social Statistics," "Theory of Population," and "The Development Hypothesis," all published around 1850, anticipate Darwin's *Origin of Species* nine years later.)

The principle of organic unity, Scott has said elsewhere, was stated in Plato's *Phaedrus* and then lay dormant for over two thousand years, resurfacing, surprisingly, in the conclusion to Spencer's essay. Scott continually argued the superiority of organic to mechanical unity, particularly in discourse.

The function of the parts, that is, of the various elements and devices of rhetoric such as figures, sentences, paragraphs, and composition generally, is inexplicable, or misapprehended, until they are given their proper place in the operation of the whole. Just what this whole, this organism in its detailed structure and function, is, cannot here be discussed at length. It is enough to say that as the content of ethics embraces all conduct in which there is adjustment of acts to ends, so the content of any adequate theory of style must embrace all manner of expression in which there is adjustment of utterance to comprehension. (xviii)

With this edition, Scott was also formulating some early notions about language, a subject that intrigued him in one form or another throughout his life. Spencer proposed that language is a hindrance to thought, demonstrated by the fact that simple ideas may be communicated by signs. For example, a finger on the lips conveys the idea "Do not speak here." But Scott explains that Spencer really was saying: "'Language is an inferior form of expression for ideas which are more easily expressed by other kinds of signs'"(3).

Scott clearly was beginning to think through the ideas he was encountering. For example, when Spencer argues that we think in particulars and thus are slowed down by abstract terms as we mentally fish for concrete illustrations of them, Scott demurs:

The trained thinker in thinking the class "horse" does not "choose from his stock" of mental horses. He thinks the concept horse, and in so doing he may attain to a perfectly definite notion of the class without having in consciousness any particular horse whatsoever. The particular image is of course present but such features as hight [*sic*], color, etc. are simply disregarded. (9)

Scott directs readers to works in psychology by both John Dewey and William James in support of his position. He also challenges Spencer's argument for the superiority of syntax which is immediately most intelligible. "But Style appeals to the emotions as well as to the intellect, and the arrangement of words which will be the most economical may not be the most musical, and the most musical may not be the most pleasurably effective" (143).

Another linguistic point which Scott questions is the argument for the superiority of English word order to French in an expression like *un cheval noir,* literally, a horse black. Spencer says that English puts the descriptive term, *black,* first, thus saving the reader loss of mental energy which would have been expended correcting an image of a specific horse which might have been spotted or brown before he learned that it was black. Scott says that (1) the Frenchman, accustomed to the substantive-adjective order, will anticipate the coming *noir,* or some other adjective, as soon as he hears the word *cheval.* Hence in his case the nascent image of a wrongly colored horse will not tend to arise. (2) In the case of the Englishman, the adjective may lead the hearer to anticipate some other substantive than "horse"; he may expect "sheep," or "man," or "eye," to follow, since all these things may possess the quality blackness. Collectively, Scott's notes and comments on Spencer's essay tell us a great deal about the quality and depth of his perceptions about language, and they illustrate his unique willingness to draw on other disciplines, especially psychology, to define rhetoric.

In 1893 Thomas DeQuincey's *Essays on Style, Rhetoric and Language* became the third in this series. As David Potter points out in his foreword to the Southern Illinois University Press Landmark Edition of DeQuincey's essays, Scott was only the second person to collect even a portion of DeQuincey's essays. According to Potter, David Masson had brought them all together in his edition of *The Collected Writings of Thomas DeQuincey* in 1889–1890. "Just three years after Masson's collection, Fred Newton Scott, recognizing the importance of DeQuincey's rhetorical theory and the need for a more generally available edition, reprinted a selection" (Potter vi). It would be sixteen years before Helen Darbishire gathered together a representative portion of these essays in *DeQuincey's Literary Criticism*. Scott's book contains the "Essay on Style," "Essay on Rhetoric," Essay on Language," and the "Essay on the English Language."

In the preface, Scott characterizes the study of rhetoric as it had been and as Scott thought it should be. His only mistake was in thinking that the revival of interest in rhetoric in the 1890s, in which he played such an important part, would continue. Two points are important: his insistence on describing rhetoric as a science and his observation that it was uncommonly late in acquiring that description. He blames textbooks for rhetoric's failure to advance, describing them as having "a depressing air of fixity and finality, which has done much to check independence of inquiry and restrict the field of research" (iii).

Scott made also a prediction about the value of DeQuincey's contribution to the literary world: he altered forever the potential impact of prose expression. "The virtues of English prose will probably remain a kind of superstition, until its history has been written from a scientific point of view. When that has been done, it may be discovered that there is no such thing as absolutely good style, any more than there is absolutely good painting, or music, or architecture" (xvi). According to Scott, "[DeQuincey] discovered capacities of prose, which, before his time, had not been known to exist; or, if they existed in isolation, no one had before woven them together and to weave together, is, in art, to make a new thing" (xvi).

For Scott, the distinctive quality of DeQuincey's prose is its musicality. DeQuincey focused on this element in his "Essay on Style": "the preparation pregnant with the future; the remote correspondence; the questions, as it were, which to a deep musical sense are asked in one passage and answered in another; the iteration and ingemination of a given effect, moving through subtle variations that sometimes disguise the theme, sometimes fitfully reveal it, sometimes throw it out tumultuously to the blaze of daylight" (4). These are the characteristics of music; why not prose, too? According to Scott, such qualities were not common in prose before DeQuincey's time.

In the "Essay on Language," Scott says DeQuincey stumbles upon two ideas of fundamental importance, neither of which he develops systematically. "The first is, that changes in language are responsive to the wants of society. The second is, that languages should be studied comparatively. Carefully worked out, the first principle would carry us far on the way to the establishment of a norm of good usage" (xxi). The second idea, says Scott, guided philological research to the present time. "But in all that time, while the foundations of the comparative method were being laid, in spite of his boasted familiarity with German thought, DeQuincey seems never even to have heard of the eminent philologist Bopp [author of *Vergleichende Grammatik*]" (xxi).

In these comments on DeQuincey's work, we see Scott's constant attempt to enlarge the scope of rhetoric. In this respect he opposed the textbooks of the time, which were drawing an ever narrowing circle around the subject. He also recognized that DeQuincey failed to appreciate the significance of his belief that changes in language are responsive to the demands of society. Scott's first professional publication expounds this principle. It is the basis of contemporary descriptive linguistics, and it is worth noting that Sterling Leonard, Ruth Weeks, and Charles Fries, all leaders in the movement to establish descriptive linguistics, were students of Scott.

The most valuable, in practical and financial terms, of Scott's publications during this decade were his textbooks. They are, in a sense, complementary to the editions just cited, which, as we have seen, were course supplements, enriched by Scott's own scholarship. The most important of these texts, and certainly the most remunerative, was *Paragraph Writing,* the first of his collaborations with Joseph Denney. In the preface to the first edition in 1893, they explain that the principles of the book were first employed in their own classrooms. Then, as knowledge of their method spread to classroom teachers, they received requests for information about the method. "Its aim is to make the paragraph the basis of a method of composition, to present all the important facts of rhetoric in their application to the paragraph" (iii).

Why would teachers so eagerly have embraced this method in the early 1890s? For one thing, when the 1892 Harvard Board of Overseers reported that students were deficient in their preparation, the popular press repeated this complaint, and hundreds of articles on the illiteracy of American boys in the early 1890s appeared. Naturally, as secondary teachers felt the pressure to prepare students to perform better on college entrance examinations, they looked for some easy means of teaching writing. Since classes were routinely large, and it was virtually impossible to assign huge numbers of papers and then grade them, teachers sought a way out of the dilemma. Scott and Denney provided it.

In explaining their rationale, Scott and Denney say that learning to write well "means learning to construct units of discourse which have order and symmetry and coherence of parts" (iii). The student needs to learn how to make such parts, put them together, and, if necessary, reassemble them if they don't cohere. They contend that the paragraph is the ideal unit of discourse for this kind of work because the sentence is too short and fragmentary, the essay too long. They quote from Bain's *Composition and Rhetoric*, making quite clear the source of the idea. They also cite an experiment Harriet Scott did in the Detroit Normal Training School in which students demonstrated their aptitude for comprehending a paragraph more quickly than separate sentences. They further invoke Aristotle, who said that the psychological principle governing the ideal structural unit is that its size be one which can be simultaneously comprehended by writer or reader. The paragraph ideally fits that criterion. They also put forth the notion that the paragraph is a theme in miniature, that students can write many more of them than essays, and that teachers can grade many more of them than essays. That makes the student's work more varied and the teacher's less burdensome.

As the table of contents reveals, this book does not exhibit the originality of Scott's conceptions about rhetoric. Scott was a practical man, and in writing texts he offered students as much as he thought they could and would learn. He also offered teachers, by nature conservative and resistant to change, as much as they would accept. Of the three sections in the book, the second, "Theory of the Paragraph," is the only one to hint at the real depth of Scott the rhetorician. It begins with an obvious theoretical question: why do we paragraph at all? First, we paragraph to break up the page, providing the reader some relief from an unbroken block of type. We paragraph, also, to represent the essential structure of an essay. Quoting William James, the authors say that thought proceeds in leaps and pauses, the pauses representing those occasions when thought, which has been shooting toward some point of interest, hesitates and amplifies certain stages. Thus, an essay is to be perceived as an organic structure, each part of which fulfills some essential place in that structure. Paragraphing of this kind is important to the essay because it contributes to its development organically, not mechanically.

Describing the way this kind of development works in an entire essay, Scott and Denney say that "the essay is the result of a sustained movement of the writer's thought toward a definite goal, but within this large development several intermediate steps are discoverable. The thought, on its way to the main conclusion, passes through many stages of transition, attains many minor conclusions, pauses for retrospective glances" (96). The paragraphs mark those stages.

Moreover, writers have options in the way they paragraph. They can "mark the articulation [of the thought] (1) at every joint, (2) at the larger joints, or (3) for the sake of variety follow now one plan, now the other. These varieties of construction may be represented diagrammatically as shown in figure 1.

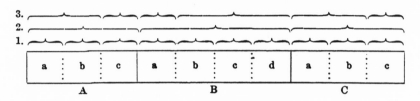

Figure 1. Varieties of Paragraph Construction. From *Paragraph Writing* 97.

The flexibility of this concept, and Scott and Denney's refusal to be dogmatic about the placement of the topic sentence—they indicate that it can come first, last, or not at all (except by implication)—suggests a liberality not present in some of their contemporaries. The conclusion to this section contains a brief history of the paragraph. In it is cited Edwin Lewis's dissertation. According to Lewis, author of *The History of the English Paragraph* (1894) and the only one in the nineteenth century to study the paragraph as a unit of discourse, "the only really new phases of rhetorical theory since Bain's 'six rules,' are Wendell's theory of Mass, and Scott and Denney's theory of Proportion" (170). He says, in addition, that "Scott and Denney's theory of Proportion is true of those writers who have a conception of the paragraph as an organic whole,—Burke, Macaulay, Arnold, for example. The principle is so strongly operative in the best prose of today that we may probably go so far as to say: in general it is true that in the best modern paragraphs the distance between periods is inversely as the emphasis on each included proposition" (170). This section offers the reader a glimpse of the scholarship and depth of Scott the rhetorician, but only a glimpse.

Without question, *Paragraph Writing* served an immediate practical need, but it also gave teachers an insight into the way scholarship could serve rhetoric. Scott and Denney's concept of the paragraph was not a presentation of the authors' biases on the subject; it was derived from the best available scholarship. And their discussion of the way paragraphs are related to thought processes reveals a merger of psychology and rhetoric that was much needed at the time.[1]

Composition-Rhetoric, another of Scott's collaborations with Denney, appeared in 1897. The book restates some now familiar ideas. For example, the joining of composition and rhetoric may have been their effort to call attention to the fact that composition, as taught by too many people then, was a degenerate offshoot of classical rhetoric, badly in need of a transfusion that would reconnect it to its historic past. This merger may also have been Scott and Denney's reaction against teaching rhetorical theory as a body of knowledge separate from its application in composition. The bibliography in this book is impressive, easily comparable to the list of works students in graduate composition and rhetoric courses now are expected to read. Among the titles are Bain's *English Composition and Rhetoric;* Buck's *Figures of Rhetoric: A Psychological Study;* Campbell's *Philosophy of Rhetoric;* DeQuincey's *Essays on Style, Rhetoric and Language;* Genung's *Outlines of Rhetoric;* Lewis's *History of the English Paragraph;* Quintilian's *Institutes of Oratory;* Spencer's *Philosophy of Style;* and Whately's *Elements of Rhetoric.*

A third textbook collaboration with Denney, *Elementary English Composition,* was published in 1900 and revised in 1908. The interesting aspect of this book is that it underscores Scott's belief in organic education. He looked at the entirety of the student's education, not merely at the contribution of the colleges, and sought the means for developing proficiency in the preparatory schools. In the preface the authors tie the indifference of students in high school composition classes to stale teaching practices, primarily review of material covered in the earlier grades. A more fundamental problem they identify is the failure of teachers to provide the sense of writing in a social context, a tenet which Scott had addressed before. As the authors explain, students have a natural impulse to express themselves which comes partly from within, partly from without. When these two impulses are balanced, students compose naturally. But at the beginning of secondary instruction, too often the teacher fails to remind the student that he is writing or speaking to another person. "He leaves them in the attitude, and the spirits, of soldiers who are firing their ammunition into the void" (iii).

Elementary English Composition sets out to challenge curiosity with attractive material, "each problem discovering to the pupil who solves it a practical principle, or a useful idiom, or a typical situation in real life" (v). The book begins with exercises for grammar review, but the questions are not traditional. They ask students when they started studying grammar, what it is about, whether or not it is of any use to anybody, whether a person working in a machine shop would find grammar or arithmetic more useful, whether or not grammar is made up of rules. The exercises apply aspects of grammar rather than demand mere repetition of rules in the abstract. For example, to demonstrate pronoun use, students read two sentences and indicate which one they prefer.

Sentence 1: "If the squirrel miss his footing and fall, he is sure to catch on the next branch; if the connection be broken, he leaps recklessly for the nearest spray or limb, and secures his hold, even if it be by the aid of his teeth."

Sentence 2: "If the squirrel miss the squirrel's footing and fall, the squirrel is sure to catch on the next branch; if the connection be broken, the squirrel leaps recklessly for the nearest spray or limb, and secures the squirrel's hold, even if it be by the aid of the squirrel's teeth." (xxi)

Other textbooks of the time were more formal, expecting the student to seek their level or fall by the wayside. Scott and Denney were not so uncompromising.

One of the most important summations Scott makes about the status of composition teaching in his time is contained in the teacher's manual to this text. "Composition in the schools has long been under a curse, and not without reason. It has lacked substance, vitality, enrichment. The stream has been so shallow that, in Ben Jonson's words, one could probe it with one's middle finger. There has been in composition teaching too much correcting of morbid English, too much metaphor mongering, too much vaporing about style, to permit it to rise to the dignity of a first-rate discipline. But now composition seems to be coming into its rights. The old superstition which made the composition teacher the Pariah of the public school system is surely passing" (see Stewart, "Rediscovering" 539).

Along with the textbooks that Scott produced at this time was the creation of a series of monographs called Contributions to Rhetorical Theory, all but one written by Scott's graduate students, and published in Ann Arbor. There would be a total of nine eventually, five before 1900. The concept itself was original, and all are valuable for different reasons. Beyond that, they are interesting because Scott's hand shows in each. Buck's *Figures of Rhetoric,* her M.A. thesis, was the first. She defines the basis of figures.

The figurative process is fundamental in the mind of man, and hence may be traced in all objective manifestations of that mind. It consists in the unification through conflict of two immediately successive precepts or concepts between which is an implicit relationship. This unification is expressed in language;

when complete, as a word, a phrase, or a "plain statement" of fact; when incomplete, as a "figure." (24)

Predictably, Buck drew on the insights of contemporary psychology. Her notes and bibliography list William James's *Principles of Psychology,* Hoeffding's *Outlines of Psychology,* John Dewey's *Psychology,* Alexander Bain's *Senses and Intellect,* Wundt's *Human and Animal Psychology,* and Ladd's *Psychology, Descriptive and Explanatory.* Although the psychology upon which she drew has obviously been supplanted by modern precepts and methods of analysis, one must not overlook the significance of her pioneering efforts to employ psychological insights to enrich aspects of rhetorical theory.

Willard Gore's *Student Slang,* published in 1895, was the second monograph in the series. It lists some eight hundred slang expressions current among University of Michigan students that year. The topic reflects Scott's lifelong preoccupation with slang (in his retirement he was compiling a dictionary of American slang). And the focus suggests Scott's attitude. In the introduction, Gore concedes that while some might prefer a normative list which indicates the degree of departure of each expression from acceptable usage, such a list is not practical because it presupposes a descriptive list from which one could make such judgments.

Joseph Denney's *Two Problems of Composition Teaching* was the third in the series. One of the two problems he identifies is the relationship between reading and composition training; the other is the nature of topics to be assigned for composition. On the latter, Denney and Scott spoke with a single voice. "If our object is to train the power of seeing and expressing relations, of grasping in imagination the meaning and total significance of a number of details, the statement of the topics should, if possible, suggest a typical situation in real life" (7). For example, instead of assigning a paper on "Foreign Missions," students should be asked to "induce a business man who has never given Foreign Missions any consideration, to contribute to their support" (7).

Scott, himself, contributed the fourth monograph: *References on the Teaching of Rhetoric and Composition.* He described it as an "advance guard of a general bibliography of rhetoric" (1). His experience with the course for teacher preparation fitted him uniquely for this task. Unlike others, at this early point in his career, he had day-to-day contact with the needs of the secondary teacher. "It is commended to the attention of those who intend to teach these subjects, and such persons are urged to form a better acquaintance with it; not with the idea that reading about teaching and methods of teaching will bring the power to teach, but with the idea that in this, as in every other line of work, the business of the scholar is to familiarize himself with the literature of his chosen field" (1, 2).

The bibliography, which runs to twenty-one pages, lists, with occasional brief annotations, books and articles by virtually everyone of importance in the latter half of the nineteenth century. Alexander Bain, A. S. Hill, Barrett Wendell, John Genung, and Scott himself are listed along with the Harvard Reports, the reports of the Committee of Ten on Secondary School Studies and the Committee of Fifteen on Elementary Education. Such a list emphasizes Scott's concern with the full range of English education from the primary grades through college. In addition, he has briefer bibliographies on the teaching of composition in German and French schools. This monograph is a valuable document not only for what change it purports to do, but for discovering the origins of Scott's tenets on the value and focus of composition teaching.

Gertrude Buck's doctoral treatise, "The Metaphor," became the fifth volume in Contributions to Rhetorical Theory (1899). It is a definitive examination of the appeal and origin of metaphor. Explaining metaphor in terms of contemporary psychology, she insists that it is not a literary "device" as it has been designated by numerous rhetoricians and philologists, but rather an organism, a "stage" in the thought process. Her main contention is that metaphor derives slowly from the consciousness, evolving through stages of blurred differentiations until it reaches distinctness. Contrary to others of the time, she finds that metaphor is *necessary* to the writer and that if it is used just to "prettify" the writing as was true in the eighteenth century, then that is "bad art." Metaphor, in Buck's analysis, emerged from a natural need to differentiate perceptions. In fact, she points out, contrary to the belief of most rhetoricians and philologists, metaphor precedes plain language, not the other way around. It is only after the user has perceived differences that he is capable of creating the metaphor to validate those differences.

Scott was by this time a figure of considerable national prominence in the profession, and as such he was beginning to speak out more forcefully on matters affecting the teaching of English. One of his first extended statements is presented in "The Report on College Entrance Requirements in English" which appeared in the *Educational Review,* October 1900. (It is not to be confused with a similar one published in June 1901 for the *School Review.*) This paper derived from remarks made at a meeting of the Michigan Schoolmaster's Club, the topic of which was the report of the Committee on College Entrance Requirements.[2] The committee, formed by the National Educational Association (NEA) in 1895, "endorsed the work of the Committee of Ten and in 1899 published an outline of a curriculum in high school English that included still another list of books that prospective college students should have studied or at least read. Such a list, its makers argued, would overcome the problem of differing requirements of various colleges" (Hook 11).

This report generated considerable opposition, particularly from Scott. Essentially, the eastern colleges, notably Harvard, were dictating high school requirements for not only their region but for the Midwest, South, and West, where, as Hook points out, many students learned their English on the job. They knew about baseball and coal mines, but not a lot about English literature. When confronted with the Harvard entrance examinations, they did poorly, as could have been predicted.

Scott praises two aspects of the report, first for simplifying the English curriculum in secondary schools: everything should be studied under either of two rubrics, English literature or English composition. That means putting such things as grammar, rhetoric, study of derivations, theory of literature, in one of the two boxes. Scott approved, for he did not believe in studying formal rhetoric in isolation from any social context, which is precisely the way it was studied. He also commends the committee for recommending that English literature and composition be studied side by side, during the four years of high school. But he found things he did not like in the report, and his scorn is barely muted. In his eyes, the committee evaded the real difficulties which they should have confronted.

[Teachers] had a right to expect that, among other things, [the report] would summarize the history of the teaching of English for the past generation; that it would classify and critically review the various methods that now compete for popular favor; that it would give the results of experiments in the teaching of literature and composition; that it would discuss the special training of teachers; that it would discriminate between elementary and advanced work in methods, in choice of subjects, and in the character of the recitation; that it would summarize and review the best of the literature on English teaching that has appeared of late; that it would treat of the methods and devices by which the labor of teaching and especially of essay-correcting may be lightened; and finally, that it would make plain in what respect this report is conceived to be an advance upon its predecessor, the report of the Committee of Ten. (291–92)

He condemns the report as a "hasty catching-up and patching together of a few general principles, a specimen program, and list of books for reading. There is nothing about it which could not have been put together on a rainy afternoon by any first-rate teacher of English working independently" (292). (In a footnote, Scott blames the situation, not the subcommittee.) Furthermore, he does not like the dogmatic tone of the report, for it treats various matters as if they were settled out of hand. English teaching "is fuller of unsolved problems than any other subject that can be mentioned. It is a kind of pedagogical porcupine. But the report ignores this. It reads as if we were all cock-sure about everything" (292). For example, although the committee says that English composition and literature should be studied side by side, they avoid the obvious, difficult question: *how* shall this be done, effectively and profitably?

Nor does the report address the fundamental question of the relation of English studies to the ultimate ends of education.

I have been reading recently in the *Revue universitaire* a series of suggestive articles by M. Jules Payot, on French composition . . . and in one of these articles M. Payot remarks that the methods of teaching composition which prevail in many of the French schools are not in harmony with the social demands which ought to guide and fashion a republican system of instruction. That seems to me to be getting down to bedrock. That is the question of prime importance. . . . *Are* our methods of instruction in English in harmony with the social demands of our great industrial community? I suspect that they are not. More than that I suspect that the hard knot of the English question lies right here—that our present ideals and methods of instruction are in large part remnants of an adaptation to a state of things which long since passed away. (293–94)

❖

Although Scott's major focus at this time was on the problems of teaching composition and rhetoric, his publications reveal a number of other interests. Between 1891 and 1895, he produced five short papers for *Modern Language Notes,* one of which was "The Russian Verb and Its Accent," a result of his recent study of the Russian language. In addition, in 1899, he collaborated with Charles Mills Gayley on one of the least well known, at this date, yet most comprehensive publications of his career, the *Introduction to the Methods and Materials of Literary Criticism: The Bases in Aesthetics* (1899). This big book (587 pages including the index) was to be his last work on aesthetics because the preoccupation with rhetoric and administrative matters was taking him away from this subject. In its linking of aesthetics and literary criticism, as well as its definitions of both, supported by extensive bibliographies, it is an impressive piece of scholarship.

In the preface the authors note that everyone who reads is now making critical judgments, and that all, from the untrained to the skilled professional, need some guidance. Scott and Gayley offer their book as a source of that guidance, but not dogmatically. It is really an introduction to two areas of study: aesthetics and comparative literature. They suggest that the person best able to profit from this book is one who knows enough psychology and rhetoric to discern the overall application of those fields to the problems of literary criticism. In addition, the reader should have some acquaintance with literary masterpieces and with the history of literature, some knowledge of art and its history, and of aesthetics. These conditions, of course, presume that Scott and Gayley themselves were comfortably familiar with this whole body of knowledge, in itself an amazing revelation.

The book contains seven large sections: (1) the nature and function of literary criticism; (2) principles of art; (3) principles of literature; (4) the theory of poetry; (5) the historical study of poetry; (6) the historical study of poetics; and (7) the principles of versification.

They divide literary criticism into types: judicial, inductive, personal or subjective, impersonal, analytic, synthetic, positive, negative, higher, lower, internal, external, static, dynamic, organic, scientific, philosophic, ethical, and aesthetic. Subsequent generations of literary critics have, of course, divided the field much differently, but the point is that, working without precedent, they attempted to give order to this subject. It was a daunting task.

When Scott and Gayley turn to the principles of literature, they divide the subject into two major subheadings: "Theory of Literature" and "Comparative Literature." The questions they pose for the latter are detailed, meticulous, and fundamental to the study of the subject:

(1) What form does the general law of art-evolution assume when it manifests itself in the growth of literature? . . . (2) How have these conditions affected the development of literature? (3) What facts of physical, social, political, or religious life will serve as permanent data to which any stage of literary growth may be referred? . . . (4) Why do certain types of literature become prominent at certain epochs in history? (5) Why should certain literary forms and ideas persist from generation to generation, or recur at intervals? (6) Is there any law governing the times of such recurrence? (7) What signs accompany the rise, the maturity, and the obsolescence of a given type? (8) Does one literary type, as epic,

ever pass into another, as drama, by a definite process of transformation? and, if so, (9) what are the modifying influences which effect such a metamorphosis? (248, 249)

"The Theory of Poetry" focuses on both theoretical and practical aspects of the production of poetic works. The first question is determining the relation of poetics to rhetoric and both of these to stylistics as defined by the Germans. The authors seem to be seeking a general theory of literature that embraces both rhetoric and poetics. In their discussion, they open up a fundamental question about poetry: is it imitative (Aristotle and his intellectual descendants) or creative (Bacon with roots in Plato)? The annotations in this section are particularly full for Aristotle's *Poetics,* Arnold's *Essays in Criticism,* Coleridge's *Literary Remains,* Dryden's *Works,* Emerson's *Works,* Goethe, Hegel's *Aesthetic,* Kant's *Critique of Judgment,* Lessing's *Laocoön,* Schiller, Shelley, Wordsworth, and Swinburne. For a comprehensive view of both poetry and its theory and practice, as perceived at the end of the nineteenth century, this chapter is an indispensable guide.

It seems fairly safe to say that the effect of this book on a modern scholar is overwhelming. It reflects an astonishing quantity of reading drawn from a familiarity with aesthetics, literary criticism, and literature in general. It is an extraordinary undertaking, combining dogged labor and unparalleled imagination.

5

Reorganization, Recognition,
and Reality

B Y THE FALL of 1901, Scott had developed those courses he
most wanted to teach and which would be best remembered
by his students. Although the number of courses he taught
had decreased somewhat, he still had too much classroom
work to do. On October 16, 1901, he wrote to the board of regents, on
Demmon's behalf, appealing for money for more help. Three of his
courses, 4, 4a, and 18, had increased by a total of ninety-one students.
"This means," Scott pointed out, "the reading and correcting of more
than 300 additional themes each week, the total number of such themes
required each week being about 800." He asked the regents to appoint
Miss Mary Plant, who graduated the previous year, to be paid $300 for
her assistance in paper grading. He was currently employing her at his
own expense (FNSP).

On June 17, 1902, Demmon made a plea for the fall term. "The Pilgrim Fellowship, which has yielded *three hundred dollars* the past year
now lapses. Mr. Maurice G. Fulton, A.M., the holder of this Fellowship,
has spent two hours a day through the year as Assistant to Professor
Scott, and his assistance is quite necessary to the proper conduct of that
work. He is a very efficient man, and I would respectfully ask that pro-
vision be made for his continuance at the same salary" (UMBR). The Pilgrim Fellowship was earned by Scott's alertness and ability as an entre-
preneur. He had persuaded A. C. Wisner of the Pilgrim Publishing
Company to offer a fellowship in rhetoric and English composition for

the purpose of investigating and improving methods of teaching those subjects in the schools.

During the 1902–1903 academic year, Scott made an adjustment in his teaching load. He converted English 21, his course in the development of rhetorical theory, into a graduate seminar, which he describes as a "Seminary in the History and Theory of Rhetoric. The subject investigated is the nature and origin of the leading types of prose structure. A few lectures are given on the general outlines of rhetorical theory, with especial attention to the sociological and psychological interpretation of rhetorical processes" (UMC, 1902–1903). That description strongly suggests that in the course Scott was combining rhetorical history and theory, and that he was anticipating modern work in sociolinguistics and the applications of psychology to rhetoric. As we have seen, the latter was already a staple of his courses.

In the spring semester Scott offered English 21a, "Problems of Rhetoric," a continuation from the fall term of English 21 and also restricted to graduate students. "Among the problems to be investigated are: the theory of economy [obviously a topic influenced by Spencer's *Philosophy of Style*]; the psychology of figures of speech; the rhythm of prose; the sociological basis of the principles of usage; the origins of prose; the morphology of publication; development of paragraph structure."

In the fall of 1903, the Department of Rhetoric was created. Available evidence suggests that the separation of Rhetoric from English had been coming for some time and that it was welcomed by all involved. Isaac Demmon wrote the regents for discussion at the April 1903 meeting:

I would again raise the question whether the time has not come for dropping the word *Rhetoric* from my title, thus leaving the sole charge of that work to Professor Scott. On account of his long service and his enthusiasm and efficiency in the conduct of the courses in Rhetoric and English Composition, I have gradually relinquished into his hands the direction of that side of the work. Furthermore, the rapid increase in the Elections in English Literature under our new system, and the need of developing still further this part of our work, have suggested to me the propriety and the desirability of turning over to Professor Scott the entire responsibility for the work he has shown such conspicuous ability to handle. (UMBR)

The division was made official by the regents, with Demmon's title changed to professor of English, and Scott's to professor of rhetoric. The men teaching in the department were given their choice of staying with English or going with Scott into rhetoric.

According to Clarence D. Thorpe, "The Department of Rhetoric came into existence as a separate unit—mainly, it is said, because Professor Scott wished it so" (Shaw, *Survey* 2:560). But he adds that there was no disturbance to the course. At this time, there existed a total of sixteen courses, four of which were new. One, "Prose Rhythms," the unique design of Scott, was included merely because of Scott's interest in literary problems. It is doubtful that there was anything injudicious in Scott's aggressive pursuit of his own department. The fact is that by 1903, the Department of English had undergone a long series of name changes, and with the gradual increase in interest in literature, offerings had become quite large, so that, in actuality, the division was both natural and advantageous to both disciplines. Scott had developed most of the advanced work in rhetoric, and his courses remained pretty much the core of the Department of Rhetoric for the next twenty-five years (561).

It is difficult, so many decades away from the event, to determine just how all the participants felt about the division of the English Department, but it was an unquestionable triumph for Scott. At forty-three, he had an academic entity that legitimized the field to which he had given so much of his time and energy. When the Rhetoric Department was formed, Scott and his colleagues moved to Old West Hall, long a landmark on the Michigan campus. The building was in poor condition, actually condemned several times, but it became a living example of the old maxim that facilities are not the measure of the quality of an education. Across the hall from the room Scott used as his office and classroom, he established a rhetoric library, the nucleus of which was provided by the Macmillan Company, a gift of some three hundred thirty volumes. Valued at $260, the collection consisted of standard works in rhetoric, literature, and psychology.

In May 1903, Scott asked the regents for an additional instructor in rhetoric in the Department of Engineering.[1] With all engineering students required to take a year's work in rhetoric—first-year students assigned to the first semester, second-year students the second semester—staffing became a problem. The entering class of 1902 numbered 240, 190 of whom took rhetoric classes. The projected increase for the entering class in 1903 would not only be higher, but the classes would include as well the 50 students who had, for various reasons, deferred their work the previous year.

We now require all students to write at least one essay a week. These essays are read and criticized by the Instructor, are returned to the student for correction and are then carefully re-examined. All of this work is now in the hands of a single Instructor. This means that during the past year one man has read, criticized and re-examined not less than five thousand manuscripts,—to say nothing of his regular classroom work and of frequent consultation with individual students. It is obviously impossible for a teacher to do satisfactory work under such conditions. (UMBR)

Two sides of Scott, the teacher and administrator, also surface at this time in incidents that occurred during the writing of entrance examinations. In October 1903, Scott wrote a letter to A. H. Pattengill of the Department of Greek, explaining why a Mr. Heller was not permitted to take the entrance examination in rhetoric. Quite clearly angry because of rumors that Heller had not been fairly treated, Scott provides Pattengill with "the cold facts." An assistant had been able to secure credentials from all but one man—Heller. When approached by Scott, "he mumbled in a sullen fashion and would not reply to my question until I had repeated it three or four times. Finally he said that he had no credentials." Scott told him he must go with him to see the dean, at which time the two discovered that the man was illiterate (FNSP).

Scott's indignation on this occasion is striking when compared to a similar episode reported by writer James Oliver Curwood in an article entitled "Son of the Forests," which appeared in *McCall's Magazine,* May 1930. An older student, Curwood tells of his first experiences in Ann Arbor where he had gone to "jimmy" himself into the University of Michigan. At the time of the entrance examination, Scott gave him a long list of printed questions which provoked intense anxiety.

I tried to cover my confusion and blankness of thought by a weak grin. Professor Scott smiled back, very pleasantly. He rose from his desk and came down among us, and when he reached me he paused for a moment and laid a kindly hand on my shoulder. Then he bent down and spoke in a low voice for me alone. *"I am glad you are not starting out too hurriedly, James. You have plenty of time!"* (33)

That little gesture, much more characteristic of the Scott one gets to know from his papers and diary entries, relaxed Curwood, who passed his exams, and even more happily, established a congenial contact with Scott.

Professor Scott had a friendly talk with me alone in which he asked all about my affairs, expressed his pleasure at the success I had already achieved in story-writing, and then said that judging from my examination papers and what I had already done he believed a very large field in newspaper work was open for me in Ann Arbor, where dozens of correspondents and special writers for outside papers were paying their expenses in that way. (33)

It was characteristic of Scott to sense a capable student in distress and then to encourage him.[2]

Scott's teaching assignments in the fall of 1903, the first year the Rhetoric Department was formed, were quite similar to those of the previous year. But he added one new course, Rhetoric 13, a seminar in newspaper writing. In September 1903, he wrote to the regents, describing the course.

Willis Abbot, editor of the *Pilgrim Magazine* offers to deliver to our students without expense to them or to the University, a course of six lectures on Modern Journalism in the United States, covering the following subjects: 1. Journalism as a Profession; 2. The Organization of a Newspaper; 3. The Collection and Treatment of News; 4. Magazines and Weekly Publications. The lectures would form a part of the course in Newspaper Writing which I have announced in the Department of Rhetoric for the coming Semester.

Mr. Abbot is a graduate of the Literary Department in the class of 1884. He has had wide experience in newspaper work and is an author of repute. The proposed lectures would doubtless be an original and a valuable contribution to a subject that is just now attracting considerable attention. (UMBR)

The description of the Rhetoric Department's program that first year reflected Scott's perception of what a total program should be. The catalogue listed three kinds of courses. The first was intended to give students practice in the leading types of prose composition (narration, description, exposition, and argument). The second was intended to familiarize students with fundamental principles of rhetoric and criticism. The third combined advanced composition with the study of rhetorical and critical theory. The teacher's course was a separate entity. What can one say of such a program? It balances theory and practice; it recognizes the limits of some students and the capabilities of others; it endorses an extremely eclectic and broad-based definition of rhetoric, one including historical, theoretical, and practical work.

That Scott continued to inspire his students is testified to in a letter from Abraham Flexner of the Flexner School in Louisville, Kentucky, written early in 1905:

I cannot defer longer telling you how delighted I am with the progress and attitude of my niece. I have never seen anything so nearly miraculous as the change that has come over her since she went to Ann Arbor. Her work at Bryn Mawr last year was most depressing and when she entered your classes, she had lost much of the faith and enthusiasm with which she had entered Bryn Mawr. She has, however, completely recovered her interest and ambition; and I attribute the change chiefly to the stimulus of your teaching and personality. . . .

I have always had confidence that Hortense would "work out," and I am profoundly grateful to you not only for your interest in her, but for your most wholesome influence over her. (FNSP)

Scott's own perceptions of his students and classes are contained in his diaries. The portrait they provide is engaging and intensely human. For example, in his appreciation class, he raised the question of whether anything was gained by studying verse technique. "Spoke with a little warmth and found myself afterwards a little excited but at the same time morose with little batteries of arguments sputtering in my mind like fire-crackers." Later, he observed, "I don't care whether they study it or not, but it is pharisaism to shy at it so" (FNSD, November 12, 1903). And there were moments when his mind drifted, as when he observed a student in his seminar in newspaper writing. "As he read, he leaned far forward and let his chair lean far back until it stood poised on its two hind legs. Only a special Providence saved him or perhaps it was the grime of the oiled floor" (FNSD, November 17, 1903). Scott got especially annoyed with this same student when he "set his neighbors to laughing by asides while I was reading. Stopped reading and asked for attention—the first time I have done such a thing. Norris considers himself a privileged character" (FNSD, January 19, 1904). Scott remembered Gayley's advice to him in 1889: "Don't let them make fun of you."

If on occasion he appears to be too harsh in his judgments on the young people with whom he worked, he reveals at others the qualities which no doubt endeared him to many: his fair-mindedness and ability to encourage genuine talent. In March 1904 he writes that "in reading a student's essay I omitted a part saying it was not in taste. The student came to me after class to protest. Said it was a 'pretty hard knockdown,' that there was nothing wrong in the essay. Looked it over afterward and found there was not."

One aspect of teaching which did not give Scott a lot of pleasure was the M.A. oral examinations. When they went well, he merely observes the fact that someone was examined. But there were occasions when his colleagues behaved like prima donnas or when students did poorly. In the former he shows barely suppressed irritation; in the latter, distance and, it almost seems, a strange lack of sympathy.

Commenting on one examination, Scott says that one examiner, Rebec, asked questions from 3:00 until 3:30, at which time Demmon came, taking the 3:30 to 4:00 time slot as he had to leave at 4:00. Rebec said he would have to be excused then as well. "Accordingly in no very good humor I carried my part of the examination. After the absurd affair was over I found myself in so excited a frame of mind that I could not control my voice in speaking to Rebec. He seemed puzzled, but whether he guessed the cause of the perturbation or not I could not determine" (FNSD, May 28, 1904). In May 1905 a Miss Blunt is in trouble. "Stuffy little room with a sargasso sea of pine tables around an iron post in the center," Scott says. "Wenley, Lloyd and Rebec the other inquisitors. Rebec and I examined till 12, then took an adjournment to the next day. Miss Blunt unable to escape from the maze of her own jargon" (FNSD, May 31, 1905). They finished her examination the next day, "the candidate very red-eyed and distraught." She subsequently wrote to Mrs. Wenley that she had failed her examination (FNSD, June 1, 1905).

As a teacher and distinguished professor, Scott was aware that many of his students held him in awe, a fact which privately amused him, not because of their naiveté, but because his own personal objectivity and modesty made him uncomfortable with the role of "the great man." During the year that Elizabeth Johnstone Phillips, then an undergraduate, served as his typist, he observes sardonically that her enjoyment of the work comes from her sense of being in touch with greatness, "as if she were having glimpses of things of great pith and moment" (FNSD, October 27, 1903). Further evidence of Scott's realistic view of his own worth is to be found in an entry for January 25, 1904, when he describes the experience of sitting for his picture. "Power of imagination illustrated by the fact that one does not burst into laughter as one sits gazing into a black funnel decorated with a saw-toothed piece of card-board. One imagines one's face displayed in public looked at by admiring students" (FNSD, January 25, 1904). So much for vanity.

❖

Between 1900 and 1905 Scott traveled twice to California, providing him with unforgettable experiences. Although his father had been dead for more than a decade, his mother, two sisters, and niece lived in Pasadena. And his former teacher, collaborator, and close friend, Charles

Gayley, was at the University of California at Berkeley. In fact, Gayley had instigated Scott's appointment to the summer staff at California. On December 4, 1901, President Benjamin Wheeler asked Scott to represent the subject of English composition, telling him that the session would last from June 27 to August 5, and informing him that he would be occupied about two hours a day for five days in each of six weeks. He offered to pay $750 for the session, pretty decent money in 1902 (UCALB). Scott required little urging, accepting Wheeler's invitation on December 9. Scott was a prize attraction for the Berkeley people, for he was internationally known by this time.

Scott offered two courses: "Analysis of English Prose" and "Methods of Teaching Rhetoric and English Composition." Forty-four enrolled in the first, with twenty-eight taking the final examination; seventy-one enrolled in the second, with thirty-three taking the examination. In addition to his teaching, Scott gave lectures open to the entire summer student body on three occasions. His July 9 lecture was entitled "The Use of Pictures in the Teaching of English Composition. (Illustrated by the stereopticon)." (Scott was quick to utilize the newly developed visual aids.) On July 16 his talk was "Essay-Correcting: Can it be made a Joy Forever?" And on July 30 he delivered what became one of his best papers: "Verbal Taboos: A Study of Hated Words" (UCALC, July 5, 12, 26, 1902).

That is the public record of his visit to Berkeley, but we learn more from his letters to Isa. Scott, flattered by the suggestion, writes that "Gayley talks frequently of inviting me out here as head of a department of rhetoric, but I do not think that there is the slightest prospect of a call. In the first place Wheeler is not particularly impressed, I think, by my peculiar ideas, especially their philosophical cast. He thinks Gayley also is too pronouncedly meta-physical. And in the second place there are serious complications in the department, Wheeler being especially favorable to a man who would be held back by the importation of such a person as I am. Then, too, I am not sure that I should want to come. It would be much better to have Gayley back at Ann Arbor" (FNSP, undated letter).

Scott's social life in Berkeley that summer was quite active. He had many dinner invitations, attended plays, and went sightseeing. He also climbed several mountains, among them Old Grizzly, located in the hills behind Berkeley. On one of his evenings Scott took a trip out to Cliff House; to the Suteo Baths to watch swimmers "gamboling" in a 500-

foot tank filled with sea water; to the beach where he sits and watches the rats come out to pick up food left by people; to Campi's for lunch; to the Bohemian Club for billiards; and finally back to the boat which will take him across the bay to Oakland. "On the way home Gayley and I agreed that this sort of dissipation was pleasant now and then, but that a steady course of it would be intolerable" (MG, letter to Isa, July 27, 1902).

Two matters, in particular, appear to have motivated Scott's second trip to California, in 1905: an invitation to lecture at Brigham Young University in Provo, Utah, and the serious illness of his sister Harriet. Although Scott refers to his correspondence with Dr. J. M. Tanner, superintendent of the Mormon Church school system, others may have been instrumental in inviting him to Utah. George Henry Brimhall, president of BYU from 1904 to 1921, picked him up in a carriage and took him to the university in the afternoon, where he lectured in a big bare room in a rear building. The audience of fifty was fairly impressive because enrollment at BYU the previous year was only fifty-eight undergraduate and two graduate students.

The *Deseret Evening News* carried a brief note that "yesterday Prof. Fred Newton Scott of the University of Michigan, delivered two of the lectures he is to give on English before the Deseret Summer Institute in this city. In the afternoon his subject was 'Verbal Taboos, A Study in Antipathies to Words,' and in the evening 'The Use of Pictures in the Teaching of English Composition.' This latter lecture was illustrated by stereopticon views of pictures. Prof. Scott is a pleasing speaker, and his lectures are very enjoyable as well as being highly instructive" (June 27, 1905, 9).

Again Scott took time for sightseeing, hiking up Provo Canyon and Mt. Timpanogos, altitude 12,000 feet, offering him a clear view into the state of Nevada. On June 30 Scott left Provo for Salt Lake City, where he met Francis Marion Lyman, Joseph Fielding Smith, and Anthon Hendrik Lund, all of whom constituted the presidency of the Mormon Church. On July 2 he reached Los Angeles, transferring to the train to Pasadena. The grammar that he wrote with Gertrude Buck was in production at this time, and a trip to the post office yielded several envelopes of proofs on which he began work almost immediately. His visit to his sister Harriet proved disappointing. She was in Esperanza, a sanitorium for patients with respiratory ailments. Unfortunately, she did not recover, and he did not see this sister again.

Scott climbed Mt. Shasta, a volcanic peak which rises 12,000 feet from the plain around it. The ascent proved to be nearly disastrous for him.

I having lagged behind, was about 100 feet below when I suddenly found myself in a place from which I could not extricate myself. The furrow I was in was so steep I could not mount it with my rubber-shod feet and the furrows on each side were still steeper and glassier. I shouted to Knowles who told me to stand up and dig in my toes. Tried this, but slipped dangerously and only saved myself by digging in my pike. Painfully removed my rubbers and put them in the strap of my camera, but the soles of my shoes were too thin and the heels set in too far to catch in the ice. Struggled vainly for perhaps 15 minutes, then began slowly pushing myself up the ice by means of the pike. I could push myself up a few inches, dig my fingers into the ice, and hold on until I struck the point of the pike in again, then push up as before. Several times I slipped back and only saved myself by a savage thrust of the pike. (FNSD, August 1, 1905)

A rock, displaced by one of the others ahead of him nearly hit him in the head. Only good fortune allowed him to return to Ann Arbor in early August.

While letters from colleagues and friends across the country and public records of his involvement in professional organizations tell us about his public life, they do not begin to give us a complete picture of the work and activities which occupied him daily. For that we must turn to his diary and daybooks which, while incomplete, do, for the years he kept them, provide a remarkably detailed and intimate account. From these we learn about his involvement in university committees and clubs, his writing and reading, his private observations on his off-campus activities, his recreations, and his family. At this point in his life Scott was serving on or was involved in fifteen different committees and clubs on campus. Some of this involvement was more or less routine, for example his duties to the university senate, the administrative board, and the graduate council, as well as his obligation to attend faculty meetings.

It is impossible to disentangle Scott's work with the *University of Michigan Daily,* the *Inlander,* and the Committee for Nonathletic Student Organizations. What went on in one frequently overlapped the other. As a result of agitation in 1903, a special senate committee was created to study nonathletic student organizations. The committee recommended the creation of a board to regulate the *Daily;* the seven-member board consisted of four senate faculty members and three students. Scott, Allen Whitney, Alfred Lloyd, and Frank Sage were the first faculty members to serve, with Scott as chair. In November 1908, the senate changed the name of the group to the Board in Control of Student Publications, and "its jurisdiction was extended to cover all periodical publications edited by members of the student body" (Shaw, *Survey* 4:1904). When the *In-lander*'s problems became entangled with the *Daily*, Scott's diary reveals considerable maneuvering and opposition. The *Inlander* was put under the control of the Quadrangle Club in 1903 and made a biweekly Sunday supplement to the *Daily* in 1905. Scott, as one of the faculty most deeply involved in the Quadrangle Club and the *Daily,* was obliged to resolve the paper's problems. The basic one was financial. In fact, Buffalo printers were suing Professors Wenley and Rebec for payment of a debt owed them.

Scott's involvement on the committee on nonathletic student activities led him into resolving similar difficulties. The committee met for the first time on June 12, 1902. Its first official act was disciplinary, recommending to the faculty of the College of Literature, Science, and the Arts the withholding of a degree from a student "guilty of irregularities in connection with the affairs of the Students' Lecture Association." Another student who was involved was dismissed by the Law School. "Their appeal to the Regents for reinstatement was denied. In that same year the University Senate resolved, 'That a committee of five members of the University faculties be established, whose duty it shall be to have general supervision of the affairs of the Students' Lecture Association, the Good Government Club, and other organizations and boards of students, excepting athletic organizations'" (minutes of the University Senate, May 26, 1902, qtd. in Shaw, *Survey* 4:1828).

Scott had to attend also to membership on the Students' Lecture Association Board where there was irregular activity in the election for positions. Students sought office in the SLA because they could use it for grafting. In April 1904, Scott wasted half an hour identifying ticketholders of the SLA. "Reed [dean of the Department of Science, Literature, and the Arts] sat at a table in the N.W. corner of the room, stamping tickets and calling off the names in a loud voice. The stamp went off every ten seconds with a noise like the crash o'doom." But the students regarded registration for the banquet and all the ticket stamping and identifying of S.L.A. members as a big joke. One candidate reportedly had a room where the students lined up for tickets just as they did at the registration. "Men with tickets stood about in the hall, gave them out where they would do the most good. One man had fifteen. They used ink erasers to remove the names of the original holders" (FNSD, April 30, 1904).

The ignominious final chapters in the life of the SLA were really rather sad. In its early history, especially before the Civil War, this association was the principal means of bringing famous speakers and artists to the campus. Its popularity was fueled by the general public's desire for self-improvement. Among those who appeared were Bayard Taylor, Horace Mann, Ralph Waldo Emerson, Theodore Parker, Wendell Phillips, Horace Greeley, Carl Schurz, Artemus Ward, P. T. Barnum, J. L. R. Agassiz, Charles Sumner, Mark Twain, Bret Harte, and Matthew Arnold.

Scott must have considered at times the irony of getting involved in both nonathletic and athletic student activities. In May 1903, a letter from Stanford President David Jordan, who was not in a good frame of mind, came to Scott in his capacity as member of the Board in Control of Athletics. This board, which consisted of five professors and four students, was charged with "full control of all questions pertaining to athletics," including "the eligibility of players, intercollegiate games, leaves of absence, the investigation of charges of misconduct on the part of players, and the hiring of coaches and trainers" (Shaw, *Survey* 4:1969-70). Jordan was angry because Michigan's football coach, Fielding Yost, had stolen a player Stanford thought belonged to them, a man named Gregory who played center. Stanford had dropped him at Christmas because of academic deficiencies, so Gregory went to the Washburn School in San José to prepare himself to enter Stanford as a regular student. Gregory was doing good work, and Jordan was assured that he would be eligible to reenter Stanford. Yost, however, went out to San José and offered Gregory a full scholarship if he would play for Michigan. He also picked up Willie Heston who became one of the great backs on Yost's powerful Michigan teams of that era.

Another time-consuming and annoying matter was the battle between two groups, one of which wanted to construct an alumni memorial hall to honor those who had served this country in its wars, the other to build a student union. Around 1903, those favoring the memorial began to warm to their task. "The usefulness of this project and the obvious need for it made a strong appeal, and many argued that the Memorial Committee and the Union Committee should combine their objectives in a plan for one building. Those who were approached for contributions, scattered as they were over the length and breadth of the country, found the two campaigns confusing and suspected a duplication of effort" (Shaw, *Survey* 4:1571).

Some idea of the friction that existed between these competing groups can be inferred from an exchange of letters between Judge Claudius Grant, who favored the memorial, and Scott. In one letter, Grant warns Scott: "Early in our correspondence you stated that you

were not in opposition to us and should not interfere with our work. If
you solicit subscriptions, it will beg such interference as may ruin both
projects" (FNSP, December 10, 1904). Before both projects were completed, there was considerable confusion and a number of bruised feelings on both sides.

Equally inflammatory was a developing battle over the issuing of
teachers' diplomas. The Literary Department had, of course, been granting teachers' diplomas for some time. After 1891, the university issued
teaching certificates to all who received the teachers' diploma. Thus,
from 1891 until 1921, when the School of Education was founded, students who met the designated requirements received three credentials at
graduation: their diploma for the work in their field; a teacher's diploma;
and a legal teacher's certificate which entitled them to teach in the
Michigan schools for the rest of their lives. The arguments were over
which persons and departments were to grant these diplomas. Faculty
concern focused on the qualifications of those giving the diplomas; they
did not want people who were intellectually suspect to do that work. In
January 1904, Scott notes that the Teacher's Diploma Committee "wran-
gled" until 11 P.M. with no result. Scott favored, if not a School of Education, at least a department that would take charge of teacher training.

In addition to his regular committee assignments, Scott was occasionally involved in other kinds of university business. For example, in
the summer of 1904, he journeyed with a colleague to Detroit to nego-
tiate for an exhibition of Whistler's paintings on the Michigan campus.[3]
Like most prominent university faculty, Scott also attended receptions
for visiting dignitaries, among them the great Danish linguist Otto Jespersen and the astronomer William Hussey.

Although all these obligations and distractions consumed a good
portion of Scott's time, he did find enjoyment in a number of his associations. He was a member of a reading club that occasionally met at his
house, of the Philological Society, and of Quadrangle. Much of Scott's
campus intellectual stimulation came from the Quadrangle Club. He
often reports leaving meetings, concerts, and other events to go to its
meetings. It was nominally a student club, but students are transient
and faculty are not, so faculty dominance of the club's activities was inevitable to some degree. The faculty members were some of the university's most distinguished people. The meetings themselves are described
by the club's founder, Clarence Morrill:

After a desultory dropping-in period, order was called by the Provost and
a paper or brief lecture was presented by some member, usually a youngster,
most often a graduate student. Once in a while we had wonderful talks from

men like Scott, Wenley, McLaughlin, Cooley. Rebec was also an unfailing fount of ideas in conversation.

    After the supper a discussion followed which, at first, was general and followed the subject; but it inevitably wandered away and broke the meeting into little groups. It was in these group conversations that the wonderful intimacies between celebrated professors and callow undergraduates sprang up which gave Quadrangle its remarkable character, and which counteracted the tendency of mere numbers to swamp the individual in a university. (Shaw, *Survey* 4:1940)

This was Scott's involvement on campus; but he was equally active off campus. On more than one occasion he mentions lecturing at Orchard Lake, where Harvey was in school. He gave his talk on verbal taboos at the Battle Creek Sanitarium where he had taken a week's vacation in July 1904, spoke in St. Paul's Chapel in Detroit in September 1904, and at St. Mary's Academy at Niles on October 27, 1905.

Scott frequently appeared before teacher's groups. C. A. Krout, superintendent of the Tiffin, Ohio, public schools, invited him to speak at the Northwestern Ohio Teacher's Association annual meeting in November 1904. They heard his illustrated lecture on "The Use of the Pictorial Art in the Teaching of English Composition." He appeared before the Ann Arbor teachers in January 1905, giving a total of three lectures in three days, not in the most comfortable physical setting—"The windows being frozen down the room was like a hot-house." In late February 1905 he was on his way to Washington, D.C., to give a talk at Central High School on Whitman's prosody. In late March 1904 he coordinated the meeting date of the North Central Association with trips to the schools in Kankakee and Blue Island, Illinois.

❖

Scott's reports of MLA meetings from 1900 to 1905 are particularly interesting because he was involved in some issues of great importance. In 1897, he had been reelected as president of the Pedagogical Section, an office he would hold until the section was dissolved. In 1900, in introducing the Pedagogical Section's report, William Mead had remarked: "About two months ago the Pedagogical Section of the Modern Language Association suddenly developed a very unusual, if not alarming energy, the credit for which belongs entirely to Professor Scott, the President of the Section" (Mead [1901] xx). He had instigated a highly significant report concerning "The Graduate Study of Rhetoric," with Scott, by means of a questionnaire, surveying college teachers from coast to coast to elicit responses to three questions: "(1) Is Rhetoric, in your opinion, a proper subject for graduate work? (2) If so, what is the proper aim, what is the scope, and what are the leading problems of Rhetoric as a graduate study? (3) If Rhetoric, in your opinion, should not be admitted to the list of graduate studies, what do you regard as the strongest reasons for excluding it?" (xx).[4]

In asking these questions, Scott was making the members of MLA face up to the basic question: were they willing to consider rhetoric in a modern and comprehensive sense, or had they relegated it to a subordinate position, limited only to freshman composition, and therefore considered of no intellectual substance? Although a majority of those responding said that rhetoric was indeed worthy of graduate study, their opinion did not prevail. It is impossible to know whether or not many of these people realized the significance of the issue, but those who might have missed it were instructed by Scott's earliest Ph.D. candidate in rhetoric at Michigan, Gertrude Buck.

In the *Educational Review,* September 1901, she told her professional colleagues that "ostensibly this report deals only . . . with the highly specialized subject of 'graduate study in rhetoric'" (197). But much more is involved. For one thing, the minority who reject rhetoric as a subject for graduate study identify it with composition or theme-writing. But the majority define it as "the science or theory of the process of communication by language." This definition is crucial, for, historically, "the act of discourse has been subject to analysis, with a view to discovering its laws" (197–98). Now, for the first time, it is being examined scientifically, which means that "the graduate study of the act of discourse need take no more account of any utilitarian purpose than does graduate study in physics or in pure mathematics" (198).

Buck points out the possibilities for research: "The nature and functions of discourse, its proper conditions and results, definition of the various kinds of discourse in psychological terms, extermination of the aesthetic basis for certain rhetorical "effects"; the nature and function of figures of speech in general, of specific figures, prose rhythms, the theory of criticism, the fundamental theory of narration, the relations of argument to formal and to real logic, the exploration of a distinct and a widespread form such as the short story, the analysis of a particular method, such as George Meredith's, and so forth" (198). She also points out the close relationship between literary criticism and rhetoric when rhetoric is defined as "a comprehensive study of communication by language" (199). This statement provides a beautiful synthesis of rhetoric as Scott conceived it, opposed to the much narrower conceptions promoted by the eastern schools.

This report of the Pedagogical Section is a watershed in Scott's professional life. He had been examining the basis for this report for over ten years. He now sought endorsement from his professional organization of this vital effort. Now widely known and respected, Scott worked to elevate rhetoric to a place of distinction, over the objections of some of his less enlightened peers, and he wanted some indication of how the profession would react.

At the meeting in Cambridge in 1901, Scott was present for the report of the Pedagogical Section. The question was whether or not literary study alone, without a course in theme writing, would be sufficient instruction in prose composition for students. Again Scott sent out questionnaires to determine "conclusive proof of the value, or the futility, of requiring freshmen to write themes steadily through the year" (Mead [1902] xi). The results suggested that, although reading is an aid to writing, theme-writing was judged necessary by the majority of the respondents. Some evidence of the significance this report was accorded is the fact that fifteen pages (and in fine print no less) were given to the responses in the 1902 *PMLA*.

In 1902, the Pedagogical Section investigated the validity of opposing views in the teaching of English. One side suggested it a mistake to try to teach "the literary art" to schoolboys; Genung, in *The Practical Elements of Rhetoric,* advocated treating schoolboy efforts, no matter how lame, as "literature in the making" (Mead [1903] viii). And again, the results of the survey were given a great deal of space in the *Proceedings.* Scott had, in all three of these studies, gone to the heart of the study of rhetoric, forcing examination of the entire foundation of the school programs. The committee of the pedagogical section issuing the report expressed the hope that the discussion generated by the reports would not cease but continue because of the importance of the issues raised. That wish was in vain. MLA revised its constitution in 1903 and while article 6 provided that "the Association may, to further investigation in any special branch of Modern Language study, create a Section devoted to that end," the practical effect of this move was to disband both the Pedagogical and Phonetic Sections of the organization *(Grandgent,* (1904), xi). There may be in this history, a further insight. Correlating with the date of the dissolution, 1903, is the establishment of Michigan's Department of Rhetoric.

Scott's services to MLA were not limited to the Pedagogical Section. In 1902, he had suggested that the Committee on Bibliography prepare a list of American contributions to the philology and literature of English, German, and the Romance languages for 1901 and 1902, and that upon its completion, it be printed in *PMLA*. In 1903, when the chairman, H. A. Todd, reported that the number of articles in English was so extensive that more help was needed for the project, Scott was selected to serve in that capacity. At the same time, the committee was considering making the American bibliography "a permanent feature of the Publications of the Association" (*Grandgent* [1904], xvi).

The 1903 MLA meeting shuttled between Ann Arbor and Detroit, combining the work of MLA and of its Central Division. The latter, an offshoot for the convenience of members distant from the Atlantic seaboard, was established in 1895.[5] Scott read his paper, "The Most Fundamental Differentia of Prose and Poetry." "Read the first part in a loud brazen and unnatural voice, the last part rather better. Eulogized by the old gentleman McGill who said the paper was 'very original scholarly and'—with a little cackle of appreciation reminiscent of something in the paper, 'curious'." Scott's personal account of this MLA meeting is most interesting because of the items he omits. He does not mention the dissolution of the Pedagogical Section, over which he has presided for three-quarters of a decade. He does not mention the election of George Lyman Kittredge as president. And he does not mention the selection of William H. Carruth of Kansas, Ruth Weeks of Missouri, and himself as vice-presidents for 1904 (FNSD, December 30, 1903).

In 1904, MLA met in Providence, Rhode Island. At the opening session, "Kittredge in his cascade of gray hair preaching on the text 'Vengeance is mine!'" (FNSD, December 28, 1904). (Scott says nothing about this speech, but it would have been helpful if he had. It was not printed in *PMLA,* it is not among the Kittredge papers at Harvard, and MLA headquarters has no record of it.) When Kittredge had to go to New York on pressing business in the middle of the convention, he asked Scott to preside at the next session. Scott spoke on Brander Matthews's paper, then "read my own and got some applause for my performance on the stringed instrument" (FNSD, December 30, 1904). His paper was "The Scansion of Prose Rhythms."

Scott has a fuller account of the 1905 meeting at Haverford. He visited with a number of people who had dealings with or personal knowledge of Walt Whitman, the subject of Scott's paper at this meeting. One of these is David McKay, who was responsible for the reissue of the seventh edition of *Leaves of Grass*. It had been published by James R. Osgood, but he backed off when threatened by the attorney general of Massachusetts because of some poems considered obscene. Whitman refused to make suggested changes, instead switching publishers. McKay "spoke of a difference with the literary executors of Whitman. They wished him to include the Peter Doyle letters in his edition of Whitman's poems, but he refused. . . . Said that a medical work refers to Whitman as an invert [homosexual] because of the Peter Doyle letters" (FNSD, December 27, 1905).

Scott met Francis Howard Williams, who told him that Whitman's voice rose and fell in each line when he recited his own poems. "Said there was a story that Whitman's last words, as taken by [Horace] Traubel—who took down everything those last days—were 'I want to—-.' Both Williams and Morris said that Whitman was a free-liver in the years at New Orleans and afterward. At New Orleans he had liaisons with women of social station, and children, or at least a child, resulted. Williams had himself seen Whitman's grandson, when the latter called on the old poet at Camden in the closing years" (FNSD, December 27, 1905).

One would think that Scott was so busy that he would have been home only to eat and sleep. But his diary is full of references to family life, and, on one occasion, clearly establishes his family as his principal priority. He also made time for recreation. In fact, it seems quite clear that his recreations provided a necessary and welcome change from his professional commitments.

Scott and Isadore were fond of music and drama. Because there was no dearth of culture in Ann Arbor by the turn of the century, his diary details many occasions when they went to concerts, plays, and lectures on campus. Major performance groups toured, stopping at Michigan, which allowed Scott to hear the Pittsburgh Symphony and to watch performances of Ben Greet's Shakespeare Company. For light diversion, Scott reports a game of bridge or whist, often with his in-laws, the Thompsons, and occasionally with friends on the faculty. Also, he loved to play golf. As often as possible, he was on the links for a round, either by himself or with whoever was available.[6] Most of the time his playing companions were colleagues. Scott's game was not always predictable. On one occasion, he lofted a ball neatly into the window of a barn "where it lay on the hay as if a hen had dropped it there." On another he recounts a "brief outing spent mainly in hunting for the ball" (FNSD, July 4, 1904; June 1, 1905).

If Scott's professional life and recreations afforded him a mixture of pleasure and pain, certainly family life did no less. In November 1903, Scott notes that he spent the day in Detroit with Isadore and the chil-

dren. While there, they bought a green canary which subsequently became the special object of attention of the family cat. He reports that
"the cat made a flying leap for the bird today. No one saw him when he
jumped, but Isadore had a snap-shot glimpse of him falling in mid-air,
the cage aswing, the bird not in the least frightened. The cat fled up-
stairs but Marion hauled him out and brought him downstairs where he
was condignly punished with accompaniment of fire-cracking spittings
and frantic scratchings" (FNSD, February 18, 1904).

But these lighter moments were tempered by more serious incidents. In June 1904, while Scott was attending a meeting of the Administration Board, he was interrupted by his colleague, Fred M. Taylor,
who whispered to him that Richard, then eight years old, had broken his
leg. The doctor was just setting Richard's leg when Scott arrived. He reports being "up all night, or most of it, reading to Richard and telling
him Tabby-dog stories. If there is not a hell, there should be one for the
person or being who causes a child unnecessary pain." He spent the next
day reading to Richard as he begins his convalescence. In fact, he spent
most of the week in Richard's room, doing what work he could. On July
4, he got up early to get Richard ready to shoot firecrackers. "Put him in
chairs by the window of the closet. Out on the roof arranged a big tin
washtub as shelter for a candle. Made a handle out of an umbrella handle and a cork that he might hold the crackers at a safe distance. Richard
jumped a little at each explosion, but gurgled afterwards with delight"
(FNSD, July 4, 1904).

6

Some Major Publications

S COTT'S PUBLICATIONS in the first decade of the twentieth century were, like his interests, prolific and eclectic. His diary entries reveal a constant string of papers and books in progress, each a response to a particular interest or need that he perceived at the time. In 1903 he collaborated with George Rice Carpenter and F. T. Baker of Columbia on *The Teaching of English*. This collaboration, initiated by Carpenter, has two parts. The first, "History and Method," was written by Carpenter and Baker. Scott wrote all of the second, "The Teacher and His Training." It is a magnificent statement of what English teachers should know and be.

The teacher who has not a passion and an aptitude for imparting instruction in English, who does not feel that it is the great thing in life to live for, and a thing, if necessary, to die for, who does not realize at every moment of his classroom work that he is performing the special function for which he was foreordained from the foundation of the world,—such a teacher cannot profit greatly by any course of training, however ingeniously devised or however thoroughly applied. (306–07)

According to Scott, the main purpose of teacher training is "to give the teacher, not knowledge of his subject, but self-knowledge; not knowledge of methods of teaching, but resources to meet the exigencies of the classroom" (307). This training will enable him to distinguish between "educational forces or educational fads" (307). More specifically, Scott designates the kind of training necessary for English teachers. First is an "ability to speak and write the English language with clearness, accuracy, and freedom from bookishness" (308). He complains that many of the teachers trained in the normal schools use a stiff, rigid, and inaccurate style of speech and writing that he calls "school-master's English." The trouble with it is that it eventually corrupts the mental faculties.

A second necessity for the English teacher is that "he should be well read in English literature and English literary history" (310). Anticipating the work of the New Critics, Scott believes that the teacher should not substitute history and biography, knowledge *about* literature for literature's "own peculiar record, which in a sense is distinct from the lives of the men who wrote it or from the times in which it appeared," closely as it is related to both (310). How much reading should the teacher have done? Scott suggests C. T. Winchester's *Five Short Courses of Reading in English Literature with Biographical and Critical References* (Ginn and Co., 1892). If the candidate is not already familiar with all the works on this list, Scott advises that he start reading.

A third and obvious requirement for the English teacher is that he should be skilled in reading and correcting themes. And in a marked departure from the conventional view, Scott advises that the proper preparation for this work is knowledge of the history and theory of rhetoric. In Scott's mind, the educated teacher is not only freed from the "tyranny" of the textbook, but "he knows ways of enriching and enlivening the subject which are denied to the teacher untrained in this respect. Above all, a thorough-going study of rhetoric absolves the teacher from the finicalness and intolerance, characteristic indeed of the sciolist in any line of thought, but peculiarly characteristic of the sciolist in rhetoric" (315–16).

A special qualification for the English teacher Scott is describing is professional knowledge of grammar. He felt it was the worst taught subject in the curriculum because teachers did not have a proper training in (1) "a study of the development of the English language from the earliest times to the present; (2) a study of the general principles of comparative philology, or the science of language; (3) a study of the psychology of speech" (316). The qualified teacher should at least have read Emerson's *History of the English Language,* Sweet's *History of Language;* and Titchener's *Primer of Psychology.* Scott summarizes: "Of the three subjects specified the first is doubtless the most indispensable, for a teacher who is ignorant of the history of his mother-tongue is disqualified for the teaching of its grammar. . . . The comparative study of language will free the student from a superstitious reverence for grammatical rules, and give him an insight into the true nature of usage and idiom. From a study of the psychology of speech he will learn through what processes the child acquires his native tongue, and how the various elements of the language present themselves to the child-mind at different stages of its development" (316).

A modern English teacher will not find these remarks extraordinary because most have been required, as undergraduates, to take courses both in the history of the English language and in modern English grammar. In the first five years of this century, however, such a stance was radical indeed.

In this work, Scott questions also whether theme correcting is intrinsically joyless or merely accompanied by factors which make it that way. In his mind, what makes it far less pleasant than it should be is that the expectations for correction are too high, that often teachers lack any aptitude or training for the job, or any real understanding of its purpose. More to the point, we need to look at the whole issue:

What is the object of composition work in the schools? . . . The teacher of composition who does no more than to cultivate in his students a facility of speech has overlooked the main point. His first and most important duty is to develop character, to bring out in the boy or girl the man or woman that is to be, to fit the student for the part he is to play in life . . . so far as his use of language is concerned. (334–35)

No one else at this time had bothered to make such a fundamental inquiry.

Another of the pedagogical projects in which Scott was involved was his collaboration with Gertrude Buck on a *Brief English Grammar,* published in 1905. In his memorial tribute upon Miss Buck's death, Scott accepts credit only for the concept, granting to Miss Buck the majority of the writing. In the preface they say that

it seems the invariable tendency of any complicated system of linguistic forms, when made a subject of study, *to cut itself off from the living processes which gave rise to it, and become in the student's mind mere matter, an arbitrary thing-in-itself, dead and meaningless* [italics mine]. The danger of this tendency has been abundantly recognized in recent text-books of English grammar and composition, which have attempted by various methods to recall the meaning to the form, to re-connect the word on the page with the thought which created it and the situation which shaped and modified it. (3)

They may not view grammar so differently from others, but the context in which they teach it is crucial. The words "communication," "social function," and "organic" are not found in other grammars.

In fact, many of their philosophical and theoretical statements about language and grammar anticipate modern descriptive linguists. For example, at the outset they establish the proposition that the spoken language is primary, the written language secondary, a position central in modern descriptive linguistics. Another position of modern descriptive linguistics taken by Scott and Buck in this book is that one cannot live by stringent rules. "And so grammar does not say to us directly, 'you must speak thus and so,' but only 'English people at the present time do speak thus and so, for the following reasons'" (13).

A third modern position taken by Scott and Buck is their insistence on constant change as a fundamental principle of language. "Even Shakespeare used some words that we do not understand without reference to a dictionary, and certain forms of speech which we call 'ungrammatical'" (12). Overall, the grammar is an interesting book, primarily for its philosophical and theoretical positions. It is important to remember that Charles Fries, who helped lead the movement for language reform, was one of Scott's students at Michigan, and that *Webster's Third International Dictionary,* which incorporated the principles articulated by Scott and Buck in 1905, ran into fierce opposition from a number of guardians of the language who felt, in 1961, that Webster's people were doing something very radical. And all this occurred over five decades after Scott and Buck wrote their brief English grammar.[1]

In 1905 Scott also collaborated with his old colleague and friend, Joseph Denney, on one of the friendliest and most inspirational books he ever wrote: *Aphorisms for Teachers of English Composition.* The beauty of this collection of wise observations about the way writing ought to be taught is that it distills Scott and Denney's teaching philosophy. Because of the nature of the book, it is difficult to summarize it. Instead, we choose to let it speak for itself, in selected aphorisms under their appropriate headings.

OF SYMPATHY

Imagine a mother saying to her sick child, "What a nuisance you are! The idea of your falling ill when I am so busy with other things. It is just your natural meanness. Here, take this medicine and get well as quick as you can. I can't afford to waste much time on you." We should know what to think of such a mother. But how much better is a teacher of English who talks to a badly

trained child in such a way as this? "What do you mean by spelling and punc-
tuating in this ridiculous fashion? Where were you brought up? You write like
a savage. How do you suppose I can take time to mark such papers as these?"
Somebody once remarked that what the teacher of English composition most
needs is a "philosophy of adolescence." The remark was laughed at, but is it not
true for the kind of teacher quoted above? (9)

❖

THE DISMAL SCIENCE

Some teachers regret that so indispensable a subject as English composition
should be so disagreeable: others have a grim satisfaction in the thought that so
disagreeable a subject has proved to be so indispensable. (11, 12)

❖

SELF AND THE OTHER SELF

When a pupil has learned to express himself, he has learned just half of the
art of composition. When he has learned to communicate himself to his fellow
beings, he has learned the other half. (15)

Scott elaborated other procedures, all including what we would
today call prewriting; he and Denney also advocate writing with a purpose. Writing with a purpose implies a specific audience, and it teaches
some general principles. "Though we are thinking all the time of the
purpose of the subject matter, we are also raising questions of art and are
teaching the laws and principles of art,—unity, selection, proportion, variety, method and the rest. These questions are most easily answered
when a particular reader is named beforehand" (20).

In none of his work does Scott's new sense of assurance appear so distinctly as in his publications on issues of interest to the profession at
large. "College Entrance Requirements in English," originally a paper
read at the sixth annual meeting of the North Central Association of
Colleges and Secondary Schools in Chicago, March 29, 1901, is Scott's
second paper on a subject which was causing a great deal of discussion
among both high school and college teachers.

Scott was ideally prepared to enter this dialogue, more so, in fact,
than almost any of his contemporaries. For one thing, he lived in an area
distant from the universities that required entrance examinations. High
school students knew about many things, but not necessarily the contents of the books on the exclusive lists that were being originated in the
more elite eastern schools. No one knew that better than Scott, who had
served long on the Committee on Entrance Requirements. In addition,
unlike some university scholars, Scott kept in close touch with the situation in the public schools. As noted, he frequently spoke at high schools

and at state English teachers' conferences, notably those in Indiana, Kansas, and Minnesota. As a member of the Michigan Schoolmasters' Club, he was in frequent contact with faculty of secondary schools. And his longtime association with Wilson Farrand, headmaster of the Newark Academy (on the Entrance Requirements Committee), and Edwin Miller, assistant superintendent and former principal in the Detroit schools, provided him ample understanding of the goals and shortcomings in the schools. Most significant of all, Scott was for years a member, and eventual president, of the North Central Association of Colleges and Secondary Schools.

According to Scott, discussion of entrance requirements had stalled on teaching methods, curriculum, and lists of required books. He wanted to start further back and ask some different questions: "What do we mean by college-entrance requirements? More particularly, what ought we to mean by entrance requirements in English?" (365). For Scott, entrance requirements imply some sort of relationship between the secondary schools and the colleges. At that time, there were two distinct conceptions of what that relationship should be: the feudal and the organic. The feudal system originated at Oxford and Cambridge and was transplanted to this country at Harvard and Yale. Under it, the university dictates to the preparatory schools arbitrary conditions under which students will be admitted for college work. Its message is: "Fit pupils to pass our examinations and the drawbridge will be lowered. If you cannot fit them, you are no longer of any interest to us. We will have none of you" (365–66).[2] Scott sees two especially undesirable consequences of this kind of attitude. First, it promotes teaching to the test regardless of the real educational needs of students. Second, it deprives teachers of necessary independence and initiative.

Speaking out of a tradition which had been developing at Michigan for more than half a century, Scott offers an alternative: the organic conception, which he calls an "emanation of the Teutonic mind. Embodied first in the school system of Prussia, it was conveyed to America by means of Cousin's famous *Report* and found its way into the Northwest Territory at a crucial period in the history of our western education" (368).[3] By "western education" Scott means primarily the schools which made up the western conference, now known as the Big Ten, plus others such as Chicago, Cornell, Colorado, and Nebraska.

Scott's metaphor for the organic conception is a living body where "the university and the schools are inseparable members." In such an organism, there is mutual dependency, each contributing to the well-being of the other. Scott recognizes that this is an ideal, of course, but as the organic conception emerges, it will not be a mere imitation of the German model; it will conform to the needs and ideals of American society. Essentially, it will offer: "(1) agreement as to what constitutes the normal course of development of young persons of high school age; (2) a trustworthy means of communication through which the university, on its part, may learn what the high schools can do, and the high schools, on their part, may learn what the university wants" (370). In one of the most salient passages he ever wrote, he responds to the question asked of universities: what are your requirements in English?

We make no formal requirements. We only point to our needs. What we want is young men and women whose literary instincts are normal and whose literary habits are good. We want students who know what good literature is and enjoy reading it; who can express themselves with a fair degree of ease and accuracy; and who have a taste for what is simple and sincere, as opposed to what is tawdry, or mawkish, or vulgar, in their own writing and the writing of their fellow students. (373)

Scott is no woolly-minded idealist, however. He knows that the organic conception of the relationship between the university and the public schools is still in a developmental stage, that while some might accept the challenge posed by the organic conception, most would, under pressure from other subjects, take the line of least resistance. He recognized as well the lack of any effective means of articulation between the university and the college. For the present, the university needs to give some idea of what it wants. On the other side, secondary school principals have to encourage the study of English and protect it from erosion, and teachers need to prepare themselves still better.

In December 1905 Scott published "The Figurative Element in Grammatical Terminology." What images, he asks, are actually aroused in the minds of children by the grammatical terms that are presented to them? To find out, he asked one of his college classes to respond to four sentences from Whitney's *Essentials of English:* "1. The parts of speech are put together to form sentences. 2. The verb governs the noun. 3. The verb is irregular. 4. The pronoun is in the objective case." He says he called attention to the terms, "parts of speech," "govern," "irregular," and "objective case," before asking his students to describe for him the images these terms evoked when they were grade school children. The responses were truly unique.

The "parts of speech," Scott discovered, to about one-third of his class, meant the organs of speech: the lips, tongue, and vocal chords. But one student supplied a marvelously vivid set of images accompanying the term: "I remember having a very lively sense of a kind of sky-rocket explosion connected with this phrase when the teacher first mentioned it to me. A 'speech' was a word; but 'parts of speech' was an explosion of the word that sent bits of sounds or perhaps letters flying in all directions. Of course some one had to gather them up again to put them into a sentence. The image still stays with me, in a somewhat faded condition, when I hear the expression" (3).

The sentence in which the verb is said to govern the noun produced an equally unusual set of images. One student imagined "a small king verb seated upon a wee throne and holding his sceptre over a frightened little noun" (4). Another came to dislike the domineering verb and developed a secret sympathy for the noun. Still another associated the verb with an aggressive father and a quiet and proper mother. If students had trouble with verbs "governing" nouns, they were totally confounded by the term "irregular" applied to verbs. Scott says almost all his students thought the irregular verb was somehow naughty. One associated it with a child who attended school irregularly. Sometimes a verb was there; sometimes it was not. Still others associated the term with malformation or disfiguration.

The terms "objective" and "case" did not produce any clearer images. Many said they had confused "objective" with "objectionable"; thus, "a pronoun in the objective cases was undesirable or out of harmony with the rest of the sentence, or it was conceived as obstinately objecting to the other words in the neighborhood" (5). The term "case" elicited varied responses. To one student the term called up images of a bad case, a case knife, and a sausage case. Another interpreted the term to mean some sort of position: "I thought that the space before a verb was the nominative case and after the verb the objective case. The sense of the word was that of a sort of socket into which a word was slipped and labeled" (5).

What conclusions can be drawn from such data? "If in a class-room where a recitation in grammar is going on one could for the briefest interval of time cast upon a screen the motley procession of images which troop through the brains even of the brightest and most thoughtful of the pupils, how empty would seem the clatter of the verbal machinery, how vain and trivial the mummery of the sentence-diagram!" (5). Equipped with such empirical evidence, Scott assigns a more decisive cause for this curious and heretofore unexplored phenomenon. The problem is not primarily with grammatical terminology: "It lies in the failure of the teacher to connect grammatical conceptions, as soon as they arise, with genuine, living interests in the minds of the pupil" (5, 6). And he reiterates a point that is basic to all his beliefs about language study: "When language is regarded as a vital bond between man and his fellows; when grammar is taught as a theory of the structure and function of that bond; when the study of grammar is at every point connected with the pupil's own use of language and with its use in literature—the teacher may employ whatsoever terms he will" (7).

In 1903 Scott had been commissioned to write the articles on rhetoric and figures of rhetoric for the *New International Encyclopedia*. "Rhetoric" contains three sections: (1) a definition of rhetoric, complete with its etymology, and its scope; (2) a brief history of rhetoric; (3) a bibliography. It is a valuable document because it reveals, in concentrated form, the breadth of Scott's conception of rhetoric, and explains the range of courses he offered at Michigan at this time. In essence, he anticipated most of the new directions rhetoric has taken in its latest revival in English departments over the past thirty-five years.

Rhetoric is, "taken broadly, the science and art of communication in language. The tendency of modern textbooks, however, has been to broaden the scope of rhetoric to include everything pertaining to the art of composition." It "properly belongs to that branch of knowledge which is concerned with the relations of men in society" (763). More specifically, it is concerned with the group of activities through which "men express themselves and convey their thoughts and feelings to their fellows" (763). Scott includes everything from gestures, picture writing, and similar activities, which he calls "primitive modes of thought conveyance," to "the most highly elaborated modes, such as the arts of architecture, sculpture, music, painting, and oral and written speech" (763). This interest in the large questions about the ways in which human beings express themselves and communicate explains the activities of Scott's personal and professional life: his love of painting and sculpture and the considerable reputation he acquired as an art critic; his love of music and his obvious interest in all kinds of written products, from what we today call "creative writing" to scholarly and nonfiction works.

He explains that "the subject matter of rhetoric is thus seen to be distinguished from that of allied sciences by the fact (1) that its medium is language and (2) that the emphasis is thrown upon the phase of communication, i.e., upon prose. But although rhetoric is primarily the science of communication, it is still concerned to a large extent with questions of expression" (763). Communication encompasses three phases: psychological, social, and formal. Psychological problems involve the very nature of a writing or speaking human being and the mental activities that characterize composing, that is, "the nature and genesis of expression," "the characteristics of genius," "the acquirement and cultivation of the speech habit," and "the factors operating in the experience of the individual to turn his self-expression into the communicative channel" (763). The first of these activities was treated by Darwin in his *Expression of the Emotions* and by his opponents. The second was addressed by Lombroso and others.[4] The third had been taken up by psychologists contemporary with Scott, but the fourth was practically unexplored. According to Scott, "it is obvious . . . that every successful writer or speaker is on one side receptive, on the other productive. As receptive he is a product of heredity and of the social environment, while as productive he exhibits the faculties of invention and social imagination" (763).

The principal questions to be examined are (1) "the typical modes of response on the part of individuals and groups of individuals in the community" and (2) the processes which determine "the formation of social or public opinion." On the second issue he cites Gideon Diall's *Psychology of the Aggregate Mind of an Audience* (Terre Haute: The Inland Publishing Company, 1897), which "has endeavored to show that the minds of an assemblage listening to a powerful speaker undergo a curious process called fusion, by which the auditors are reduced as it were to a single individual, whose characteristics are those of an impulsive youth" (764). This is a remarkable anticipation of the phenomenon observed in Nazi Germany prior to World War II. Scott warns that it is important to distinguish "as Tarde has done *(L'Opinion et la foule,* Paris, 1901), between a 'crowd' and a 'public,' the associative principle of the former being physical, of the latter psychical" (764).[5] It is obvious that in his theoretical work Scott was anticipating the work of modern psycho- and sociolinguists, and rhetoricians who have turned to cognitive psychology and social constructionism to enrich current conceptions of the nature and function of rhetoric.

Much of the history Scott presents in this brief article contains information well known to specialists in rhetoric, but his choice of individuals responsible for its evolution is, in some cases, surprising. He notes, with qualification, that rhetoric "seems" to have been invented by the Sicilian Corax and further developed by his pupil Tisias. Gorgias, while ambassador to Athens in 427 B.C., introduced rhetoric to Athens.

"It was the Athenian orator Antiphon (q.v.), however, who first combined the theory with the practice of rhetoric. The great publicist Isocrates (q.v.) founded a school of rhetoric, which he called the 'art of persuasion,' that was famous from 390 B.C. until his death" (764).

Scott acknowledges that Aristotle's *Rhetoric,* written about 322 B.C., contains contributions of greatest value, but "the system of scholastic rhetoric which finally became established was formulated principally by the practical rhetorician Hermagoras (q.v.), who wrote about 110 B.C." (764). His system was founded directly upon that of the Stoic philosophers. Scott lists the Greek Hermogenes and the Roman Quintilian as the most important representatives of this school. Other ancients he mentions as important to the tradition of rhetoric include Longinus, Dio Chrysostomus, Dionysius of Halicarnassus, Himerius, and Aphthonius, who "composed in the latter half of the fourth century exercises that were destined to supersede those of Hermogenes" (764). He considers Renaissance treatises to be based principally upon Quintilian's *Institutes of Oratory,* among them Leonard Cox's *Art or Craft of Rhetoryke* and Thomas Wilson's *Art of Rhetorique* in England and those of Tonquilin and Courcelles in France. The startling aspects of Scott's abbreviated history are his failure to mention Plato, in whose ethics of rhetoric he deeply believed, his brief treatment of Aristotle, and his omission of Cicero as a major influence on Renaissance rhetorics.

The article entitled "Rhetoric, Figures of," although briefer, is full of interesting matter and common sense. "Figures are commonly said to give strength and beauty to style, but it would perhaps be truer to say that they have the power of arousing in the reader or hearer the same emotional and imaginative processes which gave birth to them in the mind of the writer" (764). Here is a precise and meaningful explanation of stylistic distinctions which denies the notion of figures as embellishments rather than forms growing organically out of the materials and the communicative and expressive needs of a particular writer working in a particular context.

The papers he published in *PMLA* during this period straddle the gap between rhetorical and literary scholarship. As noted in the last chapter, they were first given at MLA meetings. "The Most Fundamental Differentia of Poetry and Prose" appeared in 1904 and "The Scansion of Prose Rhythm" in 1905. In the first, Scott intended, if possible, "to determine the most vital, fundamental, and essential trait which discriminates one type from the other, more particularly in the primitive stages of their development" (225; all page references are to *The Standard of American Speech.*) He begins with four assumptions. The first is that the difference between prose and poetry is fundamental, not superficial. The second is that "all literature, whether poetry or prose, is included in the circle of the arts. Literature, I mean, is cognate with architecture, sculpture, painting, and music. It is evolved from the same general sources, observes the same general laws, and manifests the same general characteristics" (225). A third is that art results from an attempt to express and convey an idea, feeling, or experience to others. A fourth assumption is that every art process "originated in some act which was at the time useful in preserving the life of man or in maintaining his social integrity" (226).

With these assumptions in mind, Scott suggests an examination of the differentia which have been proposed between prose and poetry, some having to do with content, one, at least, with form. He rejects the assertion that "poetry is the organ of the imagination, prose the organ of reason," citing numerous examples of imaginative work in the other arts and in prose, and making the point that some prose is far more imaginative than some poetry, as, for example, Burke's prose and Pope's poetry (226).

Scott also rejects the argument that poetry has greater emotional content than prose. "Wordsworth's *Excursion* pales its uneffectual fire in the presence of Carlyle's *French Revolution*" (227). He also rejects "distinguishing marks based upon the degree of some artistic quality, such, for example, as insight into man or nature, nobility of emotion, grade of pleasure aroused in the hearer, elevation of subject-matter, creative power of the writer, and so on" (227). To state his case succinctly, he says:

(1) Prose is "expression for communication's sake."
(2) Poetry is "communication for expression's sake." (233)

Scott maintains this distinction in the works of sophisticated writers, citing the differences between Bacon and Shakespeare, for example. Bacon's work is primarily expression for the sake of communication; Shakespeare's is communication for the sake of expression. His basic distinction, then, derives from context:

The difference between poetry and prose has its root in the difference between two great and ever-recurring social situations,—first, the situation in which a member of society is moved to verbal utterance mainly by a desire to communicate himself to his fellow men, the desire for expression being present but subordinate; second, the situation in which one man, or a number of men acting in concert, are moved by a desire to express or give vent to the feelings and ideas which arise in them, the desire being the natural psychological necessity that thought and feeling in simple natures must have some motor outlet. (245)

Almost alone among his contemporaries, Scott was scrutinizing fundamental issues of language which had not yet been articulated.

"The Scansion of Prose Rhythm," also written for *PMLA,* is one of Scott's more technical papers, and it both preoccupied and troubled him for a longer period of time than anything else he was working on at that period of his life. His diary is full of references to the paper, and his reading reveals the variety of sources which he examined in his search for information on the subject. He wants to discover the rhythm of prose because "to chart it and discover its law is to effect for prose what metrical scansion does for verse" (247; all page references are to *The Standard of American Speech.*) Scott is aware that a number of people, among them Robert Louis Stevenson, say quite confidently that prose rhythm is not reducible to laws because it is quite lawless, and any attempt to discover such will fail. But he nonetheless believes it is possible. He returns to the distinction he made between prose and poetry in "The Fundamental Differentia of Poetry and Prose," arguing that these two situations, the communicative and the expressive, and the mental attitudes accompanying each, account for the differences in the rhythm of poetry and of prose.

Noting the close affinity between expressive discourse and the dance, Scott says that "we may infer that what constitutes the characteristic pattern of the expressional rhythm is the recurrence of brief units of sound or motion at regular intervals, the recurring units being so grouped as to show within small compass a measured progression" (251). He calls this rhythm *nutation.*

The communicative situation exhibits a much different rhythmical pattern. Scott cites the example of one person yelling to another to save him from being hit by a train: "Get off the track." He notes a crescendo glide through "get off," then a decrescendo through "the track." One can detect the same kind of pattern in traditional calls to animals: "Co-o-o-boss" to the cow; "Whoo-ee" to pigs; "Here Vic! Here Vic!" to a dog. "The main characteristic of the communicative rhythm is a rushing, surging, gliding movement, which starting at some minimum of force, rapidity, pitch, or suspense, rises to a climax in one or all of these particulars and then falls away again." He calls this rhythm *motation.*

To discover the essential elements of motation, Scott employs routine scansion of lines, although he is well aware of the arguments against it, especially as they apply to poetry. The child, for example, will read the following line as indicated:

All night'| the dread'| less an'| gel un'| pursued'.

Admittedly, such a reading wrenches meaning badly, but defenders of this kind of scansion insist that "routine scansion is the natural form of poetry to a child" (258). Through the routine scansion, eventually the ear learns to appreciate other rhythms. (Scott has drawn from Joseph B. Mayor in *Chapters on English Metre* [London: C. J. Clay and Sons, 1886], 6.) But routine scansion of prose presents some problems that routine scansion of verse does not. The principal element of rhythm in verse (at least in languages which have Germanic origins) is stress. But the principal element of prose rhythm is pitch. With this distinction in mind, then, Scott asserts that the "organic unit of prose rhythm consists of an upward followed by a downward glide" (259), a movement identified as a *motative arc*. All prose contains such arcs arranged in sequence, with their character and interrelation determining the rhythm. (In this Scott has identified the qualities inherent in music: the difference between beat and phrase.)

Granted, a person reading prose no more emphasizes this motative arc than one reading poetry falls into the sing-song of routine scansion. Scott gets very technical in describing the complexity of motative arcs, explaining how the voice rises, pauses, and descends. He has in mind the musical terms—crescendo, intervals, cadence, and tune. There are two types of motative arcs, the suspensive and the pathetic.

In the suspensive type the voice, beginning on the natural keynote, rises in a glide or series of glides to a certain maximum. Here a pause occurs to which we may give the name *medial pause*. The voice then begins again at the altitude where it left off or slightly below (sometimes, though rarely, above), and descends in a glide or series of glides to the tonic. Usually the upward glide is marked by a crescendo of force and an increasing rate of movement, the downward glide by a decrescendo and decreasing rate of movement; but these accompaniments are subject to variation. (262)

In the pathetic arc,

The voice glides up to the apex, then, without a break, glides down again for a certain distance. The medial pause comes in the descending segment of the arc, occurring normally at an interval of a fourth (or a minor fourth) below the maximum. . . . the effect of this interval is to give to the cadence a plaintive quality. (262–63)

Scott argues that these primary types of prose rhythms, exhibiting the suspensive and the pathetic arcs, are fundamental to English prose rhythm "and by varying their constituent elements, may be produced, I think, all of the more frequent rhythms of English prose" (264). He gives examples of each, using Daniel Webster's *Second Bunker Hill Oration* for the suspensive.

The consequences of this battle | were just of the same importance as the revolution itself. (262)

Macaulay's essay on Samuel Johnson shows the pathetic.

His passions on the contrary, were violent even to ^ slaying | against all who leaned to whiggish principles. (263)

The vertical line indicates the medial pause, the caret the highest point of the arc. Obviously there are many other sub-types.

Scott concedes that "this analysis of prose rhythm, even if it be correct, has hardly stormed of this philological stronghold the outermost fortress" (270). He acknowledges that he has overlooked a great many more factors—stress, alliteration, distribution of phrasal sections, balance of word and phrase, and so on—but says he has temporarily put them aside so that he could focus on one feature: the prose foot or unit of scansion. Aware of the extremely subjective nature of his method of scanning, Scott poses this question: "If others do not scan these sentences as I have scanned them, what becomes of the theory?" Well, if his scanning agrees with that of no one else, then "I shall be forced to concede either that I have not made myself clear, because of defects in the symbolism and mode of explanation, or (reluctantly) that my sense of rhythm is defective. In the latter case this paper will have, I hope, at least a transitory interest as a document in pathological psychology" (271).

Prose rhythm is still a subject not well understood, and few individuals have had the courage to tackle it. Scott's theories are unique for his time because of the scientific focus and his attempt to take stylistic analysis beyond the intuitive.

Scott demonstrates his continued involvement in literary topics as well as the dominance of aesthetics in his understanding of literature in his paper, "Carlyle's Dante," published in the *New York Nation* in December 1903. He quotes Carlyle's depiction of Dante in *Heroes and Hero-Worship:*

After all commentaries, the Book itself is mainly what we know of him. The Book;—and one might add that portrait commonly attributed to Giotto, which, looking on it, you cannot help inclining to think genuine, whoever did it. To me it is a most touching face; perhaps of all faces that I know, the most so. Lonely there, painted as on vacancy, with the simple laurel wound round it; the deathless sorrow and pain, the known victory which is also deathless;—significant of the whole history of Dante! (279; all page references are to *The Standard of American Speech*)

As Scott points out, Carlyle could not have been looking at the Giotto portrait because it had been covered with whitewash and even its location was not known until it was "uncovered on the wall of the Bargello by Kirkup, Wilde, and Bezzi, July 21, 1840" (280–81)—Carlyle's lecture on Dante preceded that date. The reference thus raises the question, "What portrait was before Carlyle's eye, or in his mind's eye, when he composed the description?" (281). Scott got a plausible answer from Theodore Koch, who joined the Michigan library staff in 1904. In a private letter, Koch, who had an established reputation as the bibliographer of Dante, told Scott that "the search for the Bargello portrait having been going on for some three years before 1840 (eight years, according to Karus, *Dante*, 168), Giotto's name was naturally much bruited about, and Carlyle caught it up when he was describing an altogether different type of portrait" (281–82).

Then, from correspondence with Carlyle's son, Alexander, Scott learned that Carlyle had in his possession two portraits of Dante. The first was by the engraver, Stefano Tofanelli. The second is "of the Tofanelli-Morghen type, but it is much smaller and poorer than the portrait referred to above [the Tofanelli]. The design is by E. Cateni, the engraving by Lasinio Figlio" (283). Alexander Carlyle, who owned them at the time Scott wrote this paper, gave Scott descriptions of each. From these descriptions, Scott deduced that the Tofanelli engraving most closely approximated Carlyle's description, because of the laurel wreath wound about the head and other features upon which Carlyle focused. The irony is that Victorian scholars and Carlyle specialists appear to be unaware of this article. Charles Harrold and William Templeman, authors of one of the most popular Victorian prose anthologies in the mid-twentieth century, write in a footnote to the Giotto reference, "just what portrait Carlyle alludes to is not known" (183). Nor is Scott's essay included in their bibliography of works on Carlyle.

7

A Reputation Established

I N 1905–1906 AND 1907–1908, Scott, along with two of his staff members, offered courses in "Reporting and Editorial Work." They were part of Scott's effort to offer practical journalism work to students who contemplated careers in the field. Scott petitioned the regents for $15 to acquire all the materials used in producing the Sunday, October 1, 1905, edition of the *Chicago Record-Herald*. As he notes, "the collection is of considerable educative value for students who are fitting themselves for newspaper work, since it shows in a striking way the characteristic features of modern newspaper procedure" (RP). Scott also created another journalism course, first offered in the Fall of 1910, called simply "Practical Newspaper Work." He had fought the administration since December 1908 to get it instituted.

A more significant addition to his teaching schedule was Course 23, "Seminary in Advanced Composition," which appears first in the fall of 1908. The description indicates that "this course is intended for a limited number of advanced students who write with facility and are in the habit of writing, but who desire personal criticism and direction. Although the greater part of the time will be spent in the discussion of the manuscripts submitted for correction, there will be talks upon the essentials of English Composition and the principles of criticism and revision. Open only to students who receive special permission." According to Clarence Thorpe, who wrote the article on the Rhetoric Department for *The University of Michigan: An Encyclopedic Survey*, "this was destined to become one of the most prized offerings of the department. . . . The class became something like a young writers' club, and was a proving ground for many who later gained distinction in the literary field. It was, moreover, a recognition, in principle, of the importance of creative writing as a university study. To it, more than to anything else, can be traced the Hopwood prizes and the outstanding development of present advanced courses in writing at the University of Michigan" (Shaw, *Survey* 2:563).

One of the happier episodes in the Rhetoric Department's history during this period was the inception of the Field Prize for Poetry, which can be credited to Scott's influence. Nelson Field, an 1890 graduate and successful land investor in Missouri and Texas, offered a $100 cash prize for the best poem submitted by any student in the Literary Department of the university before May 1, 1909. The judges were to be the professor and assistant professors of rhetoric, in short, Scott, Joseph Thomas, and Thomas E. Rankin. The award continued until 1916–1917. It was a precursor to the more lucrative and prestigious Hopwood Awards still given by the university.

In his classes, Scott was essentially compassionate and democratic. When he spoke before the New England Teachers of English in 1901, he had said that "composition does not lie in any connection with mathematics or with the mathematical way of evaluating the ends that we want to attain. What I have before me is a set of individuals, personalities of a most interesting character to me, every one of them. Even the stupid boy on the back seat who gets most of his answers wrong is to me interesting as a personality, and everything he says is interesting, when I am in the right mood. I wish I could be in the right mood all the time. It doesn't make any difference whether it is right or wrong; it is interesting; and when I hear somebody talk about dull undergraduates, I resent it" (FNSP, Ed Miller).

Considering the recognition Scott had achieved, we should note the effect some of his publications were having on teaching at other schools. In February 1910, George Denton of the University of Illinois wrote to ask for a copy of "Rhetoric Rediviva." Denton was making a report before the Journal Club. "I shall probably not much advance the cause of rhetoric here by any thing I may say, but perhaps I shall do it no harm, if backed by your opinion" (FNSP, February 15, 1910).

From Hammond Lamont, editor of *The Nation,* came a letter dated January 1909, in which Lamont tells Scott he read "with interest" Scott's "What the West Wants in Preparatory Education." He agrees that training in literature and composition should ascend like two vertical lines, converging when they inform one another but not when they are arbitrarily forced together. He also likes Scott's description of the "pallid little essays" in criticism which immature writers produce. He has long felt these observations were correct but "for these heresies some of our English teachers in the East have flatly told me that I was an ignorant outsider who should defer to the opinion of the experts. But with your authority to shield me, I shall begin again to hold up my head in pedagogical society."[1] Edwin Miller also liked this essay. "To say nothing of its fine literary flavor, which has left a good taste in my mouth, it is an accurate expression of what I want in Detroit and am going to get, unless all signs fail. If you wish, you may say to anybody East or West that I have told our teachers of English in the Central High School here to regard the study of the college entrance books as matter which must not be allowed to interfere with the main business of the course in English, which is learning to read and write" (FNSP, January 17, 1909).

❖

From the beginning of his professional career, Scott was a traveler. In April 1906, he journeyed east, with stops at Cornell, the University of Pennsylvania, Columbia University and City College in New York, Vassar, and Ohio State. In Philadelphia he spoke with Hugo Karl Schilling, professor of German at the University of California, and Cornelius Weygandt, of the English Department at the University of Pennsylvania. He visited with "Lorch" at Drexel, very likely the Emil Lorch who was appointed head of a newly revived architecture program at Michigan in the fall of 1906. At Bryn Mawr, Scott took dinner with President M. Carey Thomas, Dr. Eleanor G. Clark, and Professor Carlton F. Brown prior to speaking before the English Club. At Columbia, he visited his old friend and collaborator, George Carpenter. After his lecture, he had dinner with Carpenter, William Peterfield Trent, Frederick Woodbridge, William Neilson, and Jefferson Butler Fletcher. He reports seeing John H. Finley, president of City College (later commissioner of education for the state of New York), then left New York for Poughkeepsie, where Gertrude Buck met his train. After dinner with her, Laura Wylie, and another, he gave another lecture. The next day he returned to New York and called on John Dewey with whom he discussed the latter's theory of emotion. Joe Denney met Scott's train in Columbus. "Lunch at [Denney's] house with President Thompson, Knight, Rhoades, Derby, Smith, and Bowa." Scott lectured here, also. This one brief swing through the East illustrates Scott's professional contacts:

scholars of reputation who were interested in him both as a person and, through his lectures, as an intellectual force.

Scott continued to speak at teachers' meetings and at individual high schools, usually in and around Ann Arbor, Detroit, and Chicago. In late October 1907, he traveled to Escanaba on Michigan's Upper Peninsula, where he read his paper on "A Substitute for the Classics" in the high school auditorium, and later spoke before the high school section. In the evening, he visited with the governor, who had come to give a talk. While in Escanaba, Scott made a third appearance, at a Michigan alumni banquet, speaking on changes in the university.

On February 20, 1908, he was on his way to New York. Isadore, in Europe with the children, writes to Marion that "Your father goes to New York next week and will go from there to Washington. He expects to deliver lectures in Cleveland and in Washington and will not be back before February 25." A month later, March 26, 1908, he was on the road again, this time to Chicago to a meeting of the North Central Association of Colleges and Secondary Schools (FNSD).

Three trips in 1910 are of especial interest. On January 27 Denney had invited him to speak before a convocation of Ohio State summer students in July or August. "You are free to read a paper, to talk, or lecture; but not to sing; and you need not make special preparation but may give something in the line of your regular university work if you prefer." Additionally, Denney wanted Scott to come for the summer session. He urges Scott to accept, writing that "everybody wants to hear you again. Don't disappoint us" (FNSP). The previous year Scott's course had drawn seven hundred students, one hundred doing graduate work.

The same day on which Denney wrote to firm up the details of Scott's visit to Columbus, he sent an additional letter to Ann Arbor: "The honor you have done me in naming me for election to the English Association, notice of which has come to me, I know not how to acknowledge in fitting terms. Sir, I will not trust myself to tell you in writing how much I appreciate this, but will try to express my obligation orally when I see you next. Sir, I am also in receipt of a letter from President Hutchins telling me that the Regents have a desire to confer an honorary degree upon me at the Commencement, June 30th. I feel, Sir, that this peculiarly grateful distinction is somehow due to our friendship, and again I find myself unable to do justice to my feelings. I can only say that I am pleased beyond measure."[2] Only a week after the trip to Columbus, Scott traveled to Boston. On July 8, 1910, "[I] read my paper, or rather gave my talk on Two Ideals of Composition Teaching before the English Round Table of the NEA" (FNSD). On July 27 he received yet another invitation to speak to a teacher's group. This one came from an MLA colleague, Edwin Hopkins of Kansas. Hopkins tells Scott that the English Round Table of the Kansas State Teachers' Association will meet in Topeka, October 20, Chancellor Strong presiding, with the following theme: "the selection of the important and the elimination of the unimportant element in our educational system." There will be discussion of three or four topics initiated by guest speakers from outside the state. "You have been elected as the first choice of the chairman and his—I should say her—advisory committee. Hence the following questions: Can you come? Will you come? Won't you come? What sum will cover your fee and expenses?" (FNSP, letter).

Hopkins has been authorized by the chair of the Round Table, Lela F. Douthart of Kansas City, Kansas, who is currently abroad, to extend the invitation. "I address you early because I am personally very desirous to have you accept; and to that end I am sending this letter to you through Professor Frank E. Bryant so that he may lend me the weight of his influence in persuading you to do so" (ibid.). Hopkins also wants Scott to make a short address at chapel service October 21, a Friday, and to be a guest of the Fortnightly Club on the night of October 22. He wants to introduce him to as many members of the faculty as possible.

Hopkins tries to persuade Scott to come by describing the program as an "English composition revival." He himself is to report on his study of composition teaching in high schools and colleges. There will also be a session on the utilitarian as well as the cultural benefit of teaching literature. He offers Scott a chance to speak on these or other topics and says he may opt for any place on the program. He urges Scott to come because state officials have not been receptive to the burden of work of high school English teachers, and he adds: "I can conceive of nobody better fitted than yourself to lend needed aid at what seems to me to be an important time" (ibid.). Scott's reply to Hopkins reveals his reservations about such invitations, and his plans, since he does accept the offer.

It has been my practice for the past two or three years to decline, on principle, all invitations such as you extend in your letter. My seeming churlishness arises from the fact that such engagements are great time consumers, however they may be in other regards, and time becomes infinitely precious as one grows older. However, your programme is alluring and I am tempted to say that I will come for the sum of $75 out of which I should expect to pay my expenses. As for a lecture, I have a talk on "Two Ideals of Composition Teaching," which I could make as short or as long as you please; or I could later join in the discussion of your paper; or I could do both. (FNSP, handwritten response to Hopkins's letter)

Scott's visit to Kansas proved to be a bit more than he had bargained for. When he reached Lawrence on October 20, Hopkins met him with some very bad news of which Scott had already been apprised by reading the *Kansas City Star:* Frank Bryant had died. Instead of a happy reunion with a former student, Scott found that he had arrived in time for a funeral at which he would be expected to take part. Bryant's death was especially poignant. A record of significant achievement already behind him, a tenured senior position in hand, and recently married, Bryant must have felt as if everything in the world was going right for him. But he contracted typhoid on his honeymoon and was dead only a month later. The chapel, where Scott was to speak, was crowded with students. He spoke first about Bryant and then on "Books That Wear."[3]

In Topeka, Scott did not have time to go over his talk, "Two Ideals of Composition Teaching," and "in consequence found myself somewhat constrained." He responded to Hopkins's report, which addressed the question "Can Good Composition Teaching Be Done Under Present Conditions?" Hopkins's negative outlook was supported by a subsequent joint investigation by MLA and NCTE which found teachers overworked at both high school and college levels (Wozniak 169–70). It may not have been his most enjoyable conference, but Scott had fulfilled his obligation to his colleague, Edwin Hopkins, and, sadly, to his "favorite pupil," Frank Bryant.

Unquestionably the most significant experience of the entire Scott family during this period was the trip abroad in 1906. Scott had obtained a leave of absence for a year, although Isadore, her mother, and the children stayed two years. In his official request, he specifies what he hopes to accomplish during the year: "If the request is granted it is my purpose to spend the year abroad, in order (1) to make a comparative study of methods of teaching composition in European Schools, and (2) to complete a work on the Science of Rhetoric, the materials for which are to be found only in foreign libraries" (UMBR, January 1906).

But, as MLA president in 1907, Scott was also much preoccupied with the speech he was to give at the annual meeting.

The stay in England that summer seems to have been a mix of work and play. After sightseeing in London, the family moved south to Seaford where they had engaged a place to live. Scott stayed in London, working in the British Museum, visiting with individuals he wanted to see, and taking in occasional lectures, concerts, and galleries which interested him, sometimes alone, sometimes with other professors who were abroad over the summer. On weekends he left London for Seaford and the family. He came in contact with numerous professors of repute, such as Stanley Hall, a pioneer educational psychologist in the United States; Sidney Webb, a founder of the Fabian Society; and Sir Israel Gollancz of the British Academy.

Scott took time out to follow up on another of his interests. In October 1906 he met with a Mr. Dudeny who was to assist him in patenting and marketing a puzzle which he had made. "[Dudeny] said that the circular tour puzzle was new so far as the ideas of shortest distances was concerned, but British public did not like strings. Thought at first he could work it out in a few minutes, but later conceded that the task might be more difficult than he had thought. Said he would send me the address of a Brighton firm that makes such things. . . . In afternoon to patent office in Chancery Lane, where I asked for and obtained printed instructions, then in search of Stationer's Hall." Later, in May 1907, he spoke with a patent-broker about a blind man's invention, a typewriter that could write letters readable by the blind as well as by people who could see (FNSD).

In line with his primary objective, however, Scott searched out materials for his MLA president's address, "The Genesis of Speech." On July 26, for example, he spent the morning reading William Henry Furness's *Borneo Head-Hunters: Its Festival and Folklore.* On July 31 he writes in his diary that he is reading "Tyler's Primitive Cultures." (He does not identify Tyler or the title of the book, but a good guess would be John Mason Tyler's *The Whence and Whither of Man: A Brief History of His Origin and Development Through Conformity to Environment.* Tyler was the author of several works on evolution.)

For several days in early August he reports his reading in the *Journal of the Anthropological Institute.* He makes other references to Laurence Austine Waddell's *Lhasa and Its Mysteries,* a record of Waddell's expedition to Tibet in 1903–1904; Theodore Koch's *Anfänge der Kunst in Urwald: Indianer Handzeichnungen auf Seinen Reisen in Brasilien Gesammelt von Dr. T. Koch-Grünberg;* George William and Elizabeth Gifford Peckham's *Wasps, Social and Solitary;* G. H. Theodore Eimer's *Organic Evolution as the Result of the Inheritance of Acquired Characters According to the Laws of Organic Growth;* and "Morgan's Behavior of Animals." (Scott's reference to Morgan is so brief that it is not possible to determine which book he was reading, or which author. Likely candidates are Conway Lloyd Morgan's *Animal Life and Intelligence* or some of the work on evolution by Thomas Hunt Morgan.) Cumulatively, Scott's reading of these authors and works reinforces the conjecture that he was looking into biology and anthropology, specifically works on evolution, for information on primitive cultures, particularly the origin of speech. This material was providing him background both for his paper on the genesis of speech and his theories on the science of rhetoric.

The Scott family crossed to Germany in late October, settling in Breit-brunn, south of Munich. Scott enrolled in the university to attend lectures by its specialists, embarked on a program of extensive reading, visited some schools, and attended a variety of concerts, meetings, and less formal sessions in which a range of topics were discussed. He also engaged a man named Jaeger to walk daily with him so that he could improve his German.

The reading is varied. On November 17 the subject is consonantal dissonance and assonance. On other occasions he is reading about art and archeology in addition to a considerable amount of material on primitive cultures, language, and biological topics. Among the latter we find references to sections on phonetics in Karl Burgman and Berthold Delbruck's *Grundriss der vergleichenden grammatik der indogermanischen sprachen* (Strassburg: K. J. Trubner, 1897–1916), an article by Jennings on the sea anemone in the 1905 volume of the *Zoologisches Jahrebericht,* Boehm's *Thierlesen* about the relations of ape mothers and children, a piece in the *Journal of Anatomy and Physiology* on the development of the alimentary canal (for which he gives no author), work by Paul and Wundt on the origin of speech in *Beilage ur Allgemeiner Zeitung*, and Bergman and Seskien's pamphlet *Ein Kritik der Künstlichen Weltsprachen.*

Art, as we know, was a major interest of Scott's, and in Munich he could not resist its attractions. One of his more interesting references on this subject occurs on May 3 when he read Benedetto Croce's review of two of Scott's papers: "The Fundamental Differentia of Poetry and Prose" and "The Scansion of Prose Rhythm" (*La Critica: Rivista Di Letteratura, Storia e Filosofia*. Diretta da B. Croce. Vol. 4, 1906. [Swets & Zeitlinger N.V. Amsterdam, 1966], 466–68). While he doesn't agree with Scott's conclusions (he is not satisfied with Scott's distinctions between expressive and communicative discourse and he doesn't think one can find a quantifiable or material basis for language such as Scott attempts), the major point is that he felt Scott's work sufficiently important to take note of it and respond to it.

In Germany he was attempting to follow through on another of the projects for which he had requested leave: observing the teaching of composition in European schools. He went to the Berlitz school in Munich on November 30 and again on December 3. He did not fare so well with the *Rektor* of the Realgymnasium in the Ludwigstrasse. Here he waited half an hour before finding the gentleman, who told Scott he could not visit the school without a permit. He "seemed glad to have me go" (FNSD, December 3, 1906).

There are a few memorable entries on the lectures he attended. The most notable lecturer he mentions is Adolph Furtwängler, a German classical archaeologist and noted authority on early Greek art. Of his manner of lecturing, Scott says that he "looked like a musician, his long hair tossed up from his forehead like spray. Much waving of hands and swaying from side to side as he spoke, in the manner of an orchestra conductor." One can only say that Scott was uncommonly prescient. Adolph was the father of Wilhelm Furtwängler, conductor of the Berlin and Vienna Philharmonics before World War II, and one of the world's great interpreters of romantic music.

Scott also heard lectures by Ivan Muller, Lepert, Supe and Schick, and Borinski. Karl Borinski spoke on the origin of speech, a subject of great interest to Scott, of course, who was by this time getting closer and closer to completing his paper. But Borinski did not impress him: "Interesting and convenient coordination of theories, but deficiency of psychological and sociological insight. Little sympathy with Darwin or Wundt. Takes 'sensible' attitude, as does Paul, whose interest is less in the truth than in the workability of his method." He went to hear Borinski again within a few days and once more was disappointed. "B. is falling back on the old device of reading extracts." A month later, "Borinski lectured on Darwin's theory of the emotions, which he handled rather superficially. He is no psychologist" (FNSD, May 11, 1906; June 19, 1907).

Scott spent many of his evenings either going to plays or concerts or enjoying the company of his German friends in Munich. He also socialized with university faculty. Interestingly, the German "Herr Doktor Professors" never intimidated Scott; in fact, it seems to have been the other way. His knowledge was something even the German scholars would have envied. For example, when Sieper invited him to call on him at his home in Mittersendling, Sieper tells Scott that he is reading *Robert Elsmere,* a novel by Mrs. Humphrey Ward. "Told him that some of the material was drawn from the Diary of H. Amiel, of which he had never heard." The ironic thing is that Amiel was a Swiss professor (1821–1881) whose *Journal* has become a classic autobiography.

Scott did not forget his children. Although he visited regularly, Richard had written to him, expressly asking if he were coming down to Breit-brunn for his birthday, July 18, since Scott would soon be leaving for Ann Arbor. Scott did, and they all had breakfast in the garden of the restaurant at Ulting. Then they took the train to Wilheim and Tuktzing and went by boat on Starnbergersee to Bernried. "Sat on the grass by the Lake front and took turns playing on Richard's mouth-organ—a birthday present. Walked through Bernried—missing the best part of it, tho' the children did not know it—and out a long dusty road to a restaurant near the station, where we had dinner. Afterward to the station where the children waited while I went back after some postcards. Went through a beautifully quiet old park with a pond where swans were swimming. By train to Diessen, then by boat to Herrsching, where I got off." The children obviously went on to Breit-brunn. It was the last real holiday they would enjoy with their father, for they were to remain in Europe the next year.

Only days later, Scott began the long trip back to Michigan. Isadore, her parents, and Harvey were touring Italy and were thus not there to see him off. Scott was to rejoin the family in July 1908 in Europe. Isadore suggests spending time in Florence and Milan. "If we could go slowly from Florence to Marseilles, stopping long enough to see the small interesting places and go north to Switzerland we could spend a very delightful two months" (MG, March 16, 1908).

Correspondence between the Scotts reveals that he apparently turned down an offer of the chairmanship of the graduate council. Isadore writes:

It seems to me that you might accept the chairmanship with the understanding that the school be reorganized in the immediate future. It seems to me that the dean of that school will have rather an enviable berth. He would rank as high as any of the other deans and probably above most of them. There is no reason, of course, why Michigan's graduate school could not be made as flourishing as any in the country. . . . If you set to work to build up a real graduate school you would have to give up almost all your teaching. Your work would be almost entirely the administration of your own department and of the school. I think you might like it for a change. The opportunity to visit other schools, to consult with other deans and presidents and to work up the right sort of a school would be very interesting and quite worth while. (MG, May 8, 1908)

The years 1905–1910 mark the high point of Scott's involvement in MLA. In 1907, after long years of service, he became MLA's president, having been nominated by Calvin Thomas of Columbia, J. B. Henneman of the University of the South, and Camillo Von Klenze of Brown at the 1906 meeting. While his family celebrated Christmas abroad, Scott was preparing for his big moment. He called the MLA meeting to order in the afternoon, presided when necessary, and, after the evening banquet, read the paper he had labored on so long. "The audience mousestill. Afterwards to very packed reception at the President's." Two months later, in a letter dated February 17, 1908, Joe Denney, in Germany, reported to Scott on the reception of his presidential address: "Word comes to me from Columbus and elsewhere that things were unusually pleasant at the meeting and that the President's address was fresh in material, mighty interesting in make-up, and invulnerable as a piece of reasoning. What more could any one desire than that?" (FNSP).

Serving the organization as its principal officer, Scott's visibility in it was further enhanced, and he became one to whom others would turn in matters political. In 1908, Joel Spingarn of Columbia challenged Charles Grandgent of Harvard over a resolution at the 1907 meeting by Professor E. C. Roedder to develop some plan to block the duplication of doctoral theses. Roedder proposed that graduate students, after one year's work, register their subjects in the *Publications* of MLA so that another could not undertake the same study for at least two years.

Spingarn, who had put in a year of graduate study at Harvard but took his Ph.D. at Columbia in 1899, was unhappy with Grandgent's editorial policies. He had, therefore, introduced a resolution at the 1908 MLA meeting to extend "the scope of the publications of the Association." With the passing of the resolution, MLA President Warren appointed Scott, Benjamin Bowen of Ohio State, Charles Bundy Wilson of Iowa, and Edward Armstrong of Johns Hopkins to the committee with Spingarn as chair. In his letter to Scott, February 26, 1909, Spingarn explains his intentions more fully: "My purpose in introducing it [the resolution] was to ascertain the opinion of American scholars as to the adequacy of the publications as they are at present. My own feeling is that they do not satisfactorily represent American scholarship, and I hoped that possibly some way might be discovered by which the publications would become the recognized organ of American scholarship, not only for our own country, but for the world" (FNSP).

As Spingarn's biographer, Marshall Van Deusen, makes clear on a

number of occasions, Spingarn was hardly the typical college professor.
He was half academic, half reformer. He was also contentious. From Van
Deusen's account, Spingarn's dismissal from Columbia in 1911 seems to
have sprung from his individuality, zeal, and outspokenness, character
traits that can be seen in this MLA transaction, and which explain, in
part, Scott's reluctance to follow Spingarn's recommendations (50).

Grandgent had tried to compromise the aims of this motion in an
earlier letter to Scott, January 3, 1909, in which he assesses Spingarn's
concerns: "I suppose you remember Spingarn's motion and the committee of five that resulted. I did not oppose it, as I think it best that any
dissatisfaction should find due utterance. There is a little group of Columbia men who would like to have our Publications made a medium
for book reviews, and perhaps would favor other changes. . . . The thing
has been suggested before, and I have repeatedly made inquiry among
the more constant and experienced members of the Association, and have
found them almost unanimously opposed to it" (FNSP). His impas-
sioned defense of the quality of the journal is more to the point in that
it directly contradicts Spingarn's assertion that the best American scholarship was not appearing in the journal.[4]

At this point, it is clear that Scott has his own ideas; he is not interested in meddling with the MLA *Publications*. At the 1909 MLA
meetings in Ithaca, Spingarn introduced a new resolution, this one pro-
hibiting the publishing of dissertations in the *Proceedings* of *PMLA* and
appointing a committee to publish periodically a bulletin. Although
adopted, the executive council subsequently pronounced both resolu-
tions unconstitutional. In making this decision, the council had polled
the members, finding that of 935, 242 favored, 297 opposed the idea of
a bulletin. Spingarn offered to finance the bulletin, but Scott was still
hesitant. "It seems best on the whole, however, to let the Treasurer have
all the rope he wants. Suppose he succeeds in stopping this scheme. The
Assoc. will then either be indiff. in which case . . ." (FNSP). This frag-
ment of a draft Scott had written on Spingarn's letter ends here but the
inference is that if the Association is indifferent, let the project drop. If
they indicate strong sentiment for it, go ahead. As observed earlier, Scott
had reservations about making a commitment to Spingarn.

At the 1909 convention, Scott read his "Rhetoric Rediviva," which
he said excited no comment, and then took part in the discussion of a
paper by Lane Cooper called "On the Teaching of Written Composition."
Philosophically and theoretically, Scott's paper had much greater weight

than Cooper's. Yet, although Cooper published his three months later in the March issue of *Education*, Scott's paper did not appear in print in his lifetime.[5]

In his work, Cooper had made three major points: (1) "Properly amplified, the subject would involve some treatment of various other topics, among them the gradual decline of interest in the disciplines of Greek and Latin, which have been essential to the development of English style in the past; and the concomitant popular demand for a kind of education in the vernacular which shall directly liberate the utterances of the masses, rather than raise up leaders in scholarship whose paramount influence might elevate and sustain the standards of taste and good usage" (421). (2) He notes that Harvard, the source of the daily theme, had made some recent adjustments so that the number of students in English literature courses now exceeds those in composition, whereas previously just the opposite situation prevailed. (3) "Since we may seldom take for granted that the immature student is in possession of a valuable truth, and since the first inquiry of the teacher should, therefore, be concerning the truth and accuracy of the pupil's communication, it follows that the teaching of expression can never safely be made the primary aim of any course" (425).

When Gertrude Buck read the published version of Cooper's paper, she wrote to Scott, observing that "it seems to me such a tissue of fallacies with such superficial plausibility that I wondered whether some answer ought not to be made by some one. If you would do this yourself of course it would have the greatest weight, but perhaps it does not seem to you necessary or advisable. I long to do so, but simply cannot undertake anything of the sort even if my answer would be effective, as it would not at all in comparison with yours" (FNSP, letter, April 23, 1910).

Scott replied that he had tried to expose some of its fallacies, "but it seems to me to be too non-sequacious to merit serious criticism. The only part to which I should care to reply is his assumption that we in this work are dependent upon Harvard for our ideas on the teaching of composition. That is a rule of course of Mr. Sanborn's men [the Benjamin Sanborn Company of Boston] that always arouses my resentment. I have written to Mr. Cooper about it, but I shall not say anything in public. If you have formulated a reply or care to formulate one, by all means publish it. The paper can at any rate serve the useful purpose of pointing a moral" (FNSP, penciled on Buck's letter). Scott did write to Cooper on the subject of Harvard's influence on composition teaching, but Cooper

politely refused to back down, saying only that he was glad to hear that
Ann Arbor "had escaped the conquest" (FNSP, May 5, 1910). All in all,
Cooper's remarks contradicted the basic tenets Scott had formulated and
espoused over the previous decade.

The following year, 1910, when MLA met in New York, John W.
Cunliffe introduced a motion "that the Chair be requested to nominate
a committee of three to submit to this meeting some course of action
with a view to the registration of subjects of doctoral dissertations in
hand." Cunliffe, Todd, and Scott were chosen. The group was identified
as the Committee on the Announcement of Subjects of Doctoral Dissertations.[6] In their report, two days later, they announced the necessity of
including the subjects of dissertations in the *Publications,* arguing that
doing so would not only prevent duplication (the original stance), but
also stimulate research. And when the committee proposed a new Committee of Three to secure unification of effort between graduate schools
in Europe as well as in the United States, the association not only approved the report, but retained Cunliffe, Todd, and Scott to carry on that
work.

The Bibliographical Section, which Scott had brought into existence
in 1902, and on which he had served, had not in subsequent years reported to the association. In fact, it may have been dissolved in 1903,
like the Pedagogical Section, with the change in the constitution. In
1910, the Bibliographical Society of America had assumed the original
tasks of the section and reported at the convention that "English, Romance, and Scandinavian studies stand in great need of a concerted effort
in order to effect needed improvements" (Day and Josephson x). The society requested that MLA appoint a committee to work cooperatively
with it to remedy the situation. Scott's perception of the need had indeed
been accurate, yet, seven years later, little progress had been made.

Scott, although dissatisfied with the direction it was taking, continued his association with MLA for the rest of his professional life, but
never again did it involve him in the ways in which it did during the period from 1905–1910. Scott's mission and the mission of MLA were no
longer in congruity. MLA had failed him in his quest to reform language
pedagogy by incorporating theory. It also was beginning to follow the
national trend of devaluing rhetoric in relation to literature studies and
to deemphasize pedagogy in favor of pure scholarship.

8

Speaking with Authority

A S WE HAVE SEEN, most of Scott's textbooks were written in collaboration with Joseph Denney and published by Allyn and Bacon, with whom he had a long-standing and comfortable relationship. But Benjamin Sanborn of Boston had approached him about collaborating with someone in the public schools, and Scott agreed to the plan. The result was *Lessons in English,* books I–II, in collaboration with G. A. Southworth. The *Lessons* were published in 1906, and Southworth, the superintendent of schools in Somerville, Massachusetts, seems to have been a thoroughly responsible and congenial partner in the enterprise.

Book I of the *Lessons* was prepared for students in grades 3–6; book II, by contrast, is described as "a systematic course in grammar and a series of lessons in composition" for more advanced students. Book I's purpose was to stimulate an appreciation for good literature. In addition, the authors provided questions "to stimulate thought, to develop clear ideas, and to enable the learner to report more readily, both orally and in writing, what he has discovered" (II:iii). Along with these elements, they insisted as well on "a definite reader or hearer to whom the pupil may address himself" (II:iii). A third stated purpose of this book was "to make children more and more observing—especially in the field of natural science—adding to their knowledge, and leading them to find out for themselves" (II:iii). These purposes, with their strong emphasis on reading and writing in a real context, reveal Scott's influence in the book.

The purpose of book II was "to place before the student an orderly and intelligible statement of the principles that determine the structure of words and sentences, and at the same time to furnish exercises for practice in the application of those principles, and to continue upon a higher plane the work in composition pursued in the lower grades" (II:iv).

Overall, this book is somewhat disappointing, considering Scott's theoretical ideas about the teaching of writing, for most of the material and the presentation is what we would now call very traditional. One must turn to the section "To Teachers" to find Scott's true attitudes. Here he says that "too many teachers think of a text-book as a kind of machine-gun, built to fire with deadly precision so many loads a minute. This is a vicious error" (II:vii). The textbook is but a supplement to "the teacher's personal enthusiasm, sympathy, and stimulus" (II:vii). He says further that "all instruction in English is growth in power of expression and appreciation. Drill which contributes to this end is good. Drill which, falling short of this end, merely fills the child's mind with rules and symbols, is a grievous waste of time" (II:viii).

The *Lessons* apparently enjoyed some commercial success—it was adopted in Kansas, Oklahoma, Texas, and West Virginia. But Scott's correspondence with Sanborn suggests that he was not particularly happy with this publisher. Shortly after Scott's return from Europe in 1907, Sanborn proposed that he collaborate in a new series of readers. His collaborator was to be a Miss Laing, an elementary school teacher.[1] Sanborn was consumed with envy at the success of the Aldine Readers, a basal reader published by Newson and Company, and wanted to cut into that market. In a later letter he refers to their success and says they are being widely adopted because, according to the superintendents, "they had a definite plan and system which was good for beginners and good to be carried out" (FNSP, September 3, 1909).

Scott's displeasure is revealed in a one-act drama called *A Question of Text Books* by Justin Frolich, the pen name Scott adopted for this *jeu d'esprit*. It was published in 1908, just after Scott's dealings with Sanborn. The setting is the office of the Central High School principal, Mr. Keene. Miss Newsome, Miss Bird, and Mr. Stripes, all English teachers, come in to discuss their choice of a new text for the school's English program. As one would expect, the characters are all abstractions for certain attitudes about the teaching of composition.

Miss Newsome argues for Inkster's *Evolutionary Composition* on the grounds that it is the latest thing, that the publishers describe it as "'thoroughly scientific—based on the psychology of the writing process—full of the most effective and fascinating devices for arousing interest—every exercise tested in one thousand schools.'" Stripes rejects Inkster's book outright because he sanctions, even uses, the split infinitive! Miss Bird doesn't much worry about the split infinitives, but dangling participles do trouble her. Miss Newsome counters by quoting a dangling modifier from *Macbeth* that Miss Bird excuses on the grounds that it is poetry.

Principal Keene calms them down and says he'll put Inkster on the *Index Expurgatorius*. So, what's the next candidate? Stripes wants Diggett's *Drill-Book* which Miss Newsome describes as "that old thing." When Stripes says it's just out, she replies: "Out of date, you mean. It's at least fifty years behind the times. And dry! It parches my throat just to look at it. Why don't you suggest Whately's 'Rhetoric'?" Stripes doesn't think that's a bad idea. He's tired of mollycoddling students. Make composition work hard and dry. Punish students who make mistakes. "If they omit a comma after co-ordinate 'which', give 'em . . . E, as they do at Harvard." In the end, the principal suggests a text that caters to the particular interests of all three. Its authors, appropriately named Shears and Snippett, its publisher, McGinn, Muffin & Co., and the publisher's representative, Smoothby, all reflect Scott's cynicism about the book trade. The company clearly has no principles: it provides a text that will sell, not one that is educationally sound.

This play is as close as we can get to understanding the enormous dichotomy between the theories Scott endorsed and the textbooks that he published. Later contacts with publishers only served to reinforce his negative attitude. In May 1909 he got a letter from Sanborn explaining their policy in handling permissions for work included in the *Lessons*. Sanborn says that the company did the work of getting them and then charged Scott and Southworth proportionately. He thinks they've done the authors a favor by saving them this labor.

It was a case where we had to have this material—the particular pieces—or cease working the Lessons in English in the entire State of New York. . . . The New York Syllabus required the memorizing of certain pieces from certain authors in six grades, and these had to go in your books, as they have now been put in all competing books, but I can not concede that you have a right to charge for the work in revising that material. I should say it was your duty to do it under the original contract, and without charge, provided it made the book any better.

From this transaction, the demands of the marketplace are very clearly disclosed.

In July 1909, Scott received a letter from Gordon Southworth telling him that the publishers wanted a special edition of the books for state adoptions. It also had to be cheaper. Agents were telling them that book I was not as good as book II. In August Scott heard from Sanborn who again emphasized the business side: "You forget that states can and do legislate on text books, both as to prices and quality. *Now,* in every state context we are obliged *before bidding,* to make oath that we have no agreement of any kind as to prices" (FNSP, August 8, 1909). Scott and Southworth did eventually revise the book, but not until 1916.

Sanborn wasn't the only publisher Scott disappointed. In February 1910 George Bacon wrote to Scott: "Three days ago I received your un-welcome letter stating that you had no time to go gallivanting about, and conveying intimations that you preferred the society of musty tomes and the seclusion of your library to active life in the haunts of men and the companionship of your fellows. If that's the kind of man you are, your case is certainly hopeless, and I am not going to waste any words on you. 'Ephraim is joined to his idols, let him alone'" (FNSP, February 11, 1910).

Bacon had wanted him to go to a school officials' meeting in Indi-anapolis and promote his textbooks. Although Scott no doubt felt satis-faction in their educational value as well as the money they were bring-ing him, there is also no question that he did not like the terms of the world of commerce.

Not surprisingly, Scott did not write any more new texts, although he and Denney did complete a revision of *Paragraph-Writing.* It was a project which occupied them for a considerable length of time, and the correspondence shows how they divided the labor. Denney writes to Scott in May 1906, before Scott went abroad:

The revised P-W must go over for another year on account of a succession of in-terferences that have kept me from it. Meanwhile Mr. Metcalf and Dr. Bacon write that it is necessary to publish a teacher's manual for the Composition-Lit-erature. I will agree to do this for them, if you will sign in blank anything that I may say in the manual, while you are gone.

The word I want from you just at present is to go ahead with the teachers' manual and with the revision of P-W. Perhaps, in regard to the last-named, it might be well for you to send me the copy for the last half of P-W before you leave, so that I shall not repeat, in what I say in the first half.

The preface to the 1909 edition which was, according to the title page, "rewritten and much enlarged," indicates the scope of that revi-sion. In fact, the revised book is 158 pages longer than its predecessors. They have opened the book with a discussion of the art of composition and the organic structure of discourse, followed by an application of the concepts developed to the paragraph and the whole composition. Second, they discuss the forms of discourse—narration, description, exposition, and argument—"at a length and with a thoroughness more nearly corresponding to their present importance in college and university classes" (vi). A third change in the revised edition was a relocation of assignments from the text proper to a separate division of the book. A fourth change was the replacement of much of the illustrative matter.

The revised edition is disappointing, a book clearly written with an eye to the marketplace. The authors have dropped the excellent section on "The Theory of the Paragraph." No doubt it had little commercial value, but it was a better representation of the kind of theoretical issues surrounding discourse that Scott examined than anything in the revised book.

On Scott and Denney's agenda also was the revision of *Elementary English Composition,* but the changes were essentially minor because, as they say in their preface to the revised edition published in 1908, the book has had a "more than kind reception . . . at the hands of teachers and school authorities" (iii). In the eight years between the first and second editions of this work, Scott and Denney had perceived "a striking change . . . in the spirit and method of composition teaching in secondary schools" (iv). Teachers were discovering ways to revitalize and enrich this instruction. And a new kind of composition teacher was appearing, "a teacher burning with enthusiasm for the once detested subject, and equipped intellectually and spiritually to attain the goal of this part of education" (iv). Scott and Denney say they feel that their book has helped to bring this situation about, a change that has stimulated those who share their principles of composition instruction and irritated those who do not. The unconventionality of their method, they feel, has provoked discussion of their methods and helped to break down the "hampering formalism" that characterized less enlightened approaches to this kind of instruction.

❖

Among Scott's professional papers are two more monographs for the series Contributions to Rhetorical Theory. In 1906 Harold Breitenbach, a member of Scott's rhetoric staff who was involved in the composition program for engineers, wrote *The Value of English to the Practicing Engineer.* Breitenbach decided to survey engineers who had been out of school for from five to ten years and were now successfully employed in their profession. They were provided with three requests: (1) to express their opinions of the value of training in English to the practicing engineer; (2) to cite any cases in which their training in English had been of special value to them; (3) to offer suggestions, on the basis of their experience, for the course in "Engineering English" given at the University of Michigan.

Responding to the first question, all the respondents said, with considerable force, that their training in English had been one of their most valuable assets. It had prepared them for writing reports, specifications, contracts, and so on. When reflecting upon what the course in English should be for engineers, they divided between those who favored practical composition work and those who argued that a good engineer should be liberally educated.

Frank Bryant's *On the Limits of Descriptive Writing Apropos of Lessing's Laocoön,* was also written in 1906. Bryant says in his preface: "My greatest obligation is to Professor Scott, who not only first interested me in the study of rhetorical problems, but who has ever since kept alive this interest with frequent encouragement, and who now, in editing this work, has done me the great service of pruning it of much extraneous material" (n.p.).

The work is an exposition of Lessing's theories about descriptive writing. Acknowledging that his arguments are logical, consistent, and fairly conclusive, Bryant insists that they are flawed because of questionable premises, that

in vision we see the separate particulars before we see the whole object, and that the mind does its work of synthesis almost instantaneously. But can this be accepted as a true theory of vision? No, I think we may answer with confidence, modern psychology will not accept any such theory as that. As all experiments tend to show, in seeing we go from the vague to the definite, and the process is often very far from being instantaneous. (11)

Furthermore, Bryant argues, the principle upon which Lessing bases his famous "chain of conclusions" is wrong and therefore invalidates everything that follows it, for both poetry and painting, contrary to Lessing's belief, are perceived temporally and spatially; and it is too simplistic to argue that "one uses articulate sounds and the other uses forms and colors" (16).

What makes this monograph so interesting is that Bryant is reflecting Scott's interest in theoretical issues in aesthetics. From Scott's seminars, Bryant was encouraged to explore a significant distinction between the types of discourse and to discover the real basis for those distinctions.

That these conclusions do not seem strikingly original today is irrele-vant; Bryant wrote his paper over ninety years ago, at a time when such problems were not even taken up in the rhetoric classes of other indi-viduals in this country.

During the first decade of the century, Scott, in his full maturity and enjoying the prestige of being a national leader in his profession, pro-duced some of his best philosophical papers. His concern was the very nature of education itself. Scott was responding to some remarkable changes in education at that time. The classical curriculum, which had dominated American education for most of the nineteenth century, was in decline because it did not serve the needs of a changing industrial so-ciety which found scientific and technological studies much more inter-esting and practical. But the defenders of Latin and Greek were still vocal.

On the other hand, as the study of modern languages became en-trenched, a split occurred between what we now call literary studies and composition. Composition was all that was left of the ancient tradition of rhetoric, and once it was reduced to concern for mechanical correct-ness, limited concepts of organization, and prescriptive but unscientific attitudes about usage and style, it became the province of inferior mem-bers of English departments. The other element of rhetoric, the oral tra-dition, barely survived. As J. N. Hook writes in *A Long Way Together,* speech teachers were often denied even a place in the English depart-ment, professors of literature considering it demeaning to offer so utili-tarian a course. Hook cites the example of Thomas Trueblood, one of Scott's colleagues, "who traveled about and 'gave short courses without credit, receiving tuition directly from the students rather than through the college administration'" (48).[2] When NCTE was formed, speech teachers were urged to join, and a Public Speaking Section was even es-tablished for them. But in 1913, the Eastern Conference decided to sep-arate themselves from English, largely at the instigation of James M. O'Neill who saw the two fields as distinctly separate.[3]

Scott addressed the problem of the split between literary studies and composition in "A Substitute for the Classics," a fantasy first presented before the Michigan Schoolmasters' Club, April 1908. It is cast as a let-ter, supposedly written in 4000 A.D. by a citizen of Timbuctoo, at this time the capital of the world republic. The writer is an English teacher who writes in Bantu, once a "despised" vernacular language of an African tribe, now the common language of the world. The letter is addressed to the superintendent for public instruction in America who has asked for suggestions in designing a secondary school curriculum.

What is education's primary goal? Scott, speaking through his fictitious letter writer, says that it is the building of character. "Moral courage, self-reliance, respect for the truth in every aspect of it, both material and spiritual, sympathy for our fellow-beings and an active desire to help them and co-operate with them, a love of justice and fair play, belief in democratic institutions, loyalty to our republic—these are the elements of character which our schools were, I believe, primarily established to develop" (89; all page references are to *The Standard of American Speech*).

It is especially important that this be the end of education in secondary schools because this is the period during which young people experience greatest emotional stress and intellectual growth, on their journey toward becoming responsible citizens. The author conjectures that the reader of his letter will expect him to produce some novel and profound doctrine for the teaching of the vernacular, a genuine substitute for the classics, but he has none. "To reveal to him [the student] the effectiveness of the tools which he already knows how to use and to show him how to sharpen them and use them more effectively, is the language teacher's first task" (96). It is difficult to recall any time at which Scott expressed more succinctly than this, his own philosophy of the teaching of English.

In 1909 Scott produced one of his most incisive professional papers: "What the West Wants in Preparatory English," published in *The School Review*. It was his opportunity to deal with a number of educational issues that raised his hackles: the nature of preparatory education, the contrast between the colleges on opposite sides of the Appalachians, and entrance examinations. He felt the term *preparatory* was responsible for one of the most serious educational fallacies of the time: that the chief purpose of English in the secondary schools is to prepare students for college. He had already spoken of the hazards of this position in previous speeches and publications. But in this piece he amplifies his views and focuses on the influence of the eastern colleges.

He makes a crucial distinction between eastern and western universities. In the West, education is perceived as "one broad highway [which] stretches from the kindergarten to the graduate school" (10). Not so in the East. But because a number of people in the West want to send their children to eastern schools, they must deal with the problem of entrance examinations. "It amazes me that the Eastern colleges do not see how perilous their footing is in the West. A half dozen determined men could in six months cause every western public high school to abandon all attempts to fit boys for the Yale or Harvard examination; and it would take very little to precipitate such a movement," Scott wrote to Wilbur Cross of Yale in 1911 (FNSP, penciled response on December 1, 1911, letter).

Now, what are the problems? The English teacher with one eye on his students and another on entrance examinations will teach to the tests, forsaking the larger and more noble goals to which he should be aspiring. What happens to the student caught in this web? Literary enjoyment and appreciation become "required reading." "To my mind the very sound of the phrase is ominous and depressing, as if one should say required wonder, required reverence, required enjoyment" (12). Equally deleterious is the effect on the course of study. Instead of increasing their reading maturity through exposure to new works, high school seniors find themselves preoccupied with questions they will be asked about books previously read for pleasure in their freshman and sophomore years.

That any great gain comes to the student either in literary appreciation or in the command of his mother-tongue from the incessant writing of outlines of plots, critical estimates which ape maturity, or characterless sketches of character, has not, I believe, been demonstrated. On the other hand, it is the experience of most teachers with whom I have discussed the question, that such essays, especially as they appear in examination papers, are for the most part the merest fluff and ravelings of the adolescent mind, revealing neither the student's independent thought, nor, except casually, his command of English. (14)

To those in the East who would regard the abandoning of the entrance examinations with horror because that would remove the principal means of holding secondary schools accountable, he says that precisely the opposite would result. The good schools would continue to turn out good students who would manage very well in the university environment. The poor schools would turn out students who could not do so, and they would be obliged to improve or go out of business. Since the problem was being studied by a joint conference on entrance requirements, Scott chose not to forestall their conclusions. But he did have some advice. "What I would suggest is that we put in one course of study literature and so much of critical theory and literary history as the pupil must have for the rational appreciation of what he reads; and that we put in another course of study training in composition, and so much grammatical and rhetorical theory as the pupil needs for the rationalizing of that discipline" (17). The entrance exam could then be devised to test two separate areas: one, the enjoyment of literature and knowledge of literary history, the other the student's ability to express himself.

The Harvard Reports of the 1890s, which were in reality primarily concerned with students' inadequate command of editorial skills, failed to recognize the young people who took the exams as human beings. Scott asks: "Where are they now, the writers of these rejected addresses? Are they in jail? Are they social outcasts? Are they editing yellow journals, or in other ways defiling the well of English? Or are they eloquent preachers, successful lawyers, persuasive insurance agents, leaders of society?" (19). In one of his clearest delineations of the value of rhetoric to society, he writes: "the main purpose of training in composition is free speech, direct and sincere communion with our fellows, that swift and untrammeled exchange of opinion, feeling, and experience, which is the working instrument of the social instinct and the motive power of civilization" (19).

Technically speaking, "Rhetoric Rediviva" is not part of the Scott bibliography. It was a paper that he read at the 1909 MLA meetings in Ithaca and then put aside, possibly because, as he noted in his diary, it "excited no comment." It opens with the observation that "although rhetoric as an art, and as a kind of theoretical obligato to the practice of composition, is now more widely taught than it ever has been before in the history of education, rhetoric as a science, especially as a subject for the most advanced study, has not yet come into its own" (413). There are three possible causes: (1) some question whether or not rhetoric can be called a science; (2) others, like J.E.C. Welldon, regard it as a closed science, begun and ended by Aristotle; and (3) still others do not consider rhetoric a subject worthy of serious scholarly investigation. Scott regrets these attitudes because the recent interest in composition work and its obvious relationship to rhetoric illuminate an old principle involving theory and practice in any discipline: applied work is intimately bound up with theoretical work.

On these grounds, then, Scott makes his plea for the revival of rhetoric as a science. He recommends examination of the following questions as a means of giving direction to graduate study of rhetoric: "What is this science? Where is it to be found? What are its principles and postulates and problems?" (414). To demonstrate what he means by the study of rhetoric as a science, he defines the characteristics of a science:

"(1) a fairly distinct and unified subject-matter of sufficient richness, depth, and interest to reward the investigator; (2) a method of research based upon accurate observation, experiment (when possible), and generalization; and (3) as the end in view, an organized body of interlocking principles, laws and classifications" (414).

Scott urges adoption of Plato's conception of rhetoric, a science which, he acknowledges, is "little more than a point of view" with "its methods . . . uncertain, its laws to be determined, [and] its problems largely unstated" (416). But, because of recent developments in a number of fields, he sees a bright future for the study of rhetoric as a science, especially the contributions in sociology and psychology.

There is hardly a topic in the traditional subject-matter of formal rhetoric which does not require reinterpretation in the light of modern psychological theory. I need only mention such researches as those in regard to internal speech, the nature of rhythm, the theory of expression, the mental images aroused by certain classes of words, the basis of motive, choice, and volition, to show how extensive and how varied is the material now lying ready for workers in the field. (417)

Scott continued to contribute brief pieces to *Modern Language Notes*. In November 1906, he published "A Primitive Short Story," a piece that reflects both his interests in literary genres and the origins of language and literary artifacts. In A. Mackenzie's "Native Australian Languages," published in the *Journal of the Anthropological Institute* (3:247), he has found three versions of "The Story of Bundoola." The first two are literal transcriptions of the story by narrators sitting around a campfire; the third is an extended version in English by an aborigine who had apparently received an English education. Scott discovers in these stories "the crude beginning of a distinct type (or sub-type) of prose composition, the humble progenitor of the modern short-story" (208). The only distinction between the primitive and the modern short story, argues Scott, is that the former is the condensation of a longer narrative while the latter is not. In all other respects, they are the same.

Two aspects of this paper are of special interest. First, he makes no distinction between fiction and nonfiction when discussing prose composition. Second, Scott was always examining origins of discourse genres, here prose composition. This paper also exemplifies Scott's eagerness to go to other fields, in this case anthropology, for material and concepts that would enrich studies in rhetoric.

"A Note on Walt Whitman's Prosody," which Scott published in

1910, examines some important aspects of Whitman's prosody. In his review of the scholarship on the subject, he finds differing positions. Barrett Wendell, among others, finds Whitman's prosody virtually nonexistent. John Burroughs, on the other hand, feels that "the music of his verse is as the music of the winds and waves. It is to be tested by open-air standards, by comparison with clouds, trees, rivers, spaces, not by comparison with works of art so called" (287; all pages references are to *The Standard of American Speech*). Scott rejects both arguments.

His concern is the relationship between art and nature. One set of critics contends that Whitman wanted art, that, in fact, his work was at its best when it eluded "the restraints of forms [and] attain[ed] the unbounded freedom of nature" (288). Scott called this an "orgiastic" view of Whitman's art, and he would have no part of it. Art and nature, like people and their government, must always be separate: "We may say that the artist never ought to be free to express himself, as nature does, in 'tufts and tussocks of grass.' He indeed achieves a freedom—all the freedom he needs, all the freedom there is for him—but he invariably achieves it by submitting himself to the restraints of artistic law" (290).

Although, as Scott points out, one may find in Whitman's poems the doctrine of formlessness expressed, one also finds passages indicating quite clearly that Whitman was a very conscious craftsman. "When he was correcting the proofs of the seventh edition of *Leaves of Grass* in 1881, he said to a reporter of the Boston *Globe,* 'This edition will complete the design which I had in my mind when I began to write. The whole affair is like one of those old architectural edifices, some of which were hundreds of years building, and the designer of which has the whole idea in his mind from the first'" (293–94).

Even more convincing proof is available in Whitman's manuscripts. Horace Traubel, one of Whitman's literary executors, had allowed Scott to examine a number of notes, outlines, preliminary drafts, and consecutive versions of some of Whitman's poems. Scott concluded from this material that "it is evident that the poet's 'spontaneity,' like that of most artists, was the result of prolonged and painful toil. The underground work which preceded the actual composition is in its extent and thoroughness amazing" (294). Thus, there is no question about Whitman's being a very conscious and painstaking craftsman, although, it may be argued, he differs from others in the poetic principles that he adopted and in his reasons for adopting them.

From "New Poetry" in Whitman's *Collect,* Scott quotes a long passage, the substance of which is that Whitman felt that the time had arrived when the boundaries between poetry and prose must be broken down. Why, Scott asks, did Whitman turn away from the forms of poetic expression which are found in the tradition of great English poets, and seek new ones? Whitman has, in short, adapted the rhythms of prose to poetry, "because the rhythm of prose, being larger and freer than the rhythm of verse, seemed nearer to the uncramped spirit of nature from which he drew his inspiration" (299).

But, having adopted the rhythms of prose for his purposes, Whitman realized that they were not completely adequate to serve his poetic needs. Consequently, he developed a hybrid form that combined both the nutative and the motative rhythms of the language (Scott's terms from "The Most Fundamental Differentia of Poetry and Prose"). Drawing on his own extensive knowledge, Scott notes that the form of Whitman's verse exists in the prose translation of the Hebrew prophets and psalmists, in the poems by Ossian, in Blake's *Prophetic Visions,* and "even in the insipid poetry of Martin Farquhar Tupper" (307).[4]

This note on Whitman's prosody, of course, would not now qualify as original scholarship, but in 1910, when Whitman scholarship was still developing and essays on his prosody were quite scarce, it constituted a major contribution to that body of work.[5]

Of all the papers Scott produced during this period, none occupied him as long or as intensely as "The Genesis of Speech." It was his presidential address, delivered before the MLA, December 26, 1907. In 1907, MLA Secretary Charles Grandgent thought it would be a feature of the convention program: "I wish the sedate traditions of the M.L.A. admitted of scare headings for your title. Even without them, it will be a drawing card."

Scott's use of materials from anthropology, biology, linguistics, and related disciplines was necessary, because he was trying to establish a physiological basis for the genesis of speech in man. He chooses the word *genesis* instead of *origin* because the latter has connotations of speech "coming into existence under the conditions and through the agencies which went to the making of Esperanto and Ido; it is almost as if they imagined some clever troglodyte saying to his fellows: 'A happy thought strikes me; let us invent a language'" (312; all pages references are to *The Standard of American Speech*). Instead, he wishes to conceive of the origin of language as a slow development.

To simplify the issue of its genesis, we may assume that whatever else it may be, "speech is, for the present purpose, primarily a mode of behavior, a significant movement of certain bodily organs—a series of co-

ordinated muscular contractions of the thorax, throat, tongue, lips, etc.
Disregarding other equally interesting questions, we may ask how these
movements are related to other bodily movements and how, in the history of early man, or his precursor, they arose, developed, and attained
their peculiar character and significance" (313).

Scott identifies what he calls covert and overt life processes which
may be both useful or life-serving and expressive-communicative. The
beating of the heart, not visible, is a covert life-serving process. A hand
reaching out to grab food is an overt life-serving process. Both, however,
are expressive-communicative, the rapidly beating heart expressive of
fear, the hand reaching out of bad manners. Citing Darwin's *Expression of
the Emotions in Man and Animals,* 1872, Scott says that expressive and
communicative functions are remnants of former life-serving functions.
For example, clenching the fist is the remnant of a knock-down blow;
clenching the teeth is a remnant of biting. While these expressive-communicative functions may have lost their original life-serving functions,
they have become life-serving in a social context. For example, if a community is hungry, it is important that he who has found food be able to
gesture to his fellows so that they will come and help in the killing of
the animal.

Scott comes, then, to his central question: "By what steps or stages
have functions originally life-serving passed over into society-serving
functions?" (318) To begin with, there is first a simple recognition-sign,
the means used by any member of a group to reveal his identity to others—the walk, pose, carriage of head, or swing of arms. The process by
which recognition signs pass into voluntary communication is complicated, technical, but very important. When the grasping for food is perceived by a mother, for example, in her child, she *completes* the gesture by
supplying food. Thus, the original image now becomes one of the child
reaching and the mother supplying. Eventually, the mere reaching out
by the child becomes the image of a request for food by the child. A level
of social cooperation is achieved.

Assuming, Scott says, that his description of the way a life-serving
movement becomes a socialized, symbolic movement is accurate, it is essential to examine the relationship of expressive-communicative movement to speech. Very simply, respiration is the life-serving function that
has evolved into speech. But the way in which this process occurred is
speculative. In general, various constrictions result in sounds that may
auger the beginning of speech. Some are caused by physiological
processes. For example, masticating and swallowing food and rejecting

it have their analogues in such expressive functions as laughing and cry-ing. There are other causes of constrictions: sneezing, snoring, coughing, spitting, groaning, hiccuping, choking, grunting, gulping, chuckling, and stuttering.[6]

Others accompany bodily strains, "such as anger, fright, suspense, and the like" (333). Fright, for example, is characterized by constriction of the throat with consequent withholding of needed air, followed by some sort of explosive opening and violent exhalation when the demand for air becomes acute.

The earliest communicative vocal utterance was, then, I conceive, a glottal stop, or some sound resembling it, followed by a voiced or voiceless sound, which in-creased in pitch and intensity to a certain point, and then diminished in these particulars to the close. . . .

I need hardly say that such an utterance as I have described was not a word. Neither was it a sentence, in any proper sense of that term, though it more nearly resembled the latter than the former. Precursor of both word and sen-tence, it was a protoplasmic speech-form in which an entire situation was in-choately expressed and communicated. Within it were embraced emotional seizure, instinctive appeal to its kind for help, discharge of feeling, conscious-ness of self, and consciousness of cooperation. (336–38)

Eventually, there is increasing specialization of the sounds made and recognition of them by members of social groups, the development of combinations of sounds into ideas, and the increased grouping of peoples who have developed more efficient primitive language systems for de-fense, food procurement, and other needs. Such an analysis is not only original and deeply provocative, but, in terms of the profession, unique in the use of materials from the social and natural sciences to enrich rhetorical theory. No contemporary conceived of rhetorical research in these terms.

Meanwhile, the profession of English was making literary study, at first philological, later New Critical, its primary business. Theoretical and philosophical work, of the kind Scott was demonstrating in this speech, was neither understood nor valued. It took the profession more than half a decade to get back on track to recognize the merit of such work.

9

Old and New Ventures

S COTT'S ATTENTION around 1911 was focused on his newspaper class, which was designed to prepare students for a vocation in journalism. He spent a good deal of energy in planning the course and then securing professional newspapermen to lecture. Scott appears to have had two motives for the latter. The obvious one was to give his students a realistic idea of what newspaper work was all about. Fortunately, he had many connections on the big city dailies in Chicago, Detroit, and New York, and was able to secure the services of some of the most interesting and distinguished newsmen of the time. His second motive was to change their attitudes. It is quite clear from letters that a number of professional newspapermen believed the universities could not train young men for their work. It was something one learned, in a hard-nosed way, on the job.

According to his diary, in January 1911 Scott was in Detroit seeing "McRae" about lecturing to his class. This very likely was Milton McRae, Edward Wyllis Scripps's business manager in one of the first newspaper chains developed in this country. Scott notes that McRae gave a very "business-like talk on a variety of subjects connected with newspapers" (FNSD, January 27, 1911). Among them was an issue which is still very much alive for journalists: should they not constrain themselves when publication of material in their possession could do real harm? A case in point involved James Garfield, the twentieth president of the United States. In private, McRae told Scott that the charges against Garfield's morals were true and that Mrs. Garfield did take steps for divorce.[1] He revealed that newspaper correspondents in Washington had met and decided not to write the story—a decision that would be unthinkable today. A tendency to the vulgar and unscrupulous was what Scott abhorred most in the newspapers of his time, and on every occasion available he railed against such excesses.

In 1911 Scott was getting some first-rate assistance from a former student, Lee White, who, in December, was working as exchange and assistant telegraph editor for the *Detroit News*. He sent Scott copies of a speech on libel in England and America by the mayor of New York City for use in Scott's class. He volunteered Mr. Pipp, the managing editor of the paper "to give a talk some time upon the subject" (FNSP, December 10, 1911). White had also lined up Jan Schmedding, Sr. of the *Detroit Journal* to talk to Scott's class about reporting in Britain and the United States or any other topic. White had no trouble getting newsmen to agree to come. He reports that "every man whom I have approached has felt highly honored by the invitation," although some felt inadequate to the task. "They all take it, as they freely tell me, as a sign that the university is not content to form its own highfalutin' conclusions about what is best for the newspaper man, but is most anxious to get a complete and effective fund of information upon the question" (FNSP, December 10, 1911).

Mr. Pipp talked to the newspaper class in December 1911 and had a surprisingly good time. White reports: "When he came back he sailed straight for Frank Kane's desk and unloaded himself of remarks to the effect that it was the swiftest hour he had ever experienced, even admitting the hour of going to press, and that he never enjoyed himself so in his life. 'Why,' he said, 'I didn't say half what I intended to. I could spend a dozen hours talking to them. I'd like to go right back there now.' . . . This from a man who confessed when he went out that he didn't believe much in a university education as a training for journalism— though more than half of his men are university or college men" (FNSP, December 20, 1911).

Among the other Detroit newspapermen Scott secured were Will Black, Kirk Alexander, and George Catlin of the *Detroit Evening News;* James Schermerhorn of the *Detroit Journal;* Clarence Kelland, assistant editor of the *American Boy;* Lee White's colleague Frank Kane; and White himself. From New York came Edwin Slosson of the *Independent;* Irvin Cobb of the *New York World,* who had won a considerable reputation and who was to distinguish himself as a war correspondent in World War I; and Paul More of *The Nation.*

What spurred this sudden renewed activity in journalism would be hard to determine. Scott had a tendency, however, to get bored with routine and to look for some new interest. Journalism was not new, but he had let it take a back seat to his work in rhetoric for a long period. Whatever the reason, in April 1911 he went to the first journalism week conference sponsored by the University of Missouri. This was a meeting Scott clearly wanted to attend, since Missouri was developing one of the finest journalism schools in the country. In fact, he was sufficiently intent on going that he had obtained reimbursement for his expenses from the regents. On Friday a national conference of teachers of journalism was held, and it was this part of the program that had drawn Scott, both as spectator and participant (S. L. Williams) (168).

At a lunch provided by Kappa Tau Alpha, a journalism fraternity, Scott spoke on the desirability of a national organization. Later, he spoke on the cultural value of a course in journalism; at a Press Club reception he also spoke for a few minutes. Oddly enough, while Scott's diary indicates that he was quite busy at this conference, the official program of the meeting does not even include his name.

The steady stream of high caliber newsmen onto the campus to speak to Scott's classes caught the attention of other faculty, administrators, and the regents. In May 1912, he got money from the regents to cover his travel expenses to New York to invite various newspapermen to Ann Arbor. In June 1912 he was in Chicago to attend a journalism educators' meeting. Scott's observations on this meeting give us a small glimpse into the mindset of a fledgling organization trying to justify itself and assert its raison d'être. In February and again in mid-October 1912, Scott went from Poughkeepsie, where he read papers on both occasions, to New York where he was again socializing with newspapermen, specifically Irvin Cobb of the *New York World,* Paul More of *The Nation,* and Norman Hapgood, editor at different times of *Collier's,* of *Harper's Weekly* and *Hearst's International*.

Scott was in New York again in April 1913 for meetings of the Associated Press and American Newspaper Publishers' Association. The meetings occurred over several days—April 22 to 25—and the *New York Times* carried numerous accounts of the various activities of differing press organizations. Mayor William J. Gaynor was the first speaker at the fifth annual dinner of the Daily Newspaper Association; more than six hundred newspapermen attended, with the secretary of the navy, Josephus Daniels, speaking at the dinner of the Associated Press/American

Newspaper Publishers' Association. It would have been an exhilarating experience for Scott with so many notables to socialize with.

In May 1914, Lee White, now in his third year as a newspaperman, wrote Scott that he wished he could hear the enthusiastic comments of Detroit newspapermen on schools of journalism. Scott's work, at least on that level, had paid off. White, who had gone to the University of Washington in the fall of 1914 to teach in the Journalism Department, wrote Scott for his views of other journalism programs, specifically Talcott Williams's course at Columbia.

Frank [Kane] thinks it's the biggest hot air course in the country. I didn't understand his criticism till I got James Melvin Lee's last news letter. I find in that the assertion that Columbia's freshmen write 1,500 words; sophomores, 2,000, juniors, 3,000, and seniors 3,500. I was flabbergasted. Frank's freshmen, who are held to two classes, three hours in reporting and one in the mechanics of printing, write at least 15,000 words. Mine in editing have had thus far this semester 22 written assignments, and I accept none of less than 300 words. (FNSP, December 22, 1914)

In summary, he asks: "Now how the deuce do they teach journalism at Columbia without making them write?"

With his successes and continued association with men of the press, it is not surprising that during 1914 and 1915, Scott was enthusiastically pursuing his interests through the newly formed American Association of Teachers of Journalism (AATJ). In December 1914, James Melvin Lee asked Scott to give the AATJ address at the convention in New York held at the Pulitzer School. For this occasion, Scott chose to speak on "Newspaper English."[2] During the summer of 1915, Scott had several reasons to return to California. One was to join representatives of the International Press Congress held in San Francisco, July 6–10. (Another was to attend the special meeting of NCTE held in conjunction with the international congress of NEA.) The gathering had been summoned by the Pan-Pacific International Exposition, which was held to prove that San Francisco had recovered from the earthquake of 1906. The business of the convention was to establish the Press Congress of the World, and out of the meetings came a constitution and the selection of officers. The first sessions of the new organization were held in Honolulu, Hawaii, in October–November 1921, with Walter Williams serving as president (W. Williams 3–5).

Present also were a number of the men Scott had come to know through AATJ and other similar press meetings. Scott was one of many who addressed the sessions, a distinguished group, among whom were William Jennings Bryan, then editor of the *Commoner* of Lincoln, Nebraska; James Schermerhorn of the *Detroit Times;* Merle Thorpe, professor of journalism at the University of Washington and later at the University of Kansas; and Talcott Williams, then director of the Pulitzer school of journalism at Columbia; as well as representatives from countries all around the world.

A number of Scott's former students simply reported back to him, telling him about their work, seeking his advice, and expressing appreciation for the experience of having been in his classes. Edgar Mowrer wrote Scott in September 1913, while he was reporting for the *Chicago News* bureau in Paris. He sent Scott an article on the educational situation in France, illustrated by material drawn from recruits to the French army. He also asked what Scott thought of Freud. Scott responded:

Freud has done good work in the analysis of dreams and other confused mental states. He has demonstrated in detail what a good many had vaguely guessed before him, namely that when the rudder of the mind is hanging loose, the vessel will be swept this way and that by the winds and currents of physiological activity or external stimuli. This reasonable explanation of mental states and processes Freud has, however, made grotesque or absurd by pushing it to the wildest extremes. His latter studies seem to me to be unbalanced and even morbid. (FNSP, penciled response on letter, September 26, 1913)

At the same time Scott was adding journalism to his professional life, he continued to engage in rhetorical concerns. In December 1911 Joseph Mauck, president of Hillsdale College, wrote to obtain Scott's views on several issues, among them whether the opinions expressed by Professor Thomas Lounsbury in *Harper's Magazine* for November 1911 had any validity. Lounsbury was one of the early critics of compulsory composition courses. He complained that under the guise of teaching students to use the English language with purity and precision, the courses had subjected students to the writing of daily themes on subjects about which they had no knowledge and in which they had no interest at all, and to the reading of handbooks and rhetorics that killed the last spark of literary sensitivity in those in which it might be found. This circumstance forced large numbers of instructors to expend energy and time in a brain-deadening process; a good many of these ill-qualified people also spread mythologies about the language that were almost impossible to root out. The problem, according to Lounsbury, is that teachers have confused the ability to learn with the ability to write. The former can be easily traced. The ability to write, however, is a much more subtle acquisition, requiring years of practice and the unconscious assimilation of a feel for the language.

Scott replied: "For my part, I should be glad to be convinced that Prof. Lounsbury is right, for the burden of essay correcting is near the limit of endurance. But, I fear there is no royal road to the mastery of so difficult an art. The question raised by Professor Lounsbury is a very old one. It has been discussed hundreds of times in print and at teachers' meetings. But the author has given it a new fillip and started what has turned out to be a very disagreeable controversy. I have no data for deciding one way or the other." Scott, with his empirical bent, thinks the best way to evaluate Lounsbury's theory is to divide students into two groups, putting one through the best course of training devised and turning the other out, so to speak, to grass. Then compare the results (FNSP, penciled response on letter, December 21, 1911).[3]

This was a tired response by Scott, who by this time would unquestionably have had a stronger opinion. Perhaps he did not care enough about Marston to grant him a longer reply, or perhaps he was simply tired of the issue. Scott had certainly spent a great deal of his life engendering support for the exact position Lounsbury was attacking. He had given his reasons, over and over, for believing that rhetoric was a legitimate intellectual pursuit, that composition was a subject worthy of respect, and he had committed himself publicly to heading a large department of rhetoric where his own reputation and the reputation of the University of Michigan would have been undermined had he, in any way, conceded that Lounsbury might have some credibility.

Clearly, Scott was sidestepping the question—for whatever reason. According to David R. Russell, the Lounsbury issue led to the founding of NCTE (134). As he concludes: "Here, then, is the central paradox of the Romantics' position: It is the study of literature, not rhetoric, that ultimately improves students' rhetoric. And the role of English departments in writing instruction is thus to teach liberal culture through imaginative literature" (136).

In September 1913, Scott wrote an editorial for the *English Journal* in which he expressed his philosophy about the teaching of composition in more detail. Because of his position as director of the rhetoric program at Michigan, he was uniquely aware of the problems in adequately staffing the standard courses in composition; part of the problem he saw was that most composition teachers were mistrained. This perception went against the attitudes of the time, which were that anyone could teach composition.

Scott notes that although teachers of freshman English should be specifically trained for teaching English composition, they are not. "With few exceptions they are trained as if they were to lecture on obscure problems of English literature to small groups of graduate students" (456). The result is that those who are hired teach for only a short time and then expect to move into the teaching of literature. Scott says there are two types of teachers, but this difference is not universally recognized. One has "the ability to pursue research in English literature, the other the ability to teach English composition." His opinion is that the two should not be intermixed, the former because they loathe the task. But the latter should not be disparaged in their choice to teach composition rather than literature.

The most notable point in this essay is his identification of the problem and his complaint that those in charge have, overall, refused to recognize it. As a national leader, Scott's words should have carried more weight and earlier brought the reforms that began halfway through the twentieth century.

In Scott's notes there are miscellaneous items on teaching which are intriguing in regard to this controversy. One set, located in his diary after October 1914, refers to the method of teaching by ideas. He says it rests on the assumption that ideas must precede writing (a belief strongly held by Lounsbury) and that thinking does not, itself, generate ideas. Such a point of view, he feels, overlooks the complexity of the composing process in which outlining and revision are as essential as writing sentences. In this respect, Scott anticipates later theorists who have pointed to the recursiveness of the composing process. In other reflections, the gist is that thinking generates ideas, as does the act of writing itself. Furthermore, these ideas grow and amplify as a result of the composing process. It is an organic conception of composing which, in 1914, would have run strongly against a segmented linear perception of composing, one which assumed that ideas preceded writing and that revision was merely a touching up of what was essentially finished.

In November 1911 Scott was in Indianapolis for a meeting of the Indiana Association of Teachers of English, where he addressed two hundred teachers. His topic was "Two Ideals of Composition Teaching," the same paper he had presented to the Kansas Association in 1910. Despite Scott's schedule and duties, he similarly honored a commitment to the

Minnesota Educational Association in October 1914. A letter from Elizabeth Hall of that organization requests "topics, photographs, material for press notices." She says, "We would like to have you speak twice that afternoon if that is not asking too much." She adds that many people "express great satisfaction upon seeing your name on the program" (FNSP, September 22, 1914). That same month, Scott also had agreed to attend the Michigan State Teachers' Association, where he "analyzed the value of poetry in a commercial age" ("News and Notes," December 1914). (This meeting was important because of the decision made to organize a Michigan branch of the National Council.)

Scott's first reported involvement with NCTE begins innocuously enough. His diary entry for November 29–30, 1911, reads: "In Chicago at organization of Council of English Teachers." That is all. However, as J. N. Hook's history of the organization indicates, "the life of almost every American who has gone to school in this country since 1911 has been touched, at least slightly, by what happened" (31). In less than a year this "Council of English Teachers" was showing uncommon life and vigor. According to the proceedings of the first annual meeting, held December 1 and 2, 1911, "the National Council of Teachers of English grew out of the work of a committee of the National Education Association. At the meeting of the English Round Table of the Secondary Department in Boston, July 1, 1910, it was voted that a committee of schoolmen be appointed to lay before the College-Entrance Examination Board the views of the high-school principals and teachers of the country in regard to the present uniform entrance requirements in English and the examinations set upon them" ("The National Council" [1912] 30). When on July 12, 1911, the Round Table met in San Francisco, the committee was asked to initiate the formation of a national society of English teachers.

When the council met in December, about sixty-five delegates and representative teachers attended, thirty-five of whom signed as charter members. Scott was elected temporary chairman at the first session and acted immediately to appoint a committee of nine to prepare a constitution and nominate officers. At the final session, Scott was officially elected president and a two-year member of the board of directors. Under the constitution, this board was in charge of the affairs of the council, with one-third being chosen for one year, one-third for two, and one-third for three so as to set up a rotation for members to serve three-year terms in the future that would allow for continuity.

The National Council announced that its aim was "'to increase the effectiveness of school and college work in English'" (Hook 17). It would coordinate the work of all the other current English groups: the state organizations, the National Conference on Uniform Entrance Requirements, MLA, and the English Round Table of the NEA. It also would represent the entire range of teachers, from elementary to college. The presence of Scott was very fortunate for the organization for reasons already noted: his association over the years with the Michigan Schoolmasters' Club, his membership in both the North Central Association and the Conference on Uniform Entrance Requirements. In addition, by this time he had become well known as a rhetorician and had established his Rhetoric Department firmly enough to have it considered by other universities as a source for faculty when they needed thoroughly grounded persons to join their programs. In other words, not only was Scott highly regarded, but his contacts both in the secondary schools and in the universities were numerous and widespread across the country.

It is important to understand that NCTE was not competitive with the other organizations. For one thing, it assisted with some of the work of MLA, as, for example, the Composition Committee and the Committee on the Revision of Grammatical Terminology. The *English Journal,* the official organ of NCTE, was proposed early in the organizational plan, and James Hosic, of Chicago Teachers' College, served as editor until 1921.

In 1912, the National Council met November 28–30, again in Chicago. Most of Scott's work at this second convention was routine—meeting with Hosic and others, attending sessions, going to luncheons and dinners. However, he did read his paper "Our Problems in Teaching Literature and Composition" at the general session. He also served as toastmaster at the annual dinner, a role that was not unfamiliar to him. About five hundred persons attended "some or all of the sessions" ("News and Notes" [1913] 61). He also was reelected or, as he put it, "re-accepted for a second term," the only NCTE president ever to achieve this distinction.[4] Scott's efforts in the early history of NCTE did not go unappreciated. J. W. Searson of Kansas State Agricultural College wrote to him, December 3, 1912: "Your skill in planning the meeting just closed and your generalship as presiding officer, entitled you to this recognition" (FNSP).

By 1913, the attendance at the council's annual meeting had increased 25 percent. Significantly, New England was the only part of the country not represented. At this time, Scott's term on the board of directors had run out, but he was reelected for another three years, now the standard period for all board members. Scott was also elected to the Executive Committee for a three-year term. This group consisted of only three members, who, along with the president and secretary, were designated by the constitution to direct the work of the council.

By now, eleven committees presented reports, among them one on pedagogical investigation. Could this latter have been a reincarnation of the Pedagogical Section of MLA on which Scott had served earlier? An identifiable continuation of Scott's work was the Committee on the Preparation of College Teachers of English, which by mid-May 1914 had sent out questionnaires to college English instructors, heads of university English departments, college presidents, and professors of education. This committee, on which Scott served, asked for five responses: (1) what preparation college teachers actually had; (2) what requirements the departments had; (3) the comparative advantage provided to advancement through higher degrees and experience; (4) specific courses offered for preparation; and (5) opinions as to the best means of preparation. In December 1914, this committee had arranged to work through the Bureau of Education at Washington with the results of the inquiries to be published in a bulletin of the bureau.

At the 1914 NCTE meeting, "the welfare of the National Council" was discussed. It was noted that although collective membership was up by 50 percent, individual membership had decreased. It was hoped that in 1914–1915 affiliations could be organized in every state. For his part, Scott stated that he was happy the Council "had undertaken the impossible, that is, the fundamental, in reforms, and can therefore never come to the end of its task, continuing from mere inertia, as such societies are likely to do" ("The National Council" [1915] 48–49).

On May 11, 1915, Scott was asked to consider accommodating the speech teachers whose meetings conflicted with those of NCTE. Thomas Trueblood explained that the timing of the NCTE meetings has caused some problems for those who belonged to the speech association. As noted, the movement which separated the composition and literature teachers also separated the English and speech teachers. This unfortunate division has never been fully reversed.

In August, as noted above, Scott attended the special meeting of NCTE at Oakland, California, held in conjunction with the international congress of NEA. On that occasion, Scott was one of a number of both high school and college representatives from all over the country who gave speeches. His was titled, "On American Speech and Speech Training." It contrasted British and American speech, emphasizing not

only the individuality of each, but also the relationship particularly of American to British speech. As will be seen, this topic preceded a similar assessment he made in his later involvement with international efforts to unify the speech habits and usage in Britain and America.

At the November 1915 meetings, Scott got involved with the speech movement of NCTE, as chairman of a committee to reform speech habits. We shall see later the direction this movement took. Also, at that time, the report of the Committee on the Preparation of College Teachers of English was given. It must be remembered that this project grew out of Scott's 1912 suggestion to the Central Division of MLA. When the results of a questionnaire survey were presented at MLA's 1912 annual convention, it was suggested that a committee should continue the investigation, and Scott was one of the members of that committee whose work was then transferred to NCTE.

Scott maintained his association with MLA despite the opportunities NCTE offered him to pursue projects that were closer to his interests and beliefs regarding both the teaching of composition and the aims and practices of rhetoric itself. One of Scott's predominant commitments to MLA in the years 1911 to 1915 was to the Committee of Fifteen on the Harmonizing of Grammatical Nomenclature, established as a response to what was termed "confusion" in the terminology associated with grammar instruction. But the committee was diverted from its original task into preparing lists of texts for reading in the schools, graded according to level of difficulty. Meanwhile, NEA had formed a committee to address grammar terminology. Seeing too many bodies at work on the same problem, W. G. Hale urged unification of the efforts of NEA, MLA, and the American Philological Association, which resulted in the Joint Committee of Fifteen.

At the 1911 meeting of the MLA, Scott read his paper "A Simple Phonetic Alphabet," his attempt to devise the "simplest visual symbols" to represent the English alphabet. The use of simplified spelling had evolved from the 1906 vote to adopt for official documents of the MLA the forms recommended by the Simplified Spelling Board. Many of the members of the Association, including Scott, utilized these spellings in their personal correspondence as well. Eventually, like the phonetic alphabet, momentum was not on the side of change, and the effort quietly subsided.

At the 1913 MLA meetings on the Harvard campus, Scott read a paper on vowel alliteration, and joined J. W. Bright, Hermann Collitz, W. A. Adams, Albert Schinz, W. G. Hale, C. E. Fay, G. L. Kittredge,

Adolphe Cohn, and L. F. Mott in discussing the report of the Committee of Fifteen on the Harmonizing of Grammatical Nomenclature. The motion to accept the report and discharge the committee was agreed upon, as was the motion to approve the report of the joint committee (MLA, NEA, American Philological Association). "The obvious trouble with such attempts is that no real uniformity is possible until there exists an almost universally accepted theory of grammar or linguistics, and that blissful state has never been attained" (Hook 53).

In 1914, when MLA met at Columbia University, Scott served on the nominating committee and announced the choices: Jefferson B. Fletcher of Columbia for president; Oliver F. Emerson of Western Reserve, Bert J. Vos of Indiana, and Mary V. Young of Mount Holyoke College for vice-presidents. Young's appointment was the source of letters suggesting a conspiracy of women members; she became the first female officer of MLA. In 1915, Scott served again on the nominating committee, which, following its innovative act of the previous year, presented Louise Pound of the University of Nebraska as one of the vice-presidents.

As to the other organizations with which Scott was involved at the time, he was in New York in both March and May 1912 for meetings of the Conference on English Requirements. The whole issue of requirements was a lengthy and protracted one. It had arisen in the late nineteenth century when increasing college enrollments, the gradual acceptance of the elective system, and the transformation of the university from an elaborate finishing school to an institution that trained national leaders—a move initiated dramatically at Harvard in 1869 by Charles Eliot—took hold. The result had been to bring to university and college campuses a much greater diversity of students than had existed in the past. Some of these were much better prepared to speak and write English than others. Further exacerbating the issue were the different philosophies of private and public universities. And the Harvard Reports of the 1890s had only intensified the situation.

Scott also continued his work within the North Central Association of Colleges and Secondary Schools, and in 1913 he was elected president of this association. Thus, by 1915, Scott had been elected to the presidencies of three organizations: MLA in 1907, NCTE from 1911 to 1913, and the North Central Association in 1913. In addition, he had established himself as an important figure in the American Association of Teachers of Journalism. It was an unparalleled achievement, bringing him prominence in language, literature, composition, journalism, and education.

This period of Scott's life is remarkable not only because he rose to such prominence, but because of the level of energy and vitality required to do so. It was not as if his work for the various organizations was all he had to do. He had other activities, interests, and obligations as well—including meeting his classes. In the early 1910s, a preoccupying issue at the University of Michigan was the organization of a graduate school and the appointment of a graduate dean. Scott was appointed to the committee on the formation of a graduate school and to the newly formed executive board of the graduate school. The official announcement of Karl E. Guthe as the choice for dean was made in June 1912. As noted in Isadore's letter from Europe in 1908, Scott was also considered a candidate, but she seemed more to favor this position than had Scott himself. Very likely, the administrative duties did not appeal to him. (Louis Strauss had noted after Scott's retirement that he was not happy doing administrative work [332]).

On campus, some of the concerns, especially those dealing with morality, are prudish by today's standards, and were addressed overzealously. As a member of the Board of Student Publications, in June 1912, Scott showed Dean John Effinger an indecent advertisement in the *Michigan Daily*. "Telephoned about it to Dilley [student business manager] who in answer to my questions said he had seen it and knew what it meant, but did not know that it was illegal" (FNSD, June 8, 1912). At the *Daily* banquet that evening Scott talked with Dilley "who said he had not appreciated the character of the advertisement and had not understood my questions."[5] At this time, as the newspaper advertising industry burgeoned, critics began to raise questions regarding obscenity and false claims. For example, patent medicines came under fire for containing cocaine, morphine, and alcohol. In 1911, a statute was enacted making untruthful, deceptive, or misleading statements in ads a misdemeanor.

Yellow journalism also was a problem, with not only the sensationalism generally ascribed to it, but also the bold type and lavish use of pictures, which some considered to be fraud in the sense of reckless and misleading information (Mott [1950] 595–96). In October 1912 Scott was upset about the vulgarities of the Omar cigarette ads, but advertisements in questionable taste were not the only things subject to faculty censure in the paper. The same month, A. R. Johnson, assistant business manager of the *Daily*, consulted Scott about inserting a notice of a political meeting in the paper. Although Scott saw no harm in it, the president said all political advertising should be kept out of the paper (FNSD, October 5, 1912).

Student discipline, a much more tightly regulated matter in the early decades of this century, probably took more of Scott's time than he would have liked. A serious case in 1913 involved one of Scott's own men, Otto Marckwardt. He was charged with misconduct in his relations with a female student, and in July he came to Scott's room to deny all the charges. "Said he knew one of the socialist girls very intimately, had known her since she was an infant, and might have spoken familiarly to her, but he was incapable of doing what he was charged with" (FNSD, July 18, 1913). A student named Joseph Richards charged that Marckwardt kissed the lady in question. He overheard a conversation. In his version, the girl said "Please don't." The man said "What's the matter?" The girl said she had a cold sore on her lip.

Scott wrote to Richards:

> You cannot expect me to take seriously the bits of trivial gossip that you quote, and so the things that you saw and heard seem to me quite inconsistent. That Mr. Marckwardt is unconventional in his manner he would himself admit. But that has nothing to do with his character.
>
> You seem to take this matter very lightly as if it were something of a joke. I assure you that it is not. Unless you have more positive evidence than you have offered thus far, I would advise you not only to refrain in your conversation from further reflections on Mr. Marckwardt's character but to assist in killing such rumors as already are in circulation. (FNSP, September 6, 1913)

Marckwardt was obviously upset. "When I think that a boy, almost a stranger in this community, should dare to call into question the good name of a man who has lived in this town for twelve years, who has been for seven years a member of the faculty, who can bring a hundred friends to testify to his honesty and moral uprightness, and when I think by what kind of facts and evidence this boy purports to prove his charges, do you wonder that I am perplexed?" (FNSP, September 11, 1913). The incident does raise some questions, however, about whether Richards fabricated the whole incident for his own reasons, or whether Marckwardt was perhaps too presumptuous about the acceptability of his behavior if the incident did, indeed, occur. Scott, himself, was prudish enough not to have accepted Marckwardt's explanation unless he was absolutely sure it was true.

Another of the time-consuming duties Scott routinely performed for the university was the squiring of visiting dignitaries. His diary contains frequent references to people who came to the campus or, in some cases, whom he met while representing the university at some local event. Among these celebrities were the Coburns, the famous acting family

(Charles Coburn is probably the best remembered today); Franklin P. Adams of the *New York Evening Mail,* one of the panelists on the old NBC radio show "Information Please"; James Kelsey of the *Chicago Tribune;* Professor Krueger of Halle; Paul E. More, editor of the *New York Nation;* Julien Bezard of Heidelberg; and the British publisher J. M. Dent, a man responsible for the Everyman's Library.

Although Scott had involved himself in more areas than many university professors, it is clear that he contributed a great deal to the university as well as to his department and classes. For recreation, which he surely needed, Scott undertook two extensive trips during the summers of 1911 and 1912.

Both are reported in considerable detail in his diary. The first was a family automobile trip from Ann Arbor to Atlantic City and return in the early summer of 1911. The car never gave them a moment's relaxation on the trip, with first a broken belt, then a lost oil pan, a damaged luggage carrier from an accident with another car, bad brakes, and a number of punctured tires. Of course, one must remember what roads, tires, and machinery in general were like in 1911. But the car wasn't the only problem. Marion Scott, then aged twenty-one, later recalled that "of all the things that happened . . . the worst was the drive across New Jersey because of the horde of mosquitoes (or flies?) that swarmed all over the car and settled on [us] when [we] slowed down or stopped. [I] never liked New Jersey much after that" (MG to Donald Stewart, May 8, 1981).

In July and August 1912 Scott traveled alone to Denver to explore the region around what is now Rocky Mountain National Park. Scott was fifty-two years old, and his goal of climbing Long's Peak, a mountain over fourteen thousand feet high, could be nothing but strenuous for him.

The ascent just stepping from one ledge to another until we came to a little ice when it was necessary to use the holes melted out around stones. The last part very straight up and then the trail came out on a shelf overhanging a dreadful gorge. The guide stepped out freely to the very edge, bringing my heart into my mouth. . . . The homestretch pretty straight up and slippery, but the bliss of approaching victory made the climb easy. (FNSD, August 21, 1912)

But in heading back to Boulder, he missed the train and wound up walking the twenty miles in late summer heat.

In the summer of 1914, Scott was determined to return to Europe. Seemingly unaware of the growing international crisis, he obtained a leave of absence from May 15 to the end of the school year so that he might have time for foreign travel and study. His purpose is revealed in a letter from S. P. Capen of the Bureau of Education, April 4, 1914, referring to Scott's "plans for studying the composition of pupils in the German elementary schools and the *Gymnasien*" (FNSP). Scott had apparently asked to be supplied with the credentials of the bureau. As Capen says, "This may possibly help you to see some of the things to which access would otherwise be difficult. If your experience in foreign schools has been anything like mine, you will be glad of any kind of an official document which will help you to open their tight-shut doors."

Scott and his family arrived in Berlin on July 15, after sightseeing in a number of places. By early August Scott had one thing on his mind: getting his family home safely. On September 15 they set off for The Hague. In Holland Scott visited a school where he saw "lively and interested pupils, boys and girls. One girl could speak English, in the British dialect." On September 22, he attended a composition class at the gymnasium and wound up discussing the formal character of teaching (FNSD).

The trip home was not exactly settling. "Heard that three English cruisers had been sunk. . . . Saw many British war vessels and two submarines. . . . Near Dover German ship towed by British tug as prize." The next night their ship was stopped twice in the night, once by a French warship, once by three English cruisers. An old German said to Scott, "There ain't no God, eh? He wouldn't let all dem peebles be killed." It had not been the summer he had planned on at all (FNSD, September 24, 1914).

10

Publications of Consequence

I N EACH OF the years between 1911 and 1915, Scott completed
at least one major work—major either in length or in substance.
But notable also in this period is his interest in Russian literature,
which resulted in two major translations, plays by Leonid Andreyeff and poetry by N. A. Nekrasov.

In reading Scott's addresses and papers, it is important to keep in
mind the dichotomy between Scott's conservative presence in the textbooks and the more innovative thinking in his theoretical papers. James
Berlin has suggested that one reason for the absence of interest in Scott's
work during much of the twentieth century is the lack of originality in
the textbooks. He attributes Scott's traditionalism in the textbooks to
his acceptance of the demands of the marketplace (Berlin, *Writing Instruction* 77). That generalization is questionable. Scott was a practical
man in his dealings with teachers at all levels of instruction. He understood that most of them were either unable or unwilling to bring the
same intellectual vigor to the study of complex rhetorical problems that
they did to the study of literature. Consequently, he took them as far as
he could, offering enough familiar matter to make them comfortable
with his books, but challenging them enough that they would not be entirely comfortable with established ways of thinking about rhetoric and
the teaching of composition.

This attitude is obvious in the paper he read before both the New
England Association in June 1910 and the Indiana Association in November 1911. Entitled "Two Ideals of Composition Teaching," it addresses the difference between the ideal the teacher holds and that which
he practices. Scott finds that the cause for this schism lies in the textbooks, in details buried or disguised so "insidiously" that the teacher unwittingly may go in the wrong direction. In his examination of what

ideals teachers should be concerned with, he finds that in the 2400 years of composition teaching, there are two, both deriving from the Greeks.

The first was the invention of Korax, a native of Sicily in the fifth century B.C. That ideal is success. Korax instructed defendants in the tricks of argument which, whether the speaker's cause was right or wrong, would allow him to prevail with the judges and juries. Naturally, these methods became very popular. Scott notes: "Literally our teaching of composition and our attitude toward composition are still controlled, whether we know it or not, by the ingenious thought of the Sicilian Korax, as elaborated by the powerful mind of Aristotle" (38; all page references are to *The Standard of American Speech*).

In Scott's mind, the ideas of Plato should have prevailed. He cites the *Phaedrus,* wherein Socrates is made to say that there are two aims to rhetoric: one that is designed to flatter and deceive, and one that "aims at the training and improvement of the souls of the citizens" (39). From this beginning Plato derives a rhetorical system that emphasizes truth and self-sacrificing devotion to the interests of the community. And this is the ideal of composition that Scott espouses. But he senses, from examining current textbooks, that teachers are not following this ideal.

Scott acknowledges that an ideal which looks beyond mere practicality is not popular. But he thinks it is necessary not only for the perpetuation of the profession, but for the good of humanity, citing the application to Christianity, "that man can save himself only by giving what is best in him to his fellow-men" (45). These are lofty and noble aims. Scott sees them as inspiring both students and teachers, rescuing them from the current drudgery inherent in the curriculum. This is a major statement by Scott, for it is a representation of his mission and his lifelong dedication to a higher plane of rhetoric.

At the 1912 meeting of the newly formed NCTE, Scott's presidential address is entitled "Our Problems." Those problems turn out to be how to assess the value of compositions and, corollary to that, the efficiency of the teaching of composition; and how to make the classics palatable and meaningful to students. On the first issue, he cites the work of Dr. Milo Burdette Hillegas, who devised a "scientific" method for ranking compositions. Hillegas took seven thousand samples of elementary composition, from which the investigators selected ten representative compositions. They then ranked these ten writings in order of increasing merit, from which they derived a scale, the lowest being the worst, the highest being "as good a piece of writing as any young person is likely to achieve" (62; all page references are to *The Standard of American Speech*). For teachers the task of grading is simplified, for all they now have to do is find the corresponding match among those sample papers for the paper they have in hand.

Scott's objection, though in general he has always admired scientific methods, is that such a scale does not recognize the many unmeasurable components in writing, such as imagination, emotion, and aesthetics. He notes that "the student's composition, as the teacher should look at it, is the expression of the student's life. To evaluate it is to evaluate life itself in one of its most delicate manifestations" (65). Additionally, Scott argues that the system overlooks the relative growth or regression of the student over time. For example, it is possible that a composition given a high ranking may be the work of a student who is regressing rather than developing, and that one given a low ranking may be the work of a student "on his way to that freedom and sincerity of speech which will one day make him a power for good" (66).

The second of "our problems" is the presentation of the classics of English literature to students who find them dull and dry, by teachers who have taught them for so long they themselves can no longer find them stimulating. He believes that the teacher must remind himself that, though the material is no longer new to him, it is new to each new group of students. He suggests that the teacher can search out a means for preserving his enthusiasm through "increased knowledge, more intimate acquaintance, leading to new methods of approach" (73). The students will, later in life, come to appreciate the classics.

Scott challenges the claim that the classics are "unrelated to life" and that they are not a "preparation for life." "Of what does [life] consist? Eating and drinking and running a typewriter and selling stocks and shoveling snow off the front walk? Is this the life for which our costly system of education is to provide? A turning over and over (to use Ruskin's simile) like that of a squirrel in a cage? If so, that is, if life means simply keeping oneself alive, our teachers are extravagantly overpaid. A little chloroform would achieve a better result at a fraction of the cost" (73). Ultimately, the integrity of the individual and generosity toward others in the community, tolerance and sincerity—the values he himself practiced—were the values he believed should direct all gainful teaching, whether in composition or literature.

In November 1913, Scott's second address as NCTE president was "The Undefended Gate." An unusual mix-up occurred with this speech, which no doubt confirmed Scott's belief that newspapermen needed rigorous schooling in the care with which they attended to fact, something he emphasized in his newspaper classes.

On November 15, Scott received a letter from Edgar T. Cutter of the

Associated Press in Chicago requesting an advance copy of the speech. On December 1, an editorial appeared in the *Chicago Tribune* titled "Cloistered Ignorance." It begins: "There has been no sadder prophet since Jonah than Professor Fred N. Scott of the University of Michigan, who was pathetic, because helpless, describing for the National Convention of Teachers of English the 'evil that comes from the newspapers.' When this academic type discloses itself, and when consideration is given to the fact that a mind so narrow is charged with the duty of broadening the horizon of young people, we almost fall into despair of the republic" (134; all page references are to *The Standard of American Speech*). What had Scott said to provoke such vilification?

Scott had begun his speech innocuously, noting that the teaching of English had not only experienced growth, but had come to be recognized as a worthy enterprise for those engaged in it. But he observes that the profession has had a problem with effecting noticeable progress in the literacy of the students. It is important to examine the causes of this situation, for they may reveal a lack of precaution against some "malign influence." There are several possibilities: the uncultured family, the carelessness of teachers of other subjects—and the newspaper.

From this summary, it is clear why the newspapers would have been so anxious to attack Scott. But they had not done their homework, missing the fact and the essence of Scott's message. He goes on to argue that the newspaper is more powerful an influence than the Bible, which "when it was read at least once a day in every Christian family, was, as an educational force, of incalculable value" (120). But the newspaper, in its evolution, discovered a vast market among the young and began printing the "funny paper." This is the culprit which Scott accuses of having corrupted young people, for it starts the child reading and then leads him beyond the cartoon page to the other areas of the paper.

Scott's objections were not those reported in the *Tribune,* but rather that the newspapers do not exercise proper manners: they scream, they swear, they tell filthy stories, they provide brutal and suggestive pictures, and, if they make mistakes, they fail to apologize. They also skew the facts "by the wording of headlines; by the size of type; by the prominence given to the article; by the comment in the editorial column" (124). Obviously suffering from an old wound, he cites an example from his own experience. He had given a speech before a society of scholars, and a reporter, though Scott had spent a good period of time with him, had been unable to grasp its meaning. In despair, Scott had finally left him to his own devices, and the speech had been misrepresented. "And

so the story, in a form which doubtless provoked laughter among my colleagues, was published in this newspaper, and was afterward circulated
about the United States in press dispatches. I still hear from it at intervals" (125).

Scott expects a newspaper to be clean and wholesome. Half seriously,
he proposes that the papers print a "filth section . . . into which might
be dumped those matters which now offend, or should offend, the eye
and nostril of the reader. Such a section might be printed in red ink or
on crimson-hued paper so that those who wanted it could readily find it
and those who did not could readily avoid it" (125–26).

Scott summarizes his indictment of journalism: "Unkempt style,
slangy diction, even bad grammar are in themselves of no great moment
when compared with violations of the great principles of amenity, truth,
sincerity, wholesomeness, and self-restraint, which are the principles of
good writing and of appreciation as they are the principles of conduct"
(126). He acknowledges that teachers cannot expect the young to quit
reading the funny papers, but a good teacher can mitigate the influence
of the newspaper. "Let us teach them what the newspaper is; what its
faults and virtues are; how the better newspaper may be distinguished
from the worse. Let us teach them also the art of reading the newspaper"
(127–28). He asserts that if the papers practice the ideals he has outlined, they can be a great power for good, eventually, in fact,
"render[ing] the teacher of English superfluous" (132).

Considering Scott's overall message in this address, there is a serious
irony in what the newspapers reported his having said. Probably the
worst perversion of his meaning in the original news release by the
Chicago City News bureau relates to this paragraph: "In time it will be
possible to cultivate the likes and dislikes of the student and by teaching him even the worst papers will conform to his tastes. The newspapers cannot be reformed right away. One way of teaching the students
the proper appreciation of the shortcomings of the newspapers is to devote one week of every month to a study of its poison and criminal reck-
lessness" (134). The writer of "Cloistered Ignorance" misconstrues
Scott's message in his zeal to attack Scott:

Into the cloistered precincts of Mr. Scott's life there should come only Walter
Pater and the only window in his wall should look into a rose garden.
    The fragrance of his thoughts and the serenity of his mood should never re-
ceive even the suggestion of the world without where pain and work, sin and
saintliness are woven into the fabric. (135)

The *Tribune* acknowledged its mistake in a strange, twisted denial:

> *The Tribune* has not changed its mind regarding what Mr. Scott was *reported* as saying, but it finds itself largely in accord with what he *did* say. The report furnished by the City Press association by its errors almost justified the condemnation of newspapers ascribed to Professor Scott. . . .
>
> The injury done Professor Scott was in attributing to him generalizations which described the production of newspapers as wholly malevolent, brutal, and vicious, and the effect as destructive of morals, taste, and decency.
>
> A protest against such statements was warranted, but it was Professor Scott's accident and *The Tribune's* misfortune to have his words as they obtained general publicity chosen not by himself but by another person. (135–36)

Scott could have taken some satisfaction from this apology had it not been so lamely stated (Scott's *accident?*), and had it not possessed the problems pursuant upon all such apologies—the impossibility of altering the original impression upon the newspaper's readers. Among his colleagues there was support for his views. An editorial in the *English Journal* in February 1914 states: "The garbling of views and the fostering of a morbid interest in crime and the baser passions have become so common on the part of the daily papers of America that it was high time for someone speaking with influence and authority to bring them to book" (124).

In 1914, in his capacity as president of the North Central Association of Colleges and Secondary Schools, Scott delivered another major address, entitled "Efficiency for Efficiency's Sake," which scrutinized teacher effectiveness. John Brereton dates the movement for modernizing the school curriculum identified as "efficiency" to the decade 1915–1925, but there is little question that this article was inspired by that movement (90, 102). As in all times, the educational concern with teaching effectiveness was well intentioned, but it had occasioned a system of testing, both of teachers and students, that Scott felt was restrictive and harmful. Simply put, he believed educational success could not be measured quantitatively.

Scott's fear was that "dazed by the brilliancy of the new conception, [the teacher] may be brought to think of himself only as a factor in the production of curves of efficiency and of his pupils only as rated units in the determination of percentages of distribution" (51; all page references are *The Standard of American Speech*). As he sees it, "the most efficient things in teaching are . . . such things as personality, sympathy, sincerity, enthusiasm, intuition of character, taste, judgment, love of truth, tact. These things are qualities, not quantities, and any judgment of them, to be adequate, must be made in terms of *quality"* (52; italics mine).

Scott's devotion to teaching borders on the spiritual. If teachers are to be tested, the tests should ask the following questions: "Is he a saver of souls? Is he a fountain of light and hope and courage? Does the spark of intelligence in the young minds before him as he addresses them shoot up into sudden flame? Do those who have sat under his ministration look back with gratitude to their contacts with him as occasions when the finest and best in them was aroused and stirred to activity? Has he been able to inspire them with the love of truth, with the ambition of being wise and good, with the growing power to enjoy what is pure and nobly fashioned?" (55). Scott succeeded in these qualities himself, according to accounts from his students. Helen Mahin writes in the *Anniversary Papers* presented to Scott in 1929: "Professor Scott did much less of imparting than of inspiring. . . . I remember the scholarly man at the table . . . speaking unobtrusively, leading us out or quietly challenging our foolish words" (2).

Carried to its logical end, testing should extend up the hierarchical ladder to the principals, superintendents, college presidents, school boards, boards of trustees, the people who elect these boards, and ultimately the testers themselves. Scott's prescription for improving the quality of teaching would be to send an errant teacher "as at once a corrective and a stimulus, Plato's beautiful vision of the ideal education: 'Then will our youth dwell in a land of health, amid fair sights and sounds, and receive the good in everything; and beauty, the effluence of fair words, shall flow into the eye and ear like a health-giving breeze from a purer region and insensibly draw the soul from earliest years into likeness and sympathy with the beauty of reason'" (60).

Often Scott had ideas that he would commit to paper and then set aside for a period of time, either to complete for some speaking engagement or, with a more seasoned view, submit for publication. One of the earliest forms of one of these papers, "Verbal Taboos," was given at the MLA meeting in 1901, at which time it was titled "A List of Hated Words." But various versions were used from time to time. There is a note in his diary in December 1903 about "Hated Words," and much later, in his diary on September 17, 1912, he notes that he "revised articles on hated words written at Longs Peak Inn and sent to Mill" (where it appeared as "Hatred of Inoffensive Words").

"Verbal Taboos," published in June 1912, became one of his most requested manuscripts, possibly because it generated a response from all those who considered themselves authorities, namely all users of the English language. After examining the meaning of *taboo* as it is defined by primitive cultures, Scott applies the term to language, saying that most negative attitudes toward particular words derived from superstitions.

He cites examples from numerous writings that mandate prohibitions, among them *The Verbalist* and G. M. Tucker's *Our Common Speech*. But of greater significance are A. S. Hill's textbooks, *The Foundations of Rhetoric* and *The Principles of Rhetoric*. "If we obey the injunctions of these books, we shall no longer speak of anything as being a *success;* we shall speak of it as being *successful* . . . we shall not think of the barn as being *back* of the house, but as being *behind* the house. According to Professor Hill we must not say 'The United States is a nation,' we must say 'The United States *are* a nation'" (168–69; all page references are to *The Standard of American Speech*).

As is typical with Scott, what troubles him is not that certain words are prohibited, but rather *why* the value judgments occur at all. His philosophical and aesthetic background was instrumental in his analysis of causation. He says that "antipathies" are instinctive and their origins both deep-seated and unreasoning. There are two classes: normal and abnormal. Normal he classifies as being common, "such, for example, as . . . [that] to snakes and to disgusting spectacles"; abnormal are those which are "peculiar to the individual and are exaggerated in intensity" (171). However, when these aversions are applied to language (such as William James's aversion to "postal card" for "post card"), in seeking the source of their origin we must consider "the nature of speech and the process of acquiring it" (173).

To test his theory, Scott designed an exercise for his students. He asked them to respond to the line from Tennyson's *Maud*, "The pimpernel dozed on the lea," assuming, correctly, that the word "pimpernel" would be unfamiliar to them.

1. The word pimpernel calls up in my mind the image of a pampered cur. He is a worthless brute who spends most of his time sleeping in the warm sunshine.

2. The pimpernel seems to me to be a small animal resembling an eel. It has short, rounded ears, and bright, beadlike eyes. As I imagine it, the pimpernel is lying half-asleep in the grass near the shore of a lake, ready to slip into the water at the slightest sound.

3. A pimpernel seems to me to be a tramp or gypsy. He lies on the bank in the sun with an old, battered hat drawn over his face.

4. I do not know what the word means, but it instantly suggests to me a small lizard covered with pimples or warts. The image flashed upon my mind as soon as the word was spoken and is still vivid and distinct. Although I never heard the word before, I seem always to have known it and to have attached this meaning to it. I am absurdly confident that this is the true meaning. (176)

Using the same analytical insight and empirical approach, Scott devised a scheme to question about a thousand persons as to what aversions they had and why they had them. His numerical breakdown is quite complex, but he notes that the results are based on the reports of only two hundred and fifty, which he selected "because they were written by persons in whose good faith, frankness, and powers of introspection I could put confidence" (177). From them he secured a total of 1,334 words. He classified these antipathies and found them to fit four main categories: a displeasing sound; offensive appearance on the page; an arousal of unpleasant images; association in childhood with a painful incident or with a person the subject disliked.

After examining numerous examples of words in each of these categories (some rather humorous, such as *surreptitious,* which calls up an image of a sticky syrup jar, or *snobbish,* a mass of slime), Scott presents his theory explaining this language phenomenon. His hypothesis is that in childhood a person receives a strongly unpleasant impression of a word; later in life his "natural aggressiveness of disposition, combined, it may be, with the elements of vanity and self-righteousness . . . leads him to assert his own preferences and override those of his fellows." If such a person attains eventually to some prominent position in society where he can prevail with his opinions to sway others, then he will, in essence, be saying, "'I don't like these words; I never did like them. Therefore, *you* shan't like them, or at any rate you shan't use them'" (186–87).

Although Scott thus views verbal taboos as part of a social hierarchy, he also responds to usage in a more modern way. Unlike others of his era, he recognized the changing nature of language and knows that one cannot legislate its usage. When he says that "words do not spring up in the mind with their dictionary values stamped upon them" (189), he forecasts the potential of words to change in their connotations and of dictionaries to reflect those changes. Given time, universal aversions to words would occasion obsolescence either of the word itself or of its meaning. This paper, because its origin can be traced back to 1901, exposes the differences between Scott's attitudes toward usage and those of the "authorities" he cites. It also substantiates how early he developed an interest in linguistics, although some of his more notable contributions did not appear until much later in his life.

In fact, between 1911 and 1915, Scott produced four other articles with linguistic bases: "The Father-Tongue"; "The Problem from the Standpoint of English"; "The Order of Words in Certain Rhythm- Groups"; and "Vowel Alliteration in Modern Poetry."

"The Father-Tongue" is a brief, informal piece deriving from his observations on the differences in English and American speech rhythms. Each group has difficulty understanding the other, especially if the speech is rapid, despite the fact that the language is one. Scott's knowledge of music was very helpful to him in his analysis of speech rhythms and metrical systems in prose and poetry. The broad range of matters relating to British and American language usage became one of Scott's deepest fascinations in the later part of his life. This little piece presages that involvement.

Scott's contribution to a symposium on reform in grammatical nomenclature in the study of languages, a program of the Michigan Schoolmasters' Club at Ann Arbor in April 1911 is "The Problem from the Standpoint of English." His focus is uniform nomenclature in relation to the elementary student. Since the student already speaks the language, "every step in the grammar should reveal to him something that he has already perceived or felt vaguely but has not perhaps seen in its proper connection" (622). Thus, he outlines general principles in arriving at useful nomenclature. The first is that a grammatical term should not be foreign to the student's own understanding. When asked about the word "govern," Scott found that "the most ridiculous ideas were entertained (by the students) regarding the power of the verb to control the fortunes of the wretched noun" (623). The second principle is that the term must match some specific category or function. He adds that using one specific correlation, even though it may not cover all uses, is better than confusing the student with the entire range that exists.

In other words, make things simple. Scott was pragmatic in this because he recognized the paralyzing confusion the elementary pupil faced when matters were too detailed. Although this was a natural view of language and language teaching for Scott, it would have been a somewhat courageous statement at this time, considering the trend toward ever more complex grammar study. One must keep in mind that Alonzo Reed and Brainerd Kellogg's books, *Graded Lessons in English* (1875) and *Higher Lessons in English* (1878), promoted sentence diagramming, a system that lingered long into the twentieth century (Murphy 173).

In "The Order of Words in Certain Rhythm-Groups," Scott offers an alternative and contradictory view of Otto Jespersen's hypothesis about the arrangement of monosyllabic and dissyllabic words in combination.[1] He thinks that Jespersen's pronouncement that "the usual practice is to place the short word first" is in error. As usual, Scott does not enter into such a discussion ill prepared. He has painstakingly created a 276 item list of "and-phrases" which in two columns contrast the patterns, in column I the short word appearing first, in column II the short word appearing last. His conclusion is that if there is any difference worthy of note, it is that "II contains more expressions of an abrupt and vehement character than does I," but even then not in every case (197; all page references are to *The Standard of American Speech*). Thus, he cautions that care must be taken not to oversimplify in linguistic matters. And not to be overlooked is his insistence, again, that language is rich in its diversity and not easily harnessed by rules or generalizations.

Finally, among this group of serious language concerns is the paper he delivered at the MLA meeting in 1913, titled "Vowel Alliteration in Modern Poetry." Characteristically, the papers for MLA were more technical, detailed, and depended heavily on research. In this paper, he dismisses the commonly held view that vowel alliteration is of no significance in modern poetry and proposes to show that it is as genuine as alliteration with consonants, that it is distinct from vowel music, and that he will have to examine vowel alliteration to determine what "constitutes the alliterating element." He opposes primarily the conclusions of George Saintsbury expressed in his *History of English Prosody*.

The paper is full of examples, notably from Milton and Tennyson. He does a statistical analysis of *Paradise Lost,* even tabulating the number of lines that contain vowel alliteration. He also clarifies the distinction between vowel music and vowel alliteration, noting that the former results from artful sequence of vowel sounds and has several distinguishing elements: the difference in vowel pitch which allows arrangement in a sort of scale, the difference in vowel quality due to overtones, the association of vowel sounds and sequences which correspond to emotional states, and the muscular action in the shift of vocal chord positions.

This is rather complex material, dependent upon Scott's familiarity with physiology, prosody, and music. Ultimately, he must settle the question of what constitutes vowel alliteration, which essentially relies upon repetition. He suggests either of two possibilities: sonority of initial sounds or the glottal catch, a recurrent sound not represented in the spelling. Noting through example that the glottal catch is universal in speech, he concludes that it becomes a substitute for consonant alliteration and thus provides the basis of vowel alliteration. This thesis is logically argued, supported by statistical evidence. This paper serves as a testament to Scott's vast knowledge of linguistics and his analytical probity in examining matters related to the field.

Among his literary scholarship of this period, is a short piece, "Keats's Missal," which originally appeared in the *New York Nation* in May 1911 and was twice reprinted. It is reminiscent of his earlier literary research, particularly "Carlyle's Dante," where he focuses on a fine point that others have overlooked. It is important here only as a reminder that Scott never restricted his research to rhetoric alone.

Scott began writing reviews of both literary and theoretical books very early in his career. His review of William Brewster's *English Composition and Style* in 1913 bears examination because it expressed very succinctly his frustration and displeasure with the lack of progress in the field of rhetoric.

It has been the misfortune of rhetoric not to have had in modern times either its Kant or its Hume. In other words, it has not had the benefit of that searching critical analysis which, by exposing inconsistencies and clearing away the lingering traditions, brings to light the permanent, underlying principles. Lacking this wholesome purgation, rhetoric has remained an accretion of loosely coordinated precepts, valuable and even indispensable as a guide to practise, but having doubtful claims to a place in the austere circle of the sciences. It follows that whereas in physics and astronomy, in chemistry and law and medicine, the writer of even the most popular or practical treatise can ground himself upon the results of profound thinking and painstaking research, the writer of rhetoric and composition must either make up his principles as he goes along or get on without them. (309–10)

Scott, as ever ahead of his time, pinpointed the flaw in the profession which was to dog it into the present day when its members still cannot decide on the definition, description, purpose, or motivating force of composition studies. Though Scott, throughout his career, had labored to elevate rhetoric to a status equivalent to that of literary studies, he was clearly disappointed that his work had had such minimal impact, even during these years when his leadership was secured in the presidencies of the principal guiding organizations.

Around 1910, Scott elected to refresh his reading in Russian literature, particularly Tolstoi, Pushkin, Chekhov, Leonid Andreyeff, and Nekrasov.[2] This was the prelude to his translation, with Clarence L. Meader, of the plays of Leonid Andreyeff. The project had a long history, beginning early in 1911 when Scott was reading *To the Stars*. By October he was in a class Meader had formed to translate *The Black Maskers*. By April 1912 he and Meader had finished a rough draft of this play, on which they had been working for ten days. At the end of January 1913, the two collaborators received a letter from Andreyeff granting permission for the translation. When the book was published, it contained three plays: *The Black Maskers, The Life of Man,* and *The Sabine Women*. Scott later published translations of three poems by N. A. Nekrasov.

All in all, Scott had plenty to do, yet in 1910 he had become involved with Elmer Crawford of *Mill Supplies,* "an Independent Monthly Journal Devoted to the Interests of the Jobbers and Manufacturers of Mill, Steam, Mine and Machinery Supplies." Scott's contributions extended monthly over the whole of 1911, missing only two months, and then irregularly during 1912. His writings were brief, but covered a wide range of practical topics having to do, as one would expect, with improving the quality of communication in the business arena.

In 1911, Scott published an edition of Thomas Hill Green's *Value and Influence of Works of Fiction*. A curiously fascinating portrait of Green is drawn by Scott, fascinating because it so parallels that of Scott himself, both as he characterized himself later at the time of his wife Isadore's death, and as his friends characterized him in their laudatory pieces at the time of his own death.

> Green's character was compounded of a variety of elements. The shyness and reserve characteristic of many cultivated Englishmen, was accentuated in his case by a natural austerity and an absorption in serious thought. But though his temper was puritanic and inclined to moroseness, there was no sourness or cynicism in it. . . . Grim though he might be outwardly, he had a keen sense of humor and a warmth of interest in his fellows that made him, for those who broke through his reserve, a charming companion. His most characteristic quality was the elevation of the mind. (11)

There is no question that the materials Scott developed between 1905 and 1915 are the most consequential among his theoretical statements. His scientific and interdisciplinary approach to research were original in the language arts. Ultimately, he worked to reform the profession, to provide rhetoric, in its broadest context, the same dignity, respect and admiration accorded all other academic fields. Scott believed he had made progress toward his goal. Unfortunately, he was overly optimistic.

The Shadow of the Great War

RED NEWTON SCOTT was fifty-six years old in 1916. He says little in his diary about the fall semester, except that he has written a paragraph to introduce the list of readings for the comprehensive examination and has prepared data for the regents "showing the number of instructors and their hours of teaching and the number of their students," information which he later revised at the request of the president. In reading his diary for 1916, one has the sense that Scott is more preoccupied with his friends and his home activities, particularly his automobile and his golf game. He rarely mentions academic affairs, except for meetings of his committees and clubs, and accounts of his reading and writing endeavors. But there were adjustments that had to be made with the coming of the Great War, for the campus environment changed enormously, seriously affecting not only admissions policy and enrollment numbers, but also the attitudes and relationships of the entire faculty and even the physical environment of the University of Michigan itself.

Among the courses other than those of primarily technical value were two courses developed in the Journalism Department. In a letter to Dean Cooley (undated, though most likely in 1917), Scott writes about these: "In reply to your letter of October 8 concerning the work of my department in connection with the war, permit me to say that while the main purpose of the Department is to cultivate a terse and vigorous English useful alike in war and peace, yet there are two particulars in which an attempt is made to contribute directly to the solution of special problems. These are: 1. The Theory and Practice of Publicity, and 2. The Methods and Principles of Government Censorship. Both of these subjects will be treated this year in the group of courses which constitute the Curriculum in Journalism" (FNSP, penciled draft).

In the catalogue for 1917–1918, there is the first hint that journalism has secured an identity of its own, for courses in journalism are listed as part of, but separate from, those of the Rhetoric Department proper. Besides a course that Scott shared with Lyman Bryson in 1916, "Seminary in the Newspaper, its Nature, Function, and Development," there are a number of separate listings, all of which were taught by Bryson: "The Newspaper"; "Editorial Writing"; "Practical Newspaper Work"; and "Reviews." At this point, it might be well to recall that both the College of Engineering's Humanities Department and the journalism offerings were outgrowths of the Department of Rhetoric under Scott's direction. By the fall of 1918, the journalism courses had been assumed by Professor John R. Brumm. At this time, also, the title and description for "The Newspaper" changed. Now called "Newspaper Organization and Methods," it is described as: "A study of the nature and function of the public press, with practice in reporting, interviewing, rewriting, and copy editing, including the writing of headlines. Particular stress will be laid upon the distinction between genuine news values and merely sensational appeals. The effect of the war on methods of newsgathering will receive proper attention."

Clearly, the direction of journalism has been irrevocably altered by events of the Great War. The function of the course in "Editorial Writing" which dealt earlier with the "writing of comment on current news," has now been expanded. "The aim of this course will be to determine the proper function of editorial writing, especially in its relation to the shaping of public opinion." "Seminary in the Newspaper" is now retitled "Seminary in Newspaper Problems," and its objectives are "to deal with the history of the newspaper and with special phases of editorial routine. Newspaper policy and responsibility will receive particular attention, together with a critical analysis of the relation of journalism to literature."

How much these changes can be attributed to any one influence would be hard to discern. Certainly the character of journalism had changed as its legitimacy was acknowledged. Certainly the occasion of World War I was a factor. And, considering Scott's writings on the function and social responsibilities of the newspaper, certainly his influence is a factor. The presence of the new man, Brumm, would also have promoted change.

By this time in his career, many students had passed through Scott's classes, some already cited who acknowledged his contributions to their lives. But these small gestures of appreciation were not enough for Georgia Jackson, Scott's former secretary and typist, a frequent correspondent who is important for the role she eventually assumed as Scott's second wife. She wanted to provide some sort of memorial gift for Scott. She wrote letters to some of his students suggesting that they acknowledge Scott's personal and professional contributions in some material way, but she was not sure what the gift should be. In November 1916, Gertrude Buck wrote to Jackson expressing her regret that nothing had come of the fund proposed for Scott to publish further monographs on rhetorical theory. According to Buck, Mary Yost had suggested a piece of permanent equipment for the new classroom or seminar room, but Buck knows little about Scott's needs. Instead, she favors securing a secretary for him, since he is still writing letters by hand (PMFNS, letter, November 13, 1916). Without question, the debt Scott's students felt was real, but they had difficulty in finding a vehicle for expressing it.

Among a number of letters from Jackson is one in which she mentions that her friend, Marjorie McKeown, had written her: "I never saw Professor Scott in better form than he was yesterday. He read a negro-love-story to 24 [his seminar] and almost disgraced himself laughing over it. He reads negro dialect to perfection." The note provides a student's vision of Scott, immersed in his material, oblivious to the undignified impression he is conveying, his enjoyment of the passages unrestrained, his enthusiasm and delight working as much to entertain himself as his students—and this despite his age and longevity in the classroom (FNSP, letter, May 23, 1917).

Praise came also from Frank McKinney, who writes in December 1916 thanking Scott for being at the dinner honoring Denney at the NCTE meetings in New York. He says that it was a success because of Scott's presence and the tribute he gave. More to the point, he adds, "We all know just what Professor Scott means to Michigan and to the Michigan students and to the Michigan alumni" (FNSP, letter, December 4, 1916).

Public recognition of Scott's contribution as a teacher was given by Talcott Williams of the Columbia School of Journalism, in his chapter "The Teaching of Journalism" in Paul Klapper's *College Teaching*. In assessing the education required for the vocation of journalism, Williams traces the development of classes or programs over the years, starting in 1870. Of Scott, he writes: "Mr. Fred Newton Scott, professor of rhetoric in the University of Michigan in 1893, began, with less newspaper notice, training in newspaper English, continuing to the present time his happy success in teaching style to his students" (536).

In January 1920, Scott received a letter from Ashley Thorndike of Columbia University, offering an appointment to the summer session. Although Scott had fought with the eastern elitists for years, he had maintained congenial relations with the faculty at Columbia. This appointment may not seem significant, but considering the eastern attitude toward Michigan, a "western" school, it was a reflection of the regard with which Scott was held at this time. Scott did accept, agreeing to give two courses. That attitudes were strongly combative between the eastern and western schools is revealed in Scott's diary entry for January 6: when he told Edward H. Kraus that he might teach at Columbia, "his face literally fell." Scott seems to have enjoyed this reaction (FNSD, January 6, 1920).

During this time, Scott had a part in the report on the preparation of college teachers of English. Spurred by Raymond Alden's article, "Preparation for College English Teaching," NCTE regularly discussed qualifications. Shortly after its founding, Scott originated a committee, within NCTE, to study conditions and find out what changes might be needed. (Scott had made this suggestion in 1912 for the MLA to undertake.) James Hosic, as chairman, sent out three short letters addressed to heads of departments in English in large universities, doctors of philosophy teaching English to undergraduates, and presidents of colleges. Questions to department heads included the following: (1) What special course, if any, do you offer for the preparation of college teachers of English? (2) What preparation have your best instructors in undergraduate English had? (3) What are your own views on the matter of preparation for teaching college English? The letter to Ph.D.'s asked: (1) What is the title of your Doctor's thesis? (2) What was the purpose of your thesis? (3) What is your judgment as to the value of your graduate work as a means of preparation for teaching undergraduates? (4) What would constitute the best preparation for that task? The questions to the presidents were: (1) What is the value of the work usually required in the graduate school of candidates for the degree of Ph.D. in English? (2) Does such work, including the thesis, constitute the best possible preparation for teaching undergraduates? (3) If not, what would you recommend? (4) What preparation have your best English instructors had?

At the annual meeting of NCTE in Chicago, November 1915, this report was presented by Professor James Hosic ("Report" 20–22). The committee concluded that "it is, of course, evident that the situation is sufficiently chaotic." The chairman then proposed other questions pertinent to this investigation, among them: agreement upon certain qualifications necessary to teach English in the freshman and sophomore years in a college or university, such as adequate scholarship and sound methods of study, acquaintance with the specific aims of the courses of composition, literature, language, familiarity with the work of secondary schools, interest in teaching as distinguished from study, and a demonstrated ability to manage and instruct college classes, knowledge of current methods of college English teaching; a special degree indicating that the holder was prepared for teaching as distinguished from higher specialized research; and additional training for oral as well as written composition, training in the effective use of books of all kinds, and training in speech sounds and other practical aspects of language study ("The National Council" 31–32).

❖

Important to consider in this period is the effect of the Great War on the total university environment. On March 30, 1917, the Michigan regents approved a resolution to provide voluntary military training under the War Department (Cross 123). Confusion reigned for a few months because no military instructor was available. But with U.S. entry into the war on April 6, 1917, students reacted spiritedly, and squads of students drilled on streets and fraternity lawns under the direction of anyone with military experience (Cross 125). The fervor reached such a level that during the April recess some three hundred students spent four hours each afternoon on the athletic field learning military maneuvers (Cross 125).

As might be expected, in the spring of 1917 hundreds of students left the university to engage either in active duty or in other important work for the government. But the students were not the only ones with patriotic spirit. Of 517 persons on the faculty, one estimate placed nearly one in four (130) in war activity ("University at War" 406). On campus, temporary buildings were set up by the men enrolled in Students' Army Training Corps or Students' Naval Training Corps because there wasn't enough space for classes and housing (Shaw, *University* 310). The semester system was abandoned in favor of a quarter system, presumably to promote faster training and education of the men (Cross 136). The administration altered requirements as well, granting a full semester's credit for military or naval service (Cross 125).

Some of the effects that were felt in the classroom had to do with the instability of the students. The officers, because of their authoritative attitudes and obligation to the war effort, were less concerned with their charges' education than with their military training (Shaw, *University* 312). As a result, the military tended to subvert the plan agreed upon between the government and the university to allow the men to continue their schooling while training for service. The program was to include forty-two hours of class work and study (fourteen hours of recitation and twenty-eight hours of preparation), and thirteen hours of drill (Shaw, *University* 312). But the military scheduled the men for duty without regard to their university obligations (Cross 137). Thus, many missed their classes and were unprepared for tests or their daily assignments. The scourge of influenza which swept through the barracks, fortified by the compact housing arrangements, also took its toll on attendance. Moreover, as classes swelled due to the increased enrollment, their management was given over to volunteers woefully unprepared both in education and experience. Equipment was scarce as well, and scheduling of rooms was nearly impossible. Instructors had an impossible task in determining the level of instruction because not only were the backgrounds of the new students markedly different, but many were not adequately prepared for college work (Cross 138).

By the fall of 1919, nearly all was back to normal except for the enrollment, which stood at a whopping 8,057. This number was larger by 1,500 than ever before, and in its own way created a new nightmare for the university. Housing was short, teachers were not available in sufficient numbers, and classroom facilities were woefully inadequate (Shaw, *University* 322).

What were the immediate effects on the Departments of English and Rhetoric? Some surviving documents suggest what they were asked to do. How much Scott would have been involved is questionable, although it is clear he would have monitored some of the changes in the basic rhetoric courses and would have assisted the Engineering Department's English program in selecting new instructors and possibly in setting up programs to satisfy the large numbers of students. Among the extant communiques is one from the depot quartermaster to the English Department chairman, dated October 15, 1918, on the subject of freshman themes. It describes a publicity campaign soon to be launched to instruct soldiers in the conservation of supplies: clothing, equipment, food, fuel, water, and so forth. The English Department is requested to assign the topic, "Why Should Soldiers Conserve?" At the end of each theme there should be a "slogan" on conservation, as, for example: "Fight

to Conserve—Conserve to Fight"; "Every Little Thing We Save Fills Another German Grave" (a rather macabre and grim slogan to suggest to
freshmen). Advanced composition classes were encouraged to participate
as well, which would have meant that Scott had a mandate to present
this particular agenda in his classes (FNSP).

On specific aspects of the teaching of rhetoric, instructions were also
provided by the War Department. R. C. MacLaurin, the educational director of the Collegiate Division, outlined the features of writing to receive attention:

1. Drill in paragraph, sentence, words, spelling, punctuation—all work
should be criticized with view of gaining mastery of the fundamentals.
2. Practice to use business letters and forms for military correspondence
correctly.
3. Should know how to do report writing—preparation of title page, table
of contents, marginal references, use charts and diagrams, divisions of headings,
summaries, and appendices.
4. Reading in history of Americanism: great speeches, literary masterpieces
in progress of Americanism.
5. Oral work—distinct enunciation, proper pronunciation and projection.
(FNSP, September 24, 1918)

Certainly more to Scott's liking would have been the communique
issued from the War Department office on September 18, 1918, by
Frank Aydelotte, a man who, though trained under A. S. Hill, had a
quite liberal outlook on work in composition. Like Scott, he had come
from Indiana, where he had taught before going into public service. In
his text, *College English,* he advocated substance before correctness. Other
qualities he insisted upon were truth and style, the latter being a reflection of the personality of the writer (Blanshard 112–13). In his letter to
the universities, Aydelotte writes:

When a discussion has proved to be of vital interest it is an easy matter to get
students to write on the topic discussed. They then have something to say, and
are concerned that what they write shall be written effectively.

Correction of the common faults in paragraphing, sentence structure, and
the use of words, comments upon the logical arrangement of material and upon
the clearness and accuracy of expression, should be made effectively, without
being allowed to occupy too large a proportion of the time. (FNSP)

Materials from the journals of the national organizations would indicate that the war did indeed influence what was going on in the class-

rooms. Articles were so directed to the teaching of patriotic subjects, to issues on the war, that in the *English Journal* for 1918, there was a notice that those interested in submitting manuscripts need not feel anxious if they did not write on patriotic topics. In 1918 as well, there is a note that attendance at the meetings, both local and national, was down in numbers. In March 1918, in the Round Table section of the *English Journal,* there is a long article by Cornelia Carhart Ward of Hunter College High School, New York, titled "A Composition Course Based on the War." Consider also an editorial in the same journal for June 1918. "Everything is now related to the world-war. How shall English teachers do their bit in making the world safe for democracy and democracy safe for the world?" (397).

The writer continues: "As the current articles in the *English Journal* show, both literature and composition are taking on new significance with the growing seriousness of the national consciousness. More and more, books and periodicals are read for their content, for their human interest, for the light they throw on what men should live for, and less for a specialized knowledge of historical facts or growth in the capacity to evaluate writing in terms of technique" (397). This altered attitude was reflected in a new direction for the teaching of composition, for "composition, meanwhile, serves more frequently as genuine communication of ideas. Obedience to conventions, no less necessary than before, is crowded into its proper subordinate place as the accessory of clearness and force in persuading one's hearers to buy Liberty Bonds or save for Thrift Stamps" (397). As can be seen, the war proved an impetus to liberalizing attitudes toward composition and composition teaching.

There is no indication in any of Scott's correspondence at this time that he was much immersed in war affairs, perhaps because of his pro-German loyalties. The commitment of the United States must have caused him a great deal of pain and personal conflict in directing his allegiances.

In the early part of 1920, Scott is involved in departmental affairs. With the expanding enrollment, he was concerned with staffing. He notes, on February 9, spending too much time in counting the registration cards of the department preparatory to making a request through the dean for more instructors (FNSD). In April, Scott is again counting numbers, recording that he worked part of the day on statistics of enrollment in rhetoric classes. Obviously, more administrative work has been necessary as the number of classes increased.

Anticipating the drop in morale of instructors in a program where class growth necessitates short tenure, Scott addressed the problem of instability. He urges higher salaries and more promotions, especially the latter, noting that it is "disheartening" to instructors to stay at that level for any length of time. Unlike others who simply consigned instructors to the level of hired hands, he sees that promotion would raise morale and thus create a superior class of instructors (FNSP, letter to Dean M. E. Cooley, September 4, 1920). This issue of status for instructors has never adequately been addressed to this day, but few have seen as clearly as did Scott in 1920 how good treatment could enhance performance.

Other documents provide clues to Scott's attitudes. In a letter to James Hosic in January 1919, Scott writes that he plans to speak at NCTE in the "symposium" on the adjustments of the teaching of English to the needs of the times (FNSP). In the proceedings of that meeting, it is recorded that "Fred N. Scott, of the University of Michigan, felt that our greatest need as a nation is the free and untrammeled flow of intelligence through the community. An enlightened public opinion is the essential factor in democracy. Whether we have great wealth does not matter so much. During the war we have had both censorship and propaganda. These were necessary because war is a hideous disease. We are now convalescing. Must censorship continue? Teachers of English have a large responsibility in the formation of national ideals. They cannot, therefore, afford to spend time trying to unsplit split infinitives or in dealing out the chaff and chicken feed of the details of rhetoric. They must make the vernacular a means for shaping the ideas and ideals of those who will be the arbiters of the future. The English teacher has a glorious opportunity in preserving our heritage of freedom" ("National Council" [1919] 263).

American Speech Week, which was launched at this same meeting, occupied Scott's attention for a period also. Better Speech Week had been initiated in September 1915 by the Eastern District High School in New York City with this description of its activities: "Typical features include the appointment of committees, the holding of contests, presenting of pageants, etc." ("National Council" [1919] 262). At the NCTE meeting, members were cautioned against the danger of setting up "narrow and pedantic standard(s)." And to this point, the members are directed to articles by Scott, George Philip Krapp, and Brander Matthews (262). Scott is listed among those serving on the Committee on American Speech as an advisor ("News and Notes," *English Journal* 4 [Nov. 1915], 612). His suggestion for a similar investment in journalism is reflected in an article by W. E. Dimorier in the *English Journal,* March 1917, which begins:

"Planning Newspaper Week without a precedent was like giving 'to airy nothing / A local habitation and a name.' I had no 'poet's eye,' neither the versatile imagination of Professor Fred N. Scott, who suggested the idea" (170). In light of these records, then, it is reasonable to assume that Scott had altered his materials and his manner of handling his classes during the war years.

In reflecting on Scott's teaching at this time, one would have to take notice of the productivity of his rhetoric students. Ada L. F. Snell's dissertation, "Pause" (1916), was published in Scott's Contributions to Rhetorical Theory in 1918, and in 1918 and 1919, she published two articles in *PMLA*. Lee White, with whom Scott carried on his most constant correspondence over the years, appeared on a program regarding the training of newspapermen via the high schools at the NCTE meeting of February 1919. In the *Proceedings* of MLA, among the papers listed as read by title only at the 1919 and 1920 meetings are two by Alice D. Snyder, then of Vassar, who had earned her Ph.D. in 1915 under Scott's tutelage. Another of Scott's students, Ruth Mary Weeks, who had earned her master's degree in 1913, produced an article published in the *English Journal* in January 1921, titled "Phrasal Prosody." Sterling Leonard had begun to make his name known; Charles C. Fries would follow in less than a decade.

With the great popularity of Walt Whitman, the issue of free verse occupied the interests of many linguists who struggled to assess its validity because they could not deny its appeal. Weeks's article, for example, takes up where Snell's left off, based on the elements of rhythm in poetry, primarily stress, time, pause, and pitch. Prose rhythm was Scott's concern, and it is possible that he influenced the direction of his students' research. In November 1916, Scott had entertained the visiting writer, Rabindranath Tagore, at his home. Eager to learn what he could, Scott questioned the accentual nature of Indian poetry. His interest focused on Tagore's recitation of a Bengalese poem. "It ran in a singsong much like that of Indian songs from Arizona, with prolongation at the end of the line a refrain. He said there was no accent in it, that it was purely syllabic, but he marked a beat with the bent forefinger of his right hand at the end (as I thought) of each line. Said this rhythmic plan from translations was instinctive. He did not know that they were rhythmic until Yeats called attention to them" (FNSD, November 16, 1916). He also read Dayton C. Miller's *The Science of Musical Sounds,* of which he noted, "I devour all such things as this with a greedy appetite," adding that "the matter is in my chosen field" (LWP, letter, July 17, 1917).

(This comment is interesting because Scott kept changing his idea about what his "chosen field" was. In 1924 he referred to "English usage" as his specialty.) (FNSP, letter, January 16, 1924.)

Scott's participation in his recreation, golf, and in his clubs, would certainly have been curtailed by the absence of many of the colleagues who had left Ann Arbor to help in some way with the war effort. But he did go golfing when he could, and some of his accounts are revealing of his personality. Of one day when he was playing with a colleague from the chemistry department, he writes: "Lost three balls and in each case found another and played it before discovering that it was not mine" (FNSD, June 30, 1916). Another time, he reports that he noticed a farmer in the meadow across the road beating his horse over the head with a pitchfork. He says, "The team then ran away dragging the great hay-load across the field until the horse that had been struck fell down. Clarkson and I went over and talked with the man. He said he had put money into the horse and the horse had to work out the worth of that money or die." Three days after the incident, worried about the horse, he discussed with Clarkson the necessity of turning in the "inhuman" farmer to the Humane Society. Clarkson wasn't interested, but Scott was. "Telephoned to Goodyear, who referred me to Ryan, the police officer" (FNSD, July 21, 1916).

On another occasion, Scott writes: "Playing the third hole . . . received a ball played off by W. square on the front of my head. My first thought was, 'How much harm has it done.' Poured cold water on my head and went home in W's car. No evil results" (FNSD, July 28, 1916).

Scott also attended to his family, now having become a grandfather. But one of his most preoccupying interests was his new automobile. He characterizes his relationship to the car for the learning period, saying that as he drove the car he felt "rather awkward as if in the hands of a willing but erratic genie." He has little confidence and notes that "I do not yet know what I should do in an emergency," but he found out when he drove down Main Street. He admits that he "did not manage backing out very well or steering in turning the corner to go out, and at the corner of State when an auto suddenly came along, pressed the accelerator instead of the brake" (FNSD, August 30, 1916; September 11, 13, 1916).

One of his incidental papers sent to *Mill Supplies* in 1916 developed from his infatuation with the automobile. "Evading the Prospect," published under his pseudonym, Justin Frolich, although totally inconsequential, is too enjoyable a piece to pass over. He tells of succumbing to an ad which in glorified terms touts the wonders of an automobile "top-raiser" now offered at a reduced price. He has to have one. After he has personally visited the garage, dispatched an order to the branch office of the company by mail, traveled to Detroit to argue with both the manufacturer and the car-maker's garage, he has met with only rudeness and stupidity. After six weeks, "Time passed. The sun rose and set. The grass grew and withered. The war in Europe continued. The first of September drew nigh. And then, suddenly . . . a circular came by mail from a supply firm a thousand miles away" (24). He placed the order, the top-raiser came, was attached and worked. The moral? "A man can buy almost anything that is offered for sale these days, if he has the price and is persistent" (24).

The growing numbers of automobiles on the University of Michigan campus soon became a problem. In fact, Scott had sustained a serious head injury in an accident. Besides, unimaginable as it may seem to us today, the university considered them a "moral risk." But the automobile remained one of Scott's grand passions—a recreational outlet that never ceased to excite him.

12

A Shift in Interest

I

N FEBRUARY 1916, Scott traveled east to Columbia University to participate, as he had regularly, in the National Conference on Uniform Entrance Requirements in English. By 1916, the problems had intensified, as the diversity of requirements among the now more numerous colleges, each vying for status, increased. Scott was one of nineteen delegates, and one of three representing the North Central Association. At the meeting, he was elected vice-chairman and also served on the committee appointed to draw up the comprehensive list for the entrance exams. Only two days later, Scott was back in Detroit, attending the joint meetings of NCTE and the Department of Superintendence of the NEA, where he spoke on "American Speech" before a gathering of superintendents.

In a complete break with tradition, the regular NCTE December meeting in 1916 was held in New York City. Much was made of this change of venue: "This was the first meeting of the Council in the eastern part of the United States and was therefore somewhat in the nature of an experiment" ("The National Council" [1917] 40). Although a number of states sent members—from Alabama, Texas, Colorado, North Dakota, Missouri, Kansas—the attendance was "nearly, if not quite, equal to the average attendance of former years" (40). This situation is a little strange, because there should have been a larger than normal number present considering the population density. Nonetheless, the members felt "the spirit of the Council was the same as in former years, and the program in its entirety probably superior to that of any previous meeting" (40). Scott, already a member of the board of directors, was appointed as well to a nominating committee.

In the course of the meetings, Scott spoke informally on the reorganization of English in the high schools, commenting that he felt the best course for training high school teachers would be to provide fundamental principles which "would enable them to evaluate the lesser details of their work" ("The National Council" [1917] 50). He stressed the importance of allowing the students to be "properly inventive," which would, in turn, reduce the work of theme-reading by two-thirds. In addressing the matter of proper teacher training for the high schools, some very impractical ideas were advanced. One teacher felt training began at birth and was stimulated by reading of the Bible, writing plays, and playing at being a teacher. Another said teachers' failings resulted from insufficient affection for books. Others seized on rather ridiculous personal qualities: the need for a fine physique and vocal equipment, good posture and handwriting. On a higher level, E. R. Barrett of Emporia Normal School opposed practice-teaching, and Sterling Leonard of Wisconsin advocated his method, whereby students became pupils in the class and then took over the lessons on occasion.

For this meeting, Scott also was chairman of the College Section; its topic was "Graduate Work in the Teaching of English." James Hosic suggested one course in the teaching of language and composition and another in the teaching of literature. The committee recognized the master's degree as essentially a teaching degree and so agreed that breadth was more essential than specialization. Joe Denney proposed the inclusion of work in all elements omitted in previous preparation and professional training for college teachers, but added that what was most essential was personality. Scott probably felt most comfortable with what Charles Sears Baldwin had to say: that assignments for writing were generally unsuitable, that there was need for greater composition training and an emphasis on content in writing, and that there was not enough use of invention or other practices advised by classic writers. Moreover, he wanted potential college teachers to be made aware that in their positions they were considered leaders of men ("National Council" [1917] 58–61).

Of course, what eventually happened was that the Ph.D. became the terminal degree, with the dreaded teaching of composition serving as the stepping stone to the ultimate reward—the teaching of literature courses. Unfortunately, by 1916, interest in composition and rhetoric was flagging. Rhetorical theory had pretty much atrophied, and composition teaching was reduced to proofreading. Most of the influential people had moved on to other things: Barrett Wendell and Gertrude Buck to literature, Scott to journalism and language, Genung to literature and biblical scholarship (Kitzhaber, *Rhetoric* 225).

At the general session, Scott was one of three speakers, following Edwin M. Hopkins, who gave the president's address. Scott's topic was "The Standard of American Speech." Earlier, in October 1916, L. N. Hines had invited Scott to deliver an address on "The Standard of American Speech" before the English section at the annual session of the Indiana State Teachers' Association. This speech became one of his better known works, a variant of "American Speech" given earlier in the year. (Later, the title would be used for the collection of his selected speeches and papers published in 1926.) It was connected as well to a paper titled "Speech and the Community," which Scott had contributed to the April edition of the *Journal of Ophthalmology, Otology, and Laryngology* in 1916.[1] In this, Scott's thesis is that the improvement of speech is primarily a social issue. We speak as our environment "compels" us to speak, our habits determined by "our parents, our playmates, our neighbors and our teachers" (33; all page references are to *The Standard of American Speech*).

By this time, a number of scholars were examining the difference between British and American speech—their rhythms, vocabulary, and even their relative status. The movement toward the formation of organizations made up of leading American and British scholars was just beginning. Eventually, a number of these would provide a forum in which to settle all kinds of linguistic issues, but also to bring together in congenial discourse the intellectual community on both sides of the ocean.

In "The Standard of American Speech," Scott details his attitudes on the relative merit of American versus British speech. He argues that, because of American democratic tradition, American speech is egalitarian, whereas British speech, in its varied levels, may assist those who aspire to the higher social strata. Thus, when American speech differs from British speech, the British view the American version as a linguistic provincialism—that is, language inferior to that spoken in England. What annoys Scott is not so much that American English is denigrated by the British as that the British argue that in America there is no standard whereas in England all educated men speak the same.

Scott questions this latter point. Since he spent considerable time in England, he could draw on a number of incidents to defend his position. He notes, in fact, that in England many of the dialects are unintelligible even to other Englishmen. In addition to anecdotes, he cites Shaw's *Pygmalion* as indisputable proof of his point. Scott also offers a number of individual words as examples of the different pronunciations in London (here, he'uh, hyah; round, rah'oond, reh'oond; door, dawr, daw, doh'uh); and in America (hog, hawg, hahg; Chicago, Chicawgo, Chicahgo; neether, nither). But, reiterating a point he made in "Speech and Community," he argues that since speech habits are learned early, a person cannot affect "superior" speech of another region for long (he cites New England as well as the mother tongue); he will revert to his natural speech when he lets down his guard.

Scott notes that although dictionaries record standard pronunciations, they are in error, for there are none. In his view, it is impossible to denigrate a given pronunciation. All are equally acceptable until, for some reason, one predominates. Scott has to defend this position, as have all liberal-minded linguists since, for it is human nature, apparently, to insist on codification in language—in grammar, pronunciation, and spelling. People don't like not knowing the "rules."

In addition to providing an intelligent and viable assessment based on historical modifications, Scott expounds on the futility of trying to adjudicate speech. (This particular pronouncement was crucial. Linguists were coming to an understanding that speech could be described, not prescribed.) Besides, he says, if we all spoke the same way, speech would be monotonous and dreary, not "intellectually alluring." Scott notes that Johnston Forbes-Robertson, a famous actor of his day, has been selected as the model for acceptable speech patterns. He ridicules this notion, saying: "I grant you at once that Mr. Forbes-Robertson's speech is admirable—in the mouth of a Forbes-Robertson—but a nation of Forbes-Robertsons, a Forbes-Robertson in the butcher shop, asking will you have ham or bacon? a Forbes-Robertson at the bank window protesting that you must be identified, a Forbes-Robertson behind the hotel register—but no, the imagination balks" (11; all page references are to *The Standard of American Speech*). Significant in all of this is Scott's progressive attitude toward language. He was foremost among linguists in recognizing the evolutionary nature of language.

The seventh annual meeting of NCTE was back in Chicago in 1917. It is noted in the records that "the attendance, doubtless on account of the war, was somewhat smaller than in previous years" ("National Council" [1918] 39). Scott participated in the discussion of the College Section on "What Can Be Done to Insure Better Preparation in English of Matriculants?" In June 1918, an editorial in the *English Journal* notes the interruption in the normal flow of activities brought about by the war (397). In November 1918, the National Council announced with disappointment that the meetings normally scheduled that month would have to be postponed, "after all arrangements for a strong meeting had been completed and the program put into type," because the influenza epidemic added to "the already difficult situation produced by the war" ("News and Notes" [1918] 608). The postponement was to March 1919 to coincide with the meetings of the Department of Superintendence.

In an editorial of February 1919, NCTE eagerly anticipated its gathering. "The armistice has been signed. The air is full of vague speculations and prophecies concerning the social changes upon which we are supposed to be entering. The period of 'reconstruction' is here" (126). And NCTE again sounds the note of idealism in looking toward the future transformation of the field of English: "Unless all signs fail, English is to be the chief humanizing agency in the schools of the future, the chief means by which the best that has been thought and said in the world shall be assimilated by our generation. . . . That is why, as we sincerely believe, the eighth annual meeting of the National Council will be memorable" (127).

Scott, who was now fifty-nine, was more than ready to enter this energetic renewal. At a symposium on February 27, on "The Adjustment of English Teaching to Present Needs," he presented his views on the importance of an enlightened public opinion to a democracy. He proclaims the teacher of English the protector of the heritage of freedom and urges use of the vernacular to shape "the ideas and ideals of those who will be the arbiters of the future" ("The National Council" [1919] 263). In his mind, the nature of the community had changed and the colleges had to be willing to change with it. There was no longer any rationale for a meritocracy. The advocates of liberal culture could no longer, practically, insist on the Arnoldian "well-rounded" man. For example, William T. Foster, president of Reed College, was out of step with the times when he declared that the democratic trend existed at the expense of intellectual standards (Russell 133).

As American Speech Week began to take hold in the imagination of the council's members, a flurry of activity emerged. According to the editorial in the September 1919 issue of *English Journal,* "several state and city associations already have active committees, and plans in many schools and clubs are already far advanced. . . . No school or club, however remote from the big centers, need hesitate to join in the celebration. . . . Slogans, posters, plays, contests, speeches, inventories, songs, and the rest should be mainly the work of the pupils of each school, the members of each club" (436–37). As preparations shifted into high gear, among the announcements about this event is one on the formation of the Committee on American Speech, listing Scott as one of the advisors.

As the year progressed, plans were formulated for the ninth annual meeting of NCTE to be held in Boston on November 24–26, 1919. In the announcement is a blunt though realistic observation: "The meeting in Boston will provide opportunity for unusual contacts. *New England does not travel and has not been largely represented in the annual conventions, not even when the gathering was centered in New York City*" ("Editorial" [1919] 507; italics mine). Scott appeared in the general session with President Joseph M. Thomas of the University of Minnesota, and Irving Babbitt of Harvard. His address, "English Composition as a Mode of Behavior," was a major statement, later to be included in *The Standard of American Speech*.

In 1920 Scott was more visible at the annual convention, doubtless because it was the decentennial of the National Council. According to preconvention publicity, "the one general session, which will be held Friday morning in Fullerton Hall at the Art Institute [in Chicago], will have as speakers Dr. Hosic, our president, Professor Rollo W. Brown, and our many times tried Professor F. N. Scott" ("News and Notes" [1920] 478). Scott's presentation was "The Anglo-American Conference of Professors of English at the University of London." Over the summer of 1920, along with Isadore, Scott had returned to England to attend this conference. In his speech, Scott, who noted that he had been seated between H. G. Wells and Gilbert Parker at one of the dinners, described the extravagant entertainment provided the group of Americans by the British government, which was anxious to strengthen the bond between the two countries. He told of how impressed the English were at what was being attempted in the teaching of literature and composition in the United States and said that they were, though ignorant of the field, anxious to join in the teaching of journalism.[2]

At the evening dinner of NCTE, Scott served as toastmaster before the one hundred assembled members. "With his usual grace and wit the toastmaster called in succession upon ten charter members of the Council to speak in this celebration of the tenth anniversary of the Council's birth. . . . The toastmaster then remarked that he had in his possession a package marked 'For the man whom the Council delights to honor.' Opening it, he disclosed a beautiful loving cup which he presented in the name of the Council to James F. Hosic, now president, but until this year secretary, of the Council" ("The National Council" [1921] 58–59).

The indebtedness of NCTE to Scott is eloquently expressed in an article by Hosic, which appeared in the January 1921 issue of the *English Journal,* a retrospective on the formation and progress of the organization. "The chairman of the first meeting, Professor Fred N. Scott of the University of Michigan, was elected president for the ensuing year, and to his constant interest and wise counsel the success of the organization is largely due" (4).

In these years, Scott was faithful in his attendance at MLA as well and read two major papers. In 1916, his address was "Accentual Structure of Isolable English Phrases," which was not published until March 1918 in *PMLA,* possibly because of the disruptions caused in the war years. Scott received an extra bit of attention in the press due to the small editorial piece in "The Conning Tower" of the *New York Tribune,* December 31, courtesy of Georgia Jackson, who had moved to New York and was working for Franklin P. Adams at the *Tribune.*

What may be the most impressive aspect of Scott's paper is the daunting number of phrases and titles he examined. Little wonder that he writes on numerous occasions of "sorting" cards (FNSD). He had used as source for the phrasal idioms, Roget's *Thesaurus of English Words and Phrases,* the total number examined being 2,494. His titles, on the other hand, came from E. A. Baker's *Guide to the Best Fiction in English;* he had worked with 4,201. Out of that mass of material, Scott's aim was to extract some sort of pattern. He explains that his concern was with "isolable" phrases entirely, and he defines these as phrasal idioms and titles that can be "detached" from the context. The former are those "permanent 'bromides' of the language," such as "in fact," "of course," "fits and starts." Titles he considered the result of conscious selection by the author, and he says that the best are both "original and pleasing to the ear."

His rules of procedure are to "recognize as accentual units all the possible permutations of accent in words of two, three, and four syllables. Another is to resolve phrases of five syllables or over into combinations of the shorter units wherever possible. The third rule is to divide the longer phrases only at a natural pause or joint" (200; all page references are to *The Standard of American Speech*). Using the terms of Greek prosody—iamb, cretic, choriamb, trochee, antibacchic, anapaest, spondee, antispast, bacchic, and Ionic a minore, epitrite, amphibrach, dactyle, paeon—Scott categorizes the variety of accent. What he discovers is that as the number of syllables increases the number of examples also increases. His conclusion is that the fiction writer "inclines on the

whole to a longer phrase than that preferred by the average intelligence."
When he turns to the classification of phrases as strong or weak according to accent, he discovers more strong endings with two, three, and four
syllables than with five or more. Scott admits he doesn't know why this
is so, but suggests that the longer phrases "partake of the nature of sentences, and so allow or demand a cadence."

The paper contains an excessive amount of statistical data, unre-
lieved by much in the way of examples or anecdotes, as is more typical
in Scott's other writings. He must have had charts made up for his oral
presentation, for there are four tables and two diagrams in the printed
version. But Scott recognizes the tedium of this overwhelming deluge of
data and cannot help but seek relief. Near the end, he states that "I will
add what, I hope, will be a pleasing divertissement, namely, an examination of the titles of the best sellers for ten years as shown by the
monthly lists in the *Bookman*" (209). Scott was, after all, not a statisti-
cian. His conclusion? That "the authors of the best sellers, whether by
craft or by instinct, chose a length suitable to the popular comprehension" (209).

In this year, 1916, Scott's formidable skills in rhetoric and linguistics were exhibited in the two remarkable papers (this one and "The
Standard of American Speech") delivered within weeks of each other, one
typical of his common sense, incisive mind, the other of the indefatigable thoroughness of his research. To his credit, he could move easily from
one arena to the other.

Like NCTE, an inability to function as usual affected MLA in December 1918. In the "Acts of the Executiv Council" for that year is
recorded a proposition "to accept the invitation of Vassar College to hold
the next annual meeting under its auspices, *provided public exigencies do not
require that there be no meeting";* later that year the Association proposed
"that the annual meeting of the Association be omitted in 1918 . . . that
the officers elected for the year 1918 be declared re-elected for the year
1919 (cxxi–cxxii; italics mine). In December 1918, the Executive Council proposed to meet on the Ohio State University campus, December
27–29, 1919. However, due to the shortage of coal and the restrictions
on travel, the meeting was postponed to March 29–31, 1920. At that
meeting, Scott read another significant paper: "The Colloquial Nasals for
Yes and *No*."

Despite this activity in NCTE and MLA, the direction of Scott's interest, it is clear, had slowly begun to shift to the field that he had long
found fulfilling—journalism—and, by comparison, his newly generated

enthusiasm for the American Association of Teachers of Journalism (AATJ) seemed more genuine. Everything he did over his years at Michigan attests to his interest: his contact with and use of practicing newspapermen in his classes, his articles for *Mill Supplies,* his reflections on the proper place of the newspaper in his paper, "The Undefended Gate," his supervision of the *Michigan Daily* and his service on the publications board, his involvement in Sigma Delta Chi (the journalism fraternity), and finally, the alteration of his department's title to Rhetoric and Journalism in 1921. His dedication is highlighted in a letter to William Marx of Holyoke, Massachusetts, where he says: "journalism offers a very unusual opportunity for influencing popular opinion and thus getting our American civilization into its proper channels." In Scott's opinion, a journalist's work was of as much importance as that of the lawyer, the doctor, or the engineer. He says: "It is in one sense more important, because it is dealing more exclusively with spiritual affairs. Journalism has, of course, its sordid aspect like any other profession, but it is the purpose of our course in journalism to subdue this feature as rapidly as possible" (FNSP, January 15, 1919).

In these years, Scott became earnestly devoted to the AATJ. When the organization was founded is not entirely clear, although in a letter of invitation dated November 18, 1912, from Willard G. Bleyer, secretary, to the Chicago conference of teachers of journalism, the conference is referred to as the third annual convention ("The Founding Years," *Journalism Monographs* 9). As has already been noted, in 1911, the University of Missouri held a Journalism Week, and the previous year there was an informal meeting of journalism faculty in California. The constitution and designation of officers first appeared in 1912, but not until 1915 had the name, American Association of Teachers of Journalism, been adopted.

Scott had presided at the 1912 conference which elected Bleyer as president. In 1914, Merle Thorpe of Kansas succeeded Talcott Williams in that position. No suitable meeting time could be found for 1915, so the University of Kansas hosted the conference in April 1916 (11–12). Kansas editors, including William Allen White of Emporia, offered a dinner and a program of eleven discussion sessions on teaching—nine on public service, and four on research. James Melvin Lee, of the New York University Department of Journalism emerged as president in 1916 and called for the next meeting to be in Chicago the following April (13). By this time, Dean Walter Williams of the University of Missouri had proposed another association for the schools of journalism, the American Association of Schools of Journalism, which then met in conjunction with the AATJ in 1917; at that meeting the name was changed to the Association of American Schools and Departments of Journalism (AASDJ) (13).

On April 11, 1917, just days after the meetings of the AATJ, James M. Lee congratulated Scott on having been selected as its next president. "The office is an honor which has long belonged to you because of your pioneer work in instruction in journalism" (FNSP). In May 1916, Hugh Mercer Blain, who had been issuing the monthly newsletter, reported that AATJ had 107 members among the 175 teachers of journalism in fifty-five colleges and universities, and that the student enrollment in journalism was 3,500 ("The Founding Years," 11).

In mid-December, James Melvin Lee, who wrote Scott in regard to setting a date for the AATJ annual meeting, comments that "the war has so altered conditions that I can see how it might be wise even to postpone the meeting until another year. . . . With the increased railroad fares and with the war tax on tickets it may be that transportation charges would be too heavy for some of our members who have been regular in attendance in the past" (FNSP).

Although Scott officially assumed the helm of the organization after the 1917 meeting, because of the war and the influenza outbreak, he was unable to convene another meeting until 1919. In April 1919, Scott is using stationery with the letterhead of AATJ, but it isn't until late July that he seems to be actively engaged in putting together the conference. He asks Lee White at that time to do a postcard canvass of the members, presumably to check whether they could come to a proposed meeting at Ann Arbor in October. During the succeeding months there is a flow of correspondence to Lee White about the meetings, the speakers, the program, and other arrangements. Scott himself has lined up William Allen White.

The conference took place on October 16–18, 1919. Although Scott was president, he seems to have taken a back seat during this important conference on his own campus once it was underway. Accounts in the *Michigan Daily* mention Scott only once, on October 17: "Prof. Fred N. Scott, head of the Rhetoric department, who is president of the American Association of Teachers of Journalism, welcomed the delegates and introduced the speakers" (1). John Brumm, not Scott, presided over the business meeting which concluded the convention. Equally interesting is the report that, while in Ann Arbor, William Allen White was entertained by Professors H. E. Riggs and T. E. Rankin, not Scott.

According to the *Daily,* this meeting, which had been coordinated with meetings of the Michigan newsmen, was the first time in the history of the AATJ when "men actively engaged in newspaper work" attended. About one hundred fifty newspapermen and teachers of journalism were expected. At the close of the convention, the state editors met to make plans for coming to the university every year. On October 29, Scott wrote to White with predictable jubilation at the success of the convention: "I also have had a number of appreciative letters. We apparently surpassed their wildest expectations. Food, shelter, amusement, art, enlightenment, and social contact—what more could man desire, especially if most of it is gratis?" Considering all this, it seems strange that Scott stayed so much in the background (LWP).

As an interesting sidelight to Scott's growing involvement with journalism, in December 1920, at the editors' and publishers' convention on the Michigan campus, the *Ann Arbor News* reported "speakers . . . went out of their way to insult their guests. Dean Alfred Lloyd said editors not only are guilty of partisanship, but they often are devoid of conscience. Prof. Fred W. [*sic*] Scott was even more insulting. He proposed that every editor and publisher be compelled to attend a graduate school of journalism where his mind and soul would be remolded better to meet the basic requirements of his profession" (December 5, 1920).

Repeating the tenets he held all his life, Scott goes on to say: "In such a school he would learn to be a gentleman, abhor lying, acquire broader sympathies, learn to suffer mental discipline and be prepared to discourage 'that cynicism which is the bane of the modern newspaperman.'" This was the same message Scott had given in "The Undefended Gate," and it met with a similar fate among the newspapermen. Yet he believed his comments to be less a criticism than a statement of what was wrong with newspaper reporting—the practices that conflicted with his own sense of decorum, honesty and fairness.

❖

Of Scott's publications between 1915 and 1920, probably his favorite was "The Congress of Letters." Scott first wrote this piece for a lecture at Vassar in February 1912. He says at the time he was working on it that he was "not sure whether it is good fun in the lighter parts or just horse play," and, as to the actual composing, that "the more serious parts [were] very hard sledding" (FNSD, February 9, 11, 1912).[3] Scott imagines the occasion of the Congress of Letters in the early history of the Chinese republic. The dearth of information about it in subsequent years is due to censorship by the Chinese government. Eventually, however, reports of the Congress "accidentally" become public in a most unlikely place, a Chinese laundry in South Chicago, from notes written on the back of old laundry bills by How Sing, one of the Chinese representatives who had escaped the bloodbath suffered by the other delegates.

The purpose of the convention of scholars and men of letters was to enact a new set of laws of literary composition and to inquire into what rules govern literary art. As the congress convenes, participants from all over the world assemble: two Englishmen, G. K. Chesterton and George Bernard Shaw; a Zulu chieftain, who engages in a dance involving wild leaps and wicked-looking knives; a German, Dr. Wehmuth-Weissacker, whose innovative apparatus mechanically measured reactions to literature; a Frenchman, M. Jules Vacour, who desires to apply scientific values to literature; and an American, "a well-fed young man from the genius belt of Indiana," who believes the road to literary success is measured in dollars; and finally, an Italian minister of war who has so little to do in his official capacity that he has devoted himself to scholarship.

This essay is an important statement of Scott's progressive attitude toward literary art. His views (both of what he promotes and what he eschews) are stated through several of the characters, in his descriptions, and in the events. For example, he casts the chairman of the meeting, Fang Chu, as the author of a work on Chinese musical instruments in five hundred volumes. The work is obviously insignificant and the length absurd. He casts G. K. Chesterton favorably, having him say that literary laws were made to be broken—Scott's view. What irreverences account for Chesterton's own failures? He doesn't attend to usage, proportion, coherence, and perspicuity. These qualities are watchwords of Wendell and Hill and their followers, and Scott obviously disapproves.

His depiction of the German representative with the mechanical apparatus to measure literary response reflects another belief of Scott's—that you cannot measure quality. He has the German describe his law: "1.72 cubic millimeters per square millimeter of 10-point type for prose and 1.89 cubic millimeters per square millimeter of 8-point type for poetry" (150; all page references are to *The Standard of American Speech*). Scott also belittles the person who worships the litterateur. He has the Russian delegate admit to dismay "at the spectacle of strong men cowering and whimpering at the feet of genius as if they were in the presence and at the mercy of an oriental despot" (153). He derides the American, whom he depicts as writing solely for monetary gain: "He had nothing against Shakespeare, but whoever saw anybody reading Shakespeare on the trolley-cars?" (155–56).

Scott speaks other of his views through the Italian. He has him voice the belief that, wrongfully, art now seems to be a by-product of life, when in actuality it is indispensable to both life and progress. Scott concludes that the genuine artist gives himself "unstintedly" so as to enjoy the wider life of the community. "It was this sacrificial flame burning purely in the breast of the poet and prose writer that had given to the world its immortal epics and lyrics and works of fiction" (160). In these propositions, the Platonic legacy reposes. Scott is able to underscore his belief that the dilettantes of the literary world, especially in the university classrooms, have the wrong notion about what constitutes the ultimate principle of literary art and the legitimate mode of literary criticism.

Among other papers Scott wrote at this time was "Familiar Quotations," read at the Classical Conference at Ann Arbor in 1919. In comparison to the technical complexity of "The Accentual Structure," "Familiar Quotations" is informal and, though persuasive, deals with the more practical matter of how to reinstate interest in the classics in the schools. For the present, he insists, teachers must use an insidious approach to spur their students to seek out the classical sources for many of the phrases that are familiar to them in their communities. Working from Bartlett's collection of quotations, Scott locates about three hundred passages, familiar in English, but taken directly from the Greek and Latin classics. Only a mind conversant with such a rich depository of literature—Greek, Latin, and English—could have accessed comparable passages. So, although this is no heavy piece, "Familiar Quotations" testifies to Scott's expansive knowledge and memory.

No other writings from this period are major statements. But some were dear to Scott. First among them were the "Inscriptions" for the *Detroit News* building, undertaken probably at the instigation of Lee White and completed in June 1916. Albert Kahn, principal architect, wrote Scott "that my inscriptions for the news building were just splendid."[4] And when he saw the building for the first time, Scott wrote Lee White: "The manner in which the inscriptions have been treated pleases me very much" (FNSP). They were carved in stone on the parapet of the *News* building and appropriately paired with full-length stone figures of famous men connected to printing, such as Johannes Gutenberg, Christophe Plantin, Benjamin Franklin, and William Caxton. Some representative examples, as quoted in the *Detroit News Sunday Magazine,* August 18, 1916, are: "Mirror of the Public Mind . . . Interpreter of the Public Intent . . . Troubler of the Public Conscience"; "Reflector of Every

Human Interest . . . Friend of Every Righteous Cause . . . Encourager of Every Generous Act"; "Promoter of Civic Welfare and Civic Pride . . . Bond of Civic Unity . . . Protector of Civic Rights."

In 1918, Scott discovered his precious inscriptions were to be included in a small volume edited by J. Madison Gathany, titled *American Patriotism in Prose and Verse, 1775–1918,* a collection of patriotic sentiment from numerous sources. Gathany's explanatory note reads: "'The Newspaper' constitutes inscriptions of ideals adopted by the well-known daily, *The Detroit News,* Detroit Michigan. The author of the ideals of 'The Newspaper' is Professor Fred Newton Scott of the University of Michigan. Of course *The Detroit News* does not claim to live up completely to these ideals, but the courage to set them forth as its ideals, and the attempt to live up to them are highly commendable, and indicate the spirit and the function of the American daily. These ideals should be learned by heart by every American citizen and transmuted into character" (286).

For a university professor to have inscriptions on the facade of a public building was indeed unusual. For Scott, it was a source of pride: they embodied every moral and ethical tenet in his emerging devotion to the world of journalism, and their endorsement by a major newspaper placed him in a position of importance in that world, a position he coveted at this point in his career.

In another of Scott's works, he returns to the field of aesthetics for an amusing experiment. He had ventured into the Ann Arbor public schools armed with large photographs of Leonardo da Vinci's *Last Supper* and *Mona Lisa* to elicit the unsophisticated responses of the children, most of whom knew nothing about the history of the paintings nor of the milieu in which they were created. The resulting article is simply a summary of the responses Scott received, many charming in their ingenuousness.

Scott writes: "In answer to the question what the people in [the *Last Supper*] were doing, one little girl said that it was a party, an opinion to which all the rest gave their assent. Why, then, it was asked, were they not eating their supper? To this one wise child replied that they were 'not hungry,' and another that they were 'all through.' A third suggested that it was because they had stopt to laugh at something. One eager mite of a girl waved a quivering small hand, and when she was given permission to speak, said solemnly, 'They have long hair'—which I thought about up to the average of contemporary art-criticism" *(The Literary Digest* (April 20, 1918), 36).

Scott drew several conclusions from this experiment. For one, "The right interpretation of a picture is a matter of education, of knowing the circumstances of its production and the trend of ideas in the time when it was painted" (37). He relates a story about three observers construing Giorgione's *Concert* as being variously: the three ages of man; a picture of Luther, Calvin, and Melanchthon; a performer who, having broken his violin string, was trying to borrow another from the man playing the organ. Scott assigns blame for such misinterpretations to the critic, not the innocent gallery visitor, arguing that these views can only be the result of "setting up art as a kind of fetish to be blindly worshiped" (37). Two points can be made about this article: one, that it is like Scott to think of such an imaginative experiment; two, that it underscores his inquisitiveness in the area of aesthetics.

From a purely historical perspective, it is interesting to note that in 1919 Scott published only a series of book reviews and "Familiar Quotations," and that there were no publications in 1920.

13

Change, Loss, and Recovery

THE 1921 academic year started off like any other. In a rare reference to his class work, Scott notes that he has been working in his office to get material ready for class, and has spent time cleaning up his desk and the tables in West Hall in preparation, as well as visiting with students. On September 27, Scott has a strange entry in his journal: "Usual sense of unreality and futility in encountering a new set of faces. Find myself counting with eagerness the number of days before the next long vacation and wondering how I shall get through with it" (FNSD). That the university had grown so rapidly in enrollment, putting pressure on all the faculty and taking away the close intimacy that had existed previously is unquestionably a factor. In 1900–1901, a total of 3,712 students were enrolled. In 1920–1921, there were 10,623, over three times as many. Within the Rhetoric Department in 1923, there are 2,600 students, 1,513 of whom are freshmen. The sections of composition are large, each averaging about thirty students. (In 1924 Rankin reports that most instructors have between seventy and eighty students.) T. E. Rankin notes on October 9, 1923 that they are trying to get by without the remedial courses by asking the instructors "to take care of their very poor students in their two hour consultation periods." They also hope to eliminate the "utterly hopeless cases" from the university "as quickly as possible" (FNSP).

Scott oversaw the work of a number of promising graduate students in rhetoric at this time, several of whom were already teaching within the Rhetoric Department: John R. Adams, Arno L. Bader, Warren Bower, Albert Conkey, Lawrence H. Conrad, Edward S. Everett, Kenneth Hoag, Robert D. Horn, Oakley C. Johnson, Amos R. Morris, Sigmund Kluss Proctor, Melvin Solve, Houghton Wells Taylor, Erich A. Walter, Carlton F. Wells (who went on to his own illustrious career at Michigan after securing his A.M. in 1922), and Cecil V. Wicker.

A number of women went through the program as well, but they do not appear among the instructors in Scott's department. In 1921 Ruth Mary Weeks wrote: "I noticed last summer that two women are now members of the Michigan faculty" (FNSP). On March 17, 1921, a Miss Sheldon "in a flower-encircled hat" appeared at Scott's office asking to be considered as a candidate for an instructorship, but "he [Dean Effinger] agreed with me that a women instructor was undesirable at present." In general, women faculty were to be found primarily in the women's colleges like Vassar or Mount Holyoke, or in small private schools. Helen Mahin was unique in finding a position at the University of Kansas, as also was Louise Pound of the University of Nebraska.

There was one big change in the Department of Rhetoric at this time. In April 1921, the regents record that Scott requested a change in his title from professor of rhetoric to professor of rhetoric and journalism at Michigan. The department name changed as well, and John R. Brumm was promoted to professor of journalism in the Department of Rhetoric and Journalism. The change reflects the growing stature of journalism. Brumm had joined the faculty in 1918 as associate professor of rhetoric, taking charge of all the journalism courses beyond those in the first two years. In 1919, he taught all of the courses (which may explain his preeminence at the AATJ meetings held then). When the department changed to Rhetoric and Journalism in 1921–1922, the curriculum was increased to twelve courses with Brumm as the director. In 1929–1930, journalism became a separate department in the College of Literature, Science, and the Arts, with Brumm as its head.[1] After his presidency in AATJ, Scott was relatively inactive. There is nothing to explain this change. He did continue attending meetings, but appeared to enjoy the affiliation with men in the field over active participation.

A letter to Scott from T. E. Rankin on November 27, 1923 indicates the situation: "I know, of course, that Mr. Brumm is very anxious to establish a School of Journalism apart from the Department of Rhetoric, and, no doubt, a good deal of work is done, in connection with the many meetings held here, in an attempt to move in that direction. I am inclined to think that the Department of Rhetoric would be better off without the present association, but, on the other hand, more especially inclined to think that Journalism is better off tied up with the Department of Rhetoric than it would be floating loose" (FNSP).

Despite Scott's lessened professional involvement in the field of journalism, in April 1925 he was elected to honorary membership in Pi Delta Epsilon, the national honorary journalistic fraternity. Indeed, when the Press Congress of the World met at Geneva, Switzerland, September 14–18, 1927, President C. C. Little appointed Scott as Michigan's official representative. At that time, Walter Williams asked Scott to participate in a discussion of education for journalism, and Scott accepted. There is, however, no evidence that Scott attended the conference, although he was in Europe that summer.

In 1921, Robert Frost came to the campus as a recipient of a fellowship in creative art established by President Marion LeRoy Burton. Burton was highly enthusiastic about this position, believing strongly that the presence on campus of a creative artist "would be stimulating to the whole college community." It was an experiment of which many were skeptical. Louis Strauss notes on April 21, 1922, that "at the outset many doubts were expressed by members of the faculty as to the wisdom of an experiment so remote from the conventional trend of educational theory and practice" (DEP).

Frost stayed the larger part of the years between 1921 and 1925. His presence drew a number of distinguished American poets to the campus for lectures and to meet with classes of students interested in creative writing, particularly poetry. Scott describes him: "a gentle, peaceful face, a bit whimsical, a voice subdued and speech a little drawling, manners quiet and natural, no tenseness or strain in anything." He records his own reaction to Frost: "Never having been exposed much to poets, the University feels, I think, a little awkward and nervous at the prospect of having Frost around. What is the etiquette of the Poetic Presence? Meeting the Poet unexpectedly as you round the corner of the South Wing, what does one do and say—to mutter a line from his poems would, I imagine, or, that failing, the poet-passage from Midsummer Night's Dream or Twinkle Twinkle Little Star . . . as if you knew them all by heart & were just running over the first lines" (FNSP, penciled on letter from Georgia Jackson, September 16, 1921). But Scott's fears were allayed. A couple of weeks after Frost's arrival, Scott called on him and was puzzled to find him, having returned from dinner at one of the sororities, dressed in what seemed to be an old flannel shirt. Scott wonders if he had made "a lightning change for the sake of an afternoon's ease"

(FNSD, October 16, 1921). Scott enjoyed Frost's company and was impressed with his opinions, principally because they were, like his own, straightforward and unpretentious.

Scott's value to the department and the devotion of his students to him is reflected in a number of incidents and letters during this period. In November 1921, Professor Laura Wylie of Vassar told him that Gertrude Buck had suffered a stroke in August. She was still recovering, and Wylie writes that Buck would have struggled to get to MLA, held at Johns Hopkins in Baltimore that year, had she known that Scott was to be there. Sadly, within a short time, Scott would be one of several offering tributes to Buck, who died on January 8, 1922.

In March 1923, Scott was elected a member of the Michigan Academy of Science, Arts, and Letters at its twenty-eighth annual meeting. Originally conceived as a means through which scientists would integrate their work, in 1921 the scope was enlarged to include arts and letters.

Over the years, numerous colleagues and students declared their appreciation for Scott's assistance in their careers. In March 1923, Dean Mortimer E. Cooley, of the engineering school, wrote to Professor John N. Weed of Ohio State University: "We are particularly fortunate here at the University in our Professor Scott of the Literary College. In the early days he was one of the cub instructors who taught English to engineers. He is in thorough sympathy with our plans in English and does everything possible to support us." Cooley explains that English in the Colleges of Engineering and Architecture is essentially a separate department, although "nominally" under the supervision of Scott. In the early years, English for engineers was "merely a course in theme writing or something of that sort," which the students regarded as a "nuisance and when finished had a bonfire and burned up everything pertaining to it" (FNSP).

Corwin Dale Willson wrote Scott in January 1923 to thank him for helping him through the period of his aspirations. "My 'poems,' turgid and filled with drum-like over-emphasis as they are, served as a catharsis of adolescent passion, a very real psychic need. Then, when this need had become less pressing, you kindly helped deflate the egoism which notice of my poems had swelled. Accordingly, I can now thank you for it and add that, in spite of one or two lapses, I have never ceased being grateful for the inspiration you helped awaken in me in those 'youthful' days" (FNSP).

In June 1925, a student, Richard Steiner, wrote him a letter which must have been greatly appreciated. "Now that the final words are about to be said over the body of the school year that has ended, I want to write and thank you for the inspiration and information you have given me during the past year. You cannot know how much I have profited from being under your instruction, and how very grateful I am to you. I think that my critical faculties, never very keen, have been sharpened, and given some solid foundation on which to grow. My creative impulse was not as active as I had hoped, but when the 'spirit did move', I felt that I was accomplishing something. But above all you have set a standard of teaching which will always be my aim to achieve, and if I succeed, to you must go the credit" (FNSP).

❖

In Scott's personal life, the changes were numerous. The family had just moved into a new home which they had taken considerable time to remodel to their satisfaction. Scott writes of the painters and carpenters being there, of rugs being placed in the rooms, and of bringing his books from the study, partly filling the shelves in the living room (FNSD, January 28, 30, 1921). On January 19, 1921, he and Isadore went to Detroit to select furnishings. Richard, the last to leave the Scott household, was married in February. On August 23, in making preparations for a short trip to Colorado, Scott and Isadore stopped briefly to make out their wills, a fortuitous decision as it turned out.

On January 6, 1922, in a letter to her daughter Marion, Isadore outlined the Scotts' plans for the summer of 1922. They are considering going to England, as Scott wants to work in the British Museum and to visit Greece. Her observations on the immediacy of taking the trip are prophetic: "I do not like to postpone it, for fear that one of us might develop rheumatism or any one of a hundred small ailments which would make it seem safer or more comfortable to stay at home, or at least in this country." She mentioned, in fact, that she had a "miserable" cold, but she was busy cleaning up the house, washing and waxing floors and washing windows (MG). Then Isadore suddenly took ill in March. On March 13, 1922, she succumbed to a staph infection.

In reflecting on her death, Scott wrote in his diary a memorable and significant panegyric to Isadore, detailing the treasured relationship. In his mood of melancholy and sorrow, Scott reveals much about his own personality.

Today at 1:15 died my dear good wife. She had a merry heart, a generous disposition, and a shrewd judgment. In almost all respects she was my opposite. I am a glum and uncommunicative owl, whereas she was light-hearted and fond of communication. I am indecisive and procrastinating, whereas she was eager to act and quick to decide. But we were, nevertheless, well-suited to each other, and neither, I believe, ever tired of the other's company. Our life in this new house was as nearly ideal as the life of two old friends can be. . . .

Her going has cost me more anguish than I supposed to exist in the whole world. It has not only torn out all the fibers of association, memory, and companionship, it has shaken and bewildered my mental world. If I have found any consolation, it has come from this reflection: Although nothing can possibly take the place of the living person—the handclasp, the kiss, the glances of mutual understanding and affection, yet I do feel that in that part of me which her influence shaped, she is still present. (FNSD)

On March 23, he wrote to Shirley Smith: "I am not going to reply to your kind letter except to say that, coming at a moment when the loneliness seemed intolerable, it saved me from futile self-abandonment" (SSP). He spent miserable days trying to find peace of mind. On March 29, he writes in his journal: "A peculiarly bad day mentally. I can propose no object to myself which is not instantly robbed of all interest in life with only a painful interest. Johnson advises Boswell if he finds any melancholy thought in his mind, to cover it up—it will then disappear; whereas if he talks about it or exhibits it, it will grow." On April 2, as he is at dinner with Richard and Marion, "the baby bright and smiling," he reflects: "The one bitter idea eating always at my heart. I can drive it away for a moment or two, but it comes back at a gallup" (FNSD).

Contained in a memo from Dean Effinger to President Marion Leroy Burton is Scott's request for leave for three weeks beginning April 19, 1922 (CLSA). He was on the verge of a nervous collapse, and wanted to go to the Battle Creek Sanitarium. His life was in disarray after the death of his wife, and letters indicate his need to reassess plans for travel abroad over the summer. He and Isadore had looked forward to going, but Scott was not sure he would follow through now that he would have to make the trip alone. But in the end, he did. In London, Scott spent most of his time in the reading room of the British Museum and looking up old friends with whom he sometimes ate or attended plays or concerts. It was a melancholy time for him; his friend J. D. Bruce departed on August 19, "leaving me quite stricken." And this melancholy is reflected as well in his record of his activities on August 22: "Drew some money and spent most of the day wandering about looking into shop windows and bidding adieu to London—a rueful employment and unprofitable. Paid a last visit—or shall I again tomorrow!—to the beloved reading-room." He departed for the United States on August 24, 1922 (FNSD).

Scott had been granted leave for 1923–24, and left immediately at the end of the school year. But he was no longer alone. Through the academic year 1922–1923, Georgia Jackson had returned to Ann Arbor to continue her studies as she had earlier proposed. Her presence in Ann Arbor, and the uninterrupted contact she had maintained with Scott over the years, led to a natural union that culminated in their marriage on June 17, 1923. Soon thereafter, Scott and his new wife embarked for the continent, residing in London through the remaining months of 1923 and traveling more extensively on the continent into the summer of 1924.

Some of Scott's itinerary can be gleaned from a letter to President Burton written in May 1924: "We have been traveling very steadily for the past few months—from Egypt to Sicily, from Sicily to Naples, Rome, Orvieto, Florence, Siena, Venice, Milan, Lucerne, Interlaken, Geneva, and finally Paris, where we hope to make a definite stand for at least the next three weeks. It is a great joy after living in our satchels for three months, to open our trunks once more" (FNSP).

In 1923 the department was moving out of West Hall (which had been scheduled for razing for a number of years) and into the new Literary Building. West Hall was one of the early ward (public) schools of Ann Arbor, and when it was originally purchased by the university "as a temporary makeshift" for classroom use in 1902, Scott took it over for the new Department of Rhetoric. It was totally inadequate, space being at a premium, and it had been condemned repeatedly over the years. It was incredible that the building did not burn down, for besides being a dilapidated wooden structure, the basement housed tons of old student themes. Even worse, the passageways were used as classrooms, office, and library.

Although the actual demolition was not carried out until 1924, the building was abandoned in 1923. But since Scott was on leave that year, he managed to avoid the commotion resulting from the move. According to T. E. Rankin, who wrote in October 1923 to keep Scott apprised of activities at Michigan while he was abroad, "The books, and pictures, and other things in your room in West Hall were stored for the latter part of the summer in the room on the first floor of the Natural Science Building, and this fall were moved to the second floor of the University High School Building" (FNSP). By May 6, 1924, Rankin was optimistic about the completion of the Literary Building, writing that "there is no question at all but that we shall be in the New Literary Building in September" (FNSP). Rankin, who has to make arrangements for Scott for the fall, questions Scott about how he wants his classroom arranged: " . . . we have assumed that you wish to use your office as a class-room just as you did in West Hall. The room, which is No. 2208 in the new building, seems a little smaller than your old room in West Hall, but I suppose you knew the dimensions when you made the arrangements with Professor Shepard" (FNSP).

Because the university published class schedules in September, there was little time for prospective students to be alerted to the changes brought about by Scott's year of leave. Rankin writes: "A number of the graduate students have been particularly disappointed because they did not know that you would not be here to give course 23" (FNSP). Since traditionally this course drew a number of creative writers, the graduate students had organized a writing club in its place.

Rankin was not alone in keeping in touch with Scott during this year of leave. In February 1924, Harold Scott wrote about conditions as he saw them. Like Rankin, he complains about the size of the courses, noting that he has 120 students in three sections. He also worries about the quality of the students he is seeing.

The American public seems to be dying to get education—yet when students arrive at the University, they apparently live to get something else, something that might be summed up in the word thrill. They get their thrills nowadays too frequently from week-end parties in Detroit and from boot-leg booze. In short, the spirit of the "outside" is really getting inside. Academic work is a sideshow now; the main show is in the Yost Field House, or in gymnasiums decorated for hopping, or in the dancehall at the Union, or in some fraternity brother's limousine parked on a cross-road a mile from town. Students do not hesitate to plead "rushing" activities as an excuse for delinquent work. (FNSP)

Another change Scott learned of was that John Brumm would be taking a leave of absence for 1924–25, and that Edwin G. Burrows, who was to take his place, had, instead, resigned. Thus, on May 10, 1924, Scott wrote to President Burton describing guidelines for the selection process: "men of powerful and compelling personality, long and successful experience in newspaper work, and teaching ability of a high order, men who would command the confidence of Michigan journalists, and give the College of Journalism, if there is to be one, instant standing and distinction in the newspaper world" (FNSP). Scott's concern, because of his continuous efforts to establish a journalism department to which he had contributed much over nearly thirty years, was legitimate.

When Scott returned to Ann Arbor in the fall of 1924, poor health prevented him from continuing through the spring semester of 1925. He had hoped to spend the summer again in England, but instead found himself writing to Sir Henry Newbolt on May 31, 1925: "I regret that I am unable to go abroad this year, but hope to do so in the summer of 1926" (FNSP).

❖

Scott was noticeably active professionally in the 1920s. In October 1921, Thomas M. Deam, secretary of the Committee on Unit Courses and Curriculum of the North Central Association, wrote to Scott on behalf of Frank G. Pickell, chairman of the committee and assistant superintendent of schools in Cleveland, requesting that he serve on an English Committee. Deam reminds Scott of the history of the organization:

Several years ago the North Central Association withdrew from the Conference on Uniform College Entrance Requirements in English. The reason for this action was a belief that the purposes and methods of the Conference were in need of changes which it could not make. Up to the present time, however, the North Central Association has done little to realize these reforms. The result is that the 1500 high schools and 200 colleges of the Association are still using the requirements laid down by the Conference, although they have no voice in its deliberations. In consequence of this situation, the Commission on Unit Courses and Curricula at its annual meeting in March, 1921, ordered the creation of a committee on college entrance requirements in English. (FNSP)

Somewhat later, with a similar mission to consider, Scott made his way to the president's office to "show him the letter from Capen." Samuel P. Capen, of the U.S. Bureau of Education, energetically forged into his work as the first director of the American Council on Education with a study of the role of the federal government in higher education, of standardization of education in colleges and universities, of the status and future of the arts and sciences, and of the costs of a college education. He chose Scott to serve as an advisor. In New York in late October 1921, Scott met with Capen, Franklin T. Baker, and Wilbur Owen Sypherd at which time they "worked out a form of letter to the General Education Board—Baker to frame it and send draft to the other members" (FNSD).

The report of this meeting, in the *English Journal,* May 1922, indicates the committee considered the following questions: "1) Shall the North Central Association permit the present situation to continue? 2)

Shall the North Central Association again seek representation in the Conference on Uniform College Entrance Requirements in English? 3) Shall the North Central Association formulate college entrance requirements of its own to meet the special requirements of North Central secondary schools and colleges?" ("News and Notes" 308). At its March 1922 meeting, the committee adopted a rather lengthy report recommending that North Central Colleges print in their catalogues a statement of college entrance requirements. The statement defined both composition teaching and literature teaching and designated the purposes of each, as well as the means by which the objectives could best be realized. Most interesting, in relation to Scott, is the stated aim of composition teaching: "to give the learner the power to communicate his ideas to others. Its subject-matter is the whole body of the pupil's ideas, emotions, and aspirations" (309). As pure embodiment of Scott's lifelong commitment, it is tempting to consider it Scott's contribution.

Busy as well on the Committee on American Speech, formed by NCTE, Scott qualified the term "better speech" to indicate the direction and focus of the movement toward "adequate expression of the best in American character" ("News and Notes" [1921] 414]). Unfortunately, like so many well-intentioned projects, the noble aims deteriorated into efforts on the part of high school teachers to improve speech by insisting on "correct" pronunciations, and the elimination of "errors" in grammar. But Scott was an idealist and had hoped for evidence in the students of education in the truest sense. He had in mind, perhaps, the successes of the renowned classic orators.

In 1922, Scott reported at NCTE on his activities with the British Society for Pure English. He indicated that a number of American scholars had wished to establish a cooperative effort with the Society, and asked that the council endorse the current work and "pledge future moral support" ("The National Council at Chattanooga" 44).

Other, more local issues emerged in this period to engage Scott's interest. At the annual meeting of NCTE held in 1921, the council decided to involve itself in what was called "essentials," appointing a committee whose first duties were to "survey the field and to report methods of determining essentials" ("Proceedings" 43). Definition of this term and the subsequent focus on it was to command the attention of the council in the next year. George Lasher, one of Scott's colleagues at the University of Michigan, indicated that while English teachers had agreed that essentials were necessary, not much had been done "to assure their mastery." He cited evidence from discussion by school representatives that the main reason for failure of freshmen in college in general was the inability to read intelligently or to use language effectively. His concern was a "thorough-going country-wide program" to assure "correct and effective expression, both written and oral." He suggested that the council's obligation was to provide a list of essentials which would be adopted as a standard for college entrance (47).

This general concern with "correctness" was apparently so intense this year that the president's address, delivered by H. G. Paul of the University of Illinois, focused on "the problem of securing better speech." Paul emphasized two things: (1) that teachers should abandon "all petty puristic scruples, ceasing to haggle over matters of divided usage and to frown upon harmless slang used in proper places"; and (2) that although they were to work for "grammatical correctness and for distinctness of articulation," the real concern should be for "effectiveness and pleasing quality in speech" ("Proceedings" 48). Thus, to those who had tried to turn the tide to an easy "list" of essentials, even indicating in which grades they should be taught, Paul proposed a freer view of language success. Throughout this convention, the dilemma of how to bring high school entrants up to college level and how to develop "systems" to measure success were issues that commanded the attention of all participants.

Scott appeared on the program of the College Section with Helen Sard Hughes of Wellesley College in an examination of "The First Two Years of College English." Hughes proposed that colleges set up a "practicable minimum for entrance into the Freshman courses in English" and provide a combined course for composition and literature in the second half of the second year. Scott took a larger view. He tied the course in composition to the total educational goal and insisted, once again, that it must serve a "cultural function." He explained that the composition course should not be considered merely "utilitarian" but would, "in the hands of the real teacher," function as a powerful cultural agent ("Proceedings" 52). He also suggested that the North Central Association would be the best group for assuring that immediate reforms in English teaching would occur.

It is interesting that this convention was so relentless in its pursuit of "correctness" and "essentials." When the last session met on Saturday morning, discussion again centered on the "mechanics which are supposed to have been mastered in the first six grades." Blame was assigned to poor college teaching and to snobbery within and between universities—especially in eastern colleges. E. M. Hopkins of the University of

Kansas looked at high costs and the lack of available funds to provide a reasonable teaching load ("Proceedings" 58–59). The problem remained unresolved—as it is yet today.

In October 1922, Karl Young, of the University of Wisconsin, wrote to Scott in response to Scott's article on "English Composition as a Mode of Behavior," which had been published in the *English Journal.* In light of the furor over essentials, minimum requirements, and the question of whose "fault" it was that writing was so poor at the freshman level, Young tells Scott: "I think your study will arouse some fresh thinking. My impression is that Freshman English needs a tonic, just now; and I feel something like a tonic in your analysis of the fundamental situation" (FNSP). In the article, Scott identified, as the sources of students' lack of proficiency in language, three main areas: the influence of spoken foreign languages; the disappearance of the isolated family unit; and the obvious schism between instinctive or natural expression and academic or school language. Of the first, he assigns the responsibility for exacerbating the problem to the teacher who does not recognize the "melting-pot" phenomenon. He points out that "more than twelve millions of our fellow-Americans . . . were born in countries where English is not the native language and have for their home speech a foreign tongue" (20–21). We cannot overlook the historical implication: "The sons and daughters of these foreign-born number at least thirteen millions more. It thus appears that there are in this country twenty-five millions of persons whose speech is either unqualifiedly foreign or is seriously influenced by the foreign speech of the home and the community" (21), and for whom English is "virtually a foreign language." In Scott's time, no one had as yet addressed this issue.

The second cause is more extensive in its influence and therefore harder to deal with. This is the disappearance of the isolated family with its inculcation of values and traditions, which effectively preserve "a certain tone and choiceness and gravity of speech" despite "provincialisms and grammatical lapses" (22). The pervasive influences that have corrupted this happy speech community are four in number: the newspaper, the telephone, the automobile, and the movie. The newspaper is responsible for cheapening the language with slang, sensationalism, flippancy, and insincerity. The telephone interrupts our "seclusion" and introduces "qualities of speech that hitherto were heard only casually" (23). The car takes us away from our community into metropolitan areas where other, presumably lesser, language forms are incorporated into the familiar speech patterns.

Scott accused overzealous teachers of forcing children to repress their natural language instincts. "And now upon this seething caldron of communicative impulses, the school, as ordinarily conducted, clamps the lid of linguistic ritual" (26). As a result, students experience a learned reticence. With an unusual visionary skill, Scott notes that "The maddening errors that students are guilty of . . . are not, in any due proportion, the product of stupidity, or malice, or even laziness. They are the outward signs of an inward lesion—of the disjunction of two phases of man's nature that can work as they should only when they work together" (28).

This essay states in unqualified terms why Scott fought so adamantly for reform in the entrance requirements, particularly for the use of theme topics that would be manageable and vital to an eighteen-year-old. Had the teachers he addressed in his many speeches and writings on this subject listened thoughtfully and followed his recommendations, the course of composition pedagogy in this country would have taken an entirely different, and very likely a happier, direction.

At the annual meeting of NCTE for 1922 held in Chattanooga, Tennessee, Scott was more active than he had been in more recent years. As member of the board of directors, he attended the early business meetings, where it was noted that the Hopkins report on "Labor and Cost of Composition Teaching" was soon to be printed. The contributors included a large number of the more distinguished members of NCTE, such as James F. Hosic, E. L. Miller, J. W. Searson, Charles G. Osgood, Allan Abbott, C. C. Certain, Rollo Brown, H. G. Paul, Edwin M. Hopkins, F. T. Baker, Sterling Leonard, W. Wilber Hatfield, as well as four large organizations—the New York City and New Jersey Associations of Teachers of English and the English Faculty of the Lewis and Clark and North Central High Schools in Spokane. Scott was one of the contributors as well.

Expressing annoyance over the inability to rectify the problems in freshman English classes, Hardin Craig suggested the appointment of a committee to survey the teaching of English from kindergarten through college. The NEA, also concerned with this issue, had asked for "a list of half a dozen people" from which would be selected a commission to formulate an American School Program. "This program is to cover the organization, administration, curriculum, and method of the American public school from the kindergarten up to the professional school" ("National Council at Chattanooga" 44). Six men were elected to this commission: Allan Abbott, C. C. Certain, Hardin Craig, J. F. Hosic, S. A. Leonard, and Scott. Scott was also selected to serve again on the editorial board of the *English Journal*.

At the open meeting of the Essentials Committee, the program indicates the questions under consideration were: What Problems Shall the Essentials Committee Attack? and How Shall It Attack Them? A number of members spoke, many providing very little that was new to the issue from the year before. When Scott's turn came, he offered a different perspective, saying that "'Essentials' is an unpleasant word, and probably misleading" ("National Council at Chattanooga" 49). He suggested that they talk of "values" and study the value of current practices. Scott was trying to turn away from "correctness" and "uniformity" to what he considered the basic uses of language. But considering the number of participants who focused on mechanical minutiae, it is obvious that teachers favored some kind of specific identification of essentials, a specific appropriation of specific elements to specific grade levels, and some valid and simple testing method to measure achievement. They may have understood what Scott meant by "values," but they clearly preferred a systematized scheme that would make teaching in English quantifiably accountable and define their role and duties. In this discussion, more than any other, may lie the clue to the lack of popularity of Scott's ideas about composition teaching.

Because he was to be on leave in 1923–1924, Scott disentangled himself from some of his obligations to NCTE as well as to other organizations. His only presence at the convention in 1923 was through a "charming letter" mailed to Ed Miller and read by him to those at the annual dinner, at which time, according to Miller, it was greeted with "great applause" (FNSP).

In 1924, the NCTE convention was held at St. Louis. Scott appeared twice on the program. At the College Section, he delivered his talk on "The Origin of the Colloquial Nasals," which he had given on several other occasions, the latest being before the Philological Section of the British Association for the Advancement of Science in December 1923. This speech is described as dealing with "pure linguistic theory." At the general session after the president's address, Scott followed up on his interest in the American-British speech controversy with his speech on "Improving the English of America."[2] He warned that the British must not assert superiority and that Americans should not be judged by "the language H. L. Mencken says is American." Of Mencken, Scott says that "to an American who is a little proud of his native speech, the reading of these pronouncements is like taking sand in the mouth. It is as if someone who professed an interest in your welfare should remark casually, that he had seen your grandfather's photograph in the rogues' gallery" ("Fourteenth Annual Meeting" 48).

He suggests five studies that could settle the issue by means of indisputable evidence. These studies would consist first of the preparation
of a list of words used in America but not in England along with English equivalents and as precise a definition as could be achieved. The second study would deal with the same thing from the other side—British
words not used in America. The third study would consist of a complete
list of grammatical constructions endemic to each nation; the fourth a
complete list of both British and American slang expressions with comparative meanings and equivalents. And the fifth would deal with into-
nations that differentiate the language use in each of the two countries.

At NCTE in 1925, Scott and Orton Lowe, director of English for the
state of Pennsylvania, discussed the report on "The Place and Function
of English in American Life" given by John M. Clapp. Scott praised the
report for its "vision and courage . . . in this attempt to find out how language actually functions in life." He recognized that this investigation
was concerned with communication and the distribution of ideas—in
essence, rhetoric as he defined it. He observed: "it plunges boldly into
the actual functioning of the language as it is employed by every member of the democracy: conversation, telephone transmission, business interchange, interviewing, listening. It tries to seize the fresh, palpitating
life of speech . . . to form . . . a picture of what I am accustomed to call
the speech community—the whole complex or interworking of society
so far as it is held together by the use of speech" ("Report of Committee" 131–32).

At the College Section meetings, the speakers were concerned with
the development of a proposed dictionary of American English. Professor Hans Kurath of Northwestern University, chairman of the Committee on a Survey of American English appointed by the Present-Day English group of MLA, explained a plan to secure investigations of the
history of the general character of American speech by examining typical communities.

Scott also participated in a discussion of a paper on "The Honors
Course in English." With Scott was O. J. Campbell, who explained that
at Michigan, students applied for the honors courses in numbers larger
than what could be accommodated, although officials at other colleges
said students were "timid" about enrolling. Campbell, of course, had in
mind the program put in place by the Department of English in 1924.
But in a January 1925 letter directed to Ernest Hatch Wilkins, dean of
the College of Arts, Literature, and Science at the University of Chicago,
Scott described the composition program. He traces the beginning to

the early nineties when he divided the freshmen classes into three sections: a delinquent section, a medium section for the majority of the students, and an advanced section. "The advanced classes were conducted on the seminar method, each class meeting for a single session of two hours a week, and the instructor following any method of instruction that seemed to him suited to the needs of the class." Scott explains that this practice was carried on for several years, until it was decided that the advanced sections required too much work from the instructors. He says that he regretted the loss of the program, "for they [the advanced classes] were a great stimulus to the better students" (FNSP).

As is obvious in this account of NCTE activities, the issue of speech, both in terms of its place and function in the school curriculum, and in the larger concern about the relative status of English and American usage, is of primary interest both for the organization as well as for Scott.

In the years between 1921 and 1925, although Scott was more active in NCTE, he still took part in most of the MLA conventions. In 1921, he served as chairman for the Section on Problems in General Aesthetics. More interesting to later developments was the work of the Present-Day English Section. The chairman, James F. Royster, suggested publication of a Present-Day English Grammar to be undertaken by MLA, designating that it should distinguish between colloquial and formal English and "should be based on scientific study of present usage apart from traditional grammatical notions" (Kenyon xxvi). This particular project eventually led to the union with the Society for Pure English and to the desire to publish the dictionary of American dialect, with Sir William Craigie leading the movement over an extended period of time.

In 1924, when MLA met in New York City, Scott read his paper "Favorite Words" before a group described as "fluctuating" in numbers because of the competition with other groups. He again appeared at the Present-Day English Section, where "Professor T. A. Knott, on behalf of the Committee on Cooperation with the Society for Pure English, made a report of Progress" (Fries xxvii). Scott's interest in the collaboration between British and American scholars had apparently led to the formation of this committee. In the same section, Professor Hans Kurath presented a tentative procedure for the survey of American English and was named chairman of a committee for proceeding with the work. As noted, Kurath had appeared also at the 1925 meeting of NCTE, along with Professor Craigie who was "in this country with the express purpose of organizing the work on the proposed dictionary of American English"

("Fifteenth Annual Meeting" 58). Thus, thanks to Scott's impetus, both NCTE and MLA had joined, along with Professor Craigie of England, in a monumental undertaking that consumed the imagination of those who had initiated the project.

Scott's involvement in the Society for Pure English (SPE) continued for a number of years. Robert Bridges, in an interview with the *New York Times* in 1924, related that the society began in 1912 when he shared his idea with Sir Walter Raleigh and L. Pearsall Smith; it was officially founded in 1913, at which time Henry Bradley was added to the group. The reasoning behind the society was Bridges's belief that because the English language was in such widespread use over the world, there needed to exist some organization that could provide guidance.

Bridges explains: "The ideal of our association is both conservative and democratic. It would aim at preserving all the richness of differentiation in our vocabulary, its nice gramatical *{sic}* usuages *{sic}*, its traditional idioms and the music of its inherited pronunciation. It would oppose whatever is slipshod and careless, and all blurring of hard-won distinctions, but it would no less oppose the tyranny of schoolmasters and grammarians, both in their pedantic conservatism and their enforcing of . . . 'rules,' based not on principle, but merely on what has come to be considered 'correct' usage" (Pope 8). Accordingly, the society arranged to publish a series of tracts on various topics relating to correct use of the language, the first issued in 1919. Among members are listed: Arthur James Balfour, Bernard Berenson, Walter de la Mare, Henry Austin Dobson, Edmund Gosse, Maurice Hewlett, Sir Arthur Quiller Couch, R. C. Trevelyan, Hugh Walpole, Mrs. Humphry Ward and Mrs. Wharton.

In 1922 a group of American scholars, including James Wilson Bright, A. S. Cook, Charles Grandgent, Robert Underwood Johnson, John Livingston Lowes, John Matthews Manly, Charles Osgood and Fred Newton Scott, proposed a permanent organization.[3] In June 1922, Bridges wrote to Scott sanctioning the principles designated by the American scholars and proposing that they, like the British group, select a five-man committee to work out the respective proposals of the SPE (FNSP). The members of the American committee, listed in a letter to Sir Henry Newbolt dated January 19, 1923 are: Henry Seidel Canby, Charles Mills Gayley, John Livingston Lowes, John Matthews Manly, and Scott—Scott serving as chairman (FNSP).

The Anglo-American Conference of Professors of English, held at Columbia University in June 1923, was composed of delegates from Oxford, Cambridge, and other British universities, and of representatives of the leading universities of the United States. Scott, who was invited to deliver the opening address and to preside over the first session, spoke on "Improving the English of America—Some Obstacles."

That Scott had now directed his energies wholeheartedly to this new movement is clear. Having involved himself in the British philological movement, it is natural that in his year of leave in 1923–1924, he would appear before one of the British groups. At a meeting of the Philological Society of the British Academy for the Advancement of Science on November 2, 1923, he delivered his speech on "American Idiom." On that same trip, he read his paper on the "The Colloquial Nasals for *Yes* and *No*" before the British Association for the Advancement of Science. His immersion in linguistic matters during this period is so intense that he himself in a letter to John o'London's *Weekly,* January 15, 1924, referred to "English usage" as his specialty. (One must remember his earlier preference in relation to Dayton C. Miller's article on the science of musical sounds; at the presentation in 1929 of the *Anniversary Papers,* Rankin defined Scott's realm as the rhythm of speech.)

Scott was determined to correct the impression H. L. Mencken had created that in America the Society for Pure English had been deterred from its noble objectives and had reduced the language to "Amerenglish." To quote Mencken: "Its [the NCTE's] whole campaign seems to be centered upon an effort to protect the grammar books against the living speech of the American people" (ix). His charges certainly could not have been upheld against Scott who had worked, along with Bridges, with sincere and earnest motives to eradicate the old air of superiority of British English and to base any assessment of the language of either nation on strictly linguistic grounds as stated in the aims of the SPE.

Scott, Bridges, and Henry Seidel Canby worked through the summer of 1924 to try to establish more firmly the logistics of the organization of the SPE. They sought the financial backing of Henry Ford, who promised assistance and then later reneged on his commitment. They also were trying to find a way to publish the findings of the SPE. Scott appealed to Canby to take on this task as part of *The Saturday Review of Literature,* which he edited, but Canby declined, suggesting instead a monthly journal—which would probably run on a deficit, at least for a while. Finally, in April 1925, Louise Pound of the University of Nebraska, described by Scott as "one of our foremost philologists," took full responsibility for the publication of a journal to be known as *American Speech,* designated the official organ of the SPE in America. For an unexplained reason, Bridges had withdrawn from the larger organization and intended issuing his tracts independently. His move left everything in a confused state. Yet Scott maintained his tie to Bridges, and in 1926, his "American Slang" was published as *Tract 24* by the SPE.

In a letter to Canby on May 11, 1925, Scott proposed the union of the English Association, the Modern Humanities Research Association, the SPE and the International Conference of Professors of English. He is concerned at the way the groups have fanned out into an amorphous mass with no particular sense of distinction in their missions. He writes: "Properly either there should be some publication in this country subordinate to the American Branch of the International English Council and a similar organ in England subsidiary to the British Branch, or else the S.P.E. should disappear on both sides of the water and the International English Council should take the place of both." He adds: "I must confess that at times the affair seems too complicated for my ingenuity" (FNSP).

During 1925, Scott's role in the movement to unite English and American scholars became intense. On January 2, 1925, he was in Washington, D.C., attending the conference of the American Association for the Advancement of Science, where he gave a speech titled, "English as Spoken in Britain and the United States." He also was active in another of the British-American organizations, the Modern Humanities Research Association, whose official organ was *Modern Language Review*.[4] In 1927, another publication emerged from this organization. Titled *Bulletin of the Modern Humanities Research Association,* it "has suddenly blossomed out into a full-blown journal, to be issued thrice yearly. . . . The journal may well become an important factor in the publishing of philological studies" ("Bibliographical Department" 79).

That both the British connection and the philological studies were central in Scott's professional life in the years between 1920 and 1925 is evidenced not only in his work and affiliations, but also in the recognition he was accorded. On May 11, 1925, he was elected a member of the British Institute of Philosophical Studies.

❖

Scott's publications continued, although they were few in number. In "Poetry in a Commercial Age," published in the *English Journal* in 1921, he endeavors to demonstrate how essential poetry is to the everyday existence of men, even those who would believe that it has no place in the world of commerce. With the overemphasis on vocational study among the rising numbers of high school graduates, who sought to bypass a college education in order to make their fortunes more quickly, there emerged an antagonistic attitude toward the arts. But Scott insists that "an industrial activity which is not the outgrowth of a sensitive intelligence, which lacks imaginative insight, which is not stimulated and sustained by right feeling, which is not guided by an intimate knowledge of human nature and by a broad sympathy with mankind is a dismal failure, no matter how many million tons of steel or gallons of oil it may turn out in the course of a year" (103; all page references are to *The Standard of American Speech*). Consequently, the exposure to poetic insights can increase the productivity of a man in business.

What then are the spiritual needs that poetry can provide? Regulated emotion, says Scott. For example, when a person is out of work, his emotions "run wild" or are channeled for him by designing men. Poetry provides a true representation of the world in which we live, which is especially important in a commercial age because, in the hurly-burly of the work world, one's perspectives become skewed. Poetry also brings us a sense of unity with those who have gone before us, of the universality of all human experience. As in "A Substitute for the Classics," Scott shows a liberalism toward change; in both, he defends the humanizing influence of art and literature in the educational forum.

"English and American Vernacular" was published in May 1925. Previously titled "American Idiom," it had been given as a speech before the British Philological Society in 1923. In this work, Scott hypothesizes about the degree of difference between English and American vernacular, discovering it to be directly proportional to the type of subject matter addressed. When dealing with trivial ideas the languages are very far apart; with practical subject matter there is very little difference between the two; and with philosophical concepts, there is virtually no distinction.

He cites sample words from American and British slang. "I skun up the stairs," "kid those roughnecks along," "attaboy," "it's time to hit the hay," and others are in no way understandable to an Englishman, who at no level of his language can find a counterpart. These expressions, he says, spring up spontaneously from strictly American experiences. In the same way, the British expressions "ripping," "top hole," "not arf" and "bloody" mean nothing to an American.

In the second grouping, Scott finds that "a spade is a spade in both countries." Only in a few ways are there differences. Because of these few words, however, there is an impression prevalent in language users in both countries that the speech is largely different. Unlike others, Scott turns to statistical data drawn from empirical study. He finds that of at least two hundred thousand words in current use in England, only 1.4 to 1.95 percent, or about four hundred words, would be unfamiliar in the United States. The number of English words unfamiliar to Americans would be about the same. Thus, either an American or Englishman, having committed some four hundred to six hundred words to memory before making a trip to the nonnative country, would encounter no impediments in his business or social life.

In the third area, however, that of concepts, even less divergence is observable. Scott says: "In all the forms that must be employed in debating the crucial questions of life, thought, and conduct, the two languages differ slightly, if at all" (145). Consequently, in his judgment, the only cause for concern is that as time passes and the two users of the English language grow apart in habits, there may ultimately be differences in meaning in words that apply to "temper, ideals, and national aspirations." Such a likelihood is remote, but we should remain alert, for such diversification could render international speech unintelligible and "set back the timepiece of civilization a century and a half" (145).[5]

In these years, Scott produced one other work with significant ramifications for the study of speech origins, "The Colloquial Nasals."[6] He wanted to tie the group of nasal vocal expressions to some basic origin, for he had observed that they appeared in numerous cultures. For that reason, he began to suspect that they were somehow part of the semiarticulate sounds of beginning language. Basically, he was interested in only the nasals for yes and no. He sought by his study to do two things: (1) identify their component elements and (2) account for their origin.

The first part of this endeavor consists of describing inhalation and exhalation of breath, combined with the formation of a nasal voiced continuant (m) and a soft-palate nasal (ng). The two responses, yes and no, are somewhat the same except that the utterance for no is the reverse of that for yes. The sounds would be familiarly recognized as "uh-huh" or "nh-nh." In accounting for their origin, Scott refers to his own earlier work, "The Genesis of Speech," of which this study was, in actuality, a continuation. His theory was that "the vocal utterances which we call speech are modifications of ordinary breathing." Through observation, he concludes that the forms under consideration are both connected with suckling, one when food is accepted, the other when it is rejected. He writes: "Thus the nasal form for *yes* is a remnant or reminiscence of the

innervation of the infant's vocal passages involved in the processes of taking food into the mouth, swallowing, and releasing the breath" (276; all
page references are to *The Standard of American Speech*).

After offering a similar explanation for the other nasal, no, Scott indicates how the interpretation of meaning became attached to both.
When the baby is sounding the yes, his head nods up and down, that
being the result of first leaning forward to take the food and then moving backward to swallow. On the other hand, with no, the baby throws
its head from side to side to avoid taking the food. Thus the sounds for
both nasals, yes and no, "are in their origin almost purely physiological,
both arising from instinctive and habitual innervations of the vocal region" (277). He cites four authorities: Darwin, who has noticed his own
children behaving in this manner, and Truman Michelson, John R.
Swanton, and Edward Sapir, all of whom attest to the presence of these
nasals in American-Indian languages.

Scott observes wryly that it is harder to secure data from civilized
people than from the uncivilized because the former are unaware of their
use of these words. Upon asking a friend whether he thought Scott's theory was sound, the friend replied, "'Uh-huh, but I never use those forms
myself'" (278). He notes that we also do not find them often in writing,
probably because writers do not know how to represent them in written
symbols. As in "The Genesis of Speech," Scott utilizes interdisciplinary
research, drawing from biology, anthropology, and physiology.

From the small group of writings within the years 1920 to 1925,
three of the publications—"Poetry in a Commercial Age," "English Composition as a Mode of Behavior," and "The Colloquial Nasals"—were
granted high praise by his contemporaries. They constitute consequential interdisciplinary scholarship when placed in the historic context of
linguistic studies of that time, which concentrated more on the historical origins and descriptive patterns of language.

14

Retirement

URING SCOTT'S period of leave in 1923–1924, many changes occurred in the Department of English and the Department of Rhetoric and Journalism that were to rock Scott's comfortable empire. Foreshadowing events that brought about the eventual amalgamation of the English and Rhetoric Departments, Harold Scott wrote in March 1924 of some problems: "The department of English literature is trying, I believe, to get required courses, and at the same time plotting against us. As I figure it out, the new blood in that department, all outsiders, have really got the whip hand there. They believe that rhetoric and literature should be taught together, because they were taught together in the schools from which they came. They believe further that, because they have always put rhetoric in second place, it rightfully belongs in second place. To me it is laughable that although they can see the practical value of literature, they cannot see the practical value of rhetoric" (FNSP). He was referring to James Holly Hanford and Oscar James Campbell, Ph.D.s from Harvard who had been hired by the English Department in 1921. Along with Louis Strauss, this triumvirate agitated to absorb Scott's department.

In April 1925, T. E. Rankin wrote to Scott, who had fled to Florida because of failing health, referring to "the silly letter [Dean] Effinger wrote you under date of the 14th., a copy of which he sent to me (for my disciplining, I suppose)." But, more important, he pleads for Scott to return for the following school year: "Please come back for next year's work. I wish you would, and the whole Rhetoric group and hosts of other people would be glad, indeed." He sees Effinger's letter as an attempt to pressure Scott into retiring. He adds that Campbell's proposal to the administration recommended "that all of the rhetoric teaching be thrown out." Before ending his letter, he renews his plea: "I'm sure that now the situation has so developed, due to standing pat, that you would not be hounded to death by the ill-mannered politicians in this building" (FNSP).

Scott was now sixty-five years old. It was clear that he was being badgered by those in power within the English Department who were supported by the shortsighted views of a new president, C. C. Little, called in upon the sudden death of President Burton in the spring of 1925, a death Scott called "an appalling loss" (FNSP).

At the beginning of 1926, Scott was encountering the factors which within the next two years would lead to his exit from the academic arena. Besides the attack on the Rhetoric Department, which had been his alone for so many years and which he had molded to suit his philosophical notions, other changes that affected him nearly as severely were the loss of longtime friends and colleagues, and the shift from the cozy atmosphere of a relatively small college to a campus crowded with hordes of students. Forever at an end was the camaraderie of earlier times. Scott's age brought with it difficulties as well, for he suffered from a variety of chronic physical ailments. There are, then, increasingly over this two-year period, a decline in his publications and in his participation in academic and professional life.

In examining the record of meetings from 1926 on, the atypical absence of Scott from all the professional organizations is evident. In November 1926, he was scheduled to serve as toastmaster at what was to be an eventful gathering of NCTE because it had joined with the sesquicentennial celebration of the English Language Congress. But his place was taken by Orton Lowe. He also did not attend the December meetings of MLA, nor those of AATJ. By 1927, he had virtually dropped out of sight except for his attendance at the 1927 meetings of the International Council for English held in London.

Similarly, Scott's publication days were essentially over. In 1926, *The Standard of American Speech,* a collection of his most distinguished and substantial writings, was published. The book included his presidential addresses and the major speeches delivered at NCTE, and MLA, as well as articles published in the influential journals over the span of his career. A publicity notice provided by the *Montreal Journal of Commerce* announced that it was "a superb and scholarly collection of brilliant essays and reprints of addresses" (FNSP). John Clapp summed up perhaps more succinctly than any other what the small volume represented.

He wrote to Scott: "You have gone ahead of us on many roads, and cap-
tured and pinned down on the page the ideas which most of us have just
caught sight of now and then in the distance" (FNSP). The book was cor-
dially received and highly lauded, but it represented Scott's past.

Other than the book, there was but one new piece, "American
Slang" (a mere listing of slang expressions), which appeared in the *Soci-
ety for Pure English Tracts,* and a brief review of Will Durant's *The Story of
Philosophy* in the *Michigan Alumnus.*

The moves taken against Scott's program by O. J. Campbell and
others to achieve the amalgamation of the English and Rhetoric Departments are important to explain the changes in Scott's routine. From early
in 1926, evidence in letters reveals the intensity of this battle. In February, Oakley Johnson wrote that he has learned that Scott, who was again
in Florida, was considering retirement. Like Rankin, Johnson pleads
with him to reconsider. "I think that amalgamation with the Department of English need not be the inevitable result of your resignation,
and your presence next year will help the staff to demonstrate that"
(FNSP). Johnson foresaw that once Scott was gone, the department
would be absorbed; the alternative, to replace Scott and retain the department, was apparently not under consideration. The seriousness of
Scott's loss to the others within the Rhetoric Department had occasioned
the drafting of a letter in February 1926, signed by most of his colleagues, urging against Scott's early retirement (FNSP).

In a letter to the president and board of regents written on May 26,
1926, by Effinger, some sense of the pressure exerted by O. J. Campbell
is made clear. Campbell had been offered $9,000 to chair the English
Department at the University of Wisconsin. To counter that offer, Effinger proposed that Campbell be awarded a salary of $7,500 and, more im-
portantly, that "the Departments of English and Rhetoric be combined,
the combined departments to be known as the Department of English,
this action to be effective July 1, 1927" (CLSA). That date is significant
because it became the actual date on which Scott activated his retirement. Further proposed was a committee to work out the details of the
amalgamation: two professors from the Rhetoric Department and two
from the English Department with a time frame of July 1, 1926, only a
little more than a month away. Scott and Rankin from Rhetoric and
Strauss and Campbell from English were designated to serve on this
committee.

There was evidence that something underhanded might be occurring. Effinger proposed to President Little: "Would it not be advisable

that the Department of Rhetoric be so informed? Professor Campbell and I have talked over the situation and are inclined to think that there should be a perfect understanding of the whole situation on the part of all concerned" (CLSA). The question of who knew what and when they knew it is important to consider. In response to Effinger's charge, Little wrote on June 10 that he agreed that the Rhetoric Department should know that the amalgamation is "in process." But he suggests that "it would be better to do this informally than to have any action taken by the Board of Regents, since it may be that the combination which you finally decide upon as advisable, will need some method of treatment and description which we can not foresee at the present time" (CLSA). Time was passing, and the Department of Rhetoric's only knowledge about this "process" was hearsay.

On June 18, President Little finally wrote to Scott as chairman of the Department of Rhetoric and Journalism: "I want to tell you officially what I believe you already understand, that negotiations looking toward an amalgamation of the present Departments of English and Rhetoric have been authorized by action of the Regents. The understanding is that during the year 1926–1927 there shall be a joint committee on English, with a fair and equitable representation from those departments, and that *Professor O. J. Campbell will serve as executive secretary*" (italics mine) (FNSP). Little's letter is carefully written. His final sentence contains words that later would occupy much of the committee's time, for his statement of the purpose of the merger was vague and nonspecific: "The committee is authorized to consider the policies and problems of the two departments, *with a view to increasing the efficiency of both and effecting their closer association*" (FNSP; italics mine).

T. E. Rankin wrote Scott on June 22, 1926, that when he sent Harris Fletcher to Dean Effinger on another matter, Effinger confided that he "had a statement in writing from the President saying that amalgamation of the two departments would be accomplished before the end of the coming year." Rankin's apprehension for the future shows the extent to which his opposition and his rancor have risen. "I could not teach well next fall if I were to lend myself to helping to administer this great department into the inferiority which is sure to follow operation of such plans as Mr. Campbell, Mr. Strauss, and Mr. Effinger have proposed in recent months" (FNSP).

Scott's response to President Little is puzzling in its restraint. He said he favored any change that would "improve the teaching of English in the University." Yet, later, he defended his department and fought against the change. He adds polite remarks that would, rhetorically, carry some argumentative edge: "I am greatly comforted by your assurance that nothing will be done to weaken the Rhetoric staff. They are a splendid body of teachers, loyal to the core, and full of a fine enthusiasm for a kind of work that is commonly regarded as drudgery or worse. It would be a great economic loss to the University if anything were done to dishearten or humiliate them" (FNSP).

These words about the economic loss to the University would serve as his primary defense when Scott got into the fray. His reference to "drudgery or worse" was intentional. Now that the teaching of literature—not just at Michigan, but at all major universities and colleges—had insinuated itself in the curriculum, it was clearer each day that those who taught rhetoric or composition were subject to growing disdain. On July 19, C. D. Thorpe wrote Scott: "Campbell assured me that there would be no curtailment of our work, that no one of our staff who was 'any good' need fear anything." But even Thorpe, distant as he seems to have been from the action, senses something amiss. "Just how liberal the interpretation of that phrase [any good] will be remains to be seen" (FNSP).

In a July 28 letter, Rankin writes that he has firsthand evidence that two of the regents "most familiar with the details of the University are opposed to the plan" (FNSP). Why had Little earlier written that the board of regents had authorized the change? Rankin predicts that the president is in for trouble in the upcoming year because of conflicts with both the regents and the state. He himself sees Little as "a charming man, of considerable ability," but notes that, increasingly, Little is charged with incompetence because he does not "know the University." In August, Rankin explains why the situation so profoundly torments him. "I fear the whole affair over amalgamation is University politics and not University business" (FNSP).

On October 2, 1926, the members of the committee—Scott, Rankin, Strauss, and Campbell—received formal notification from Dean Effinger of the action that had been taken over the summer. In his letter, Effinger repeats Little's words, which became the watchwords of the administration's efforts: "the consideration of policies and problems of the two departments with a view to increasing the efficiency of both and effecting a closer association between them" (FNSP). Penned on the bottom of this letter is a note by Scott which made its way to Effinger. "The present policy, which is the result of 25 years of trial and error, if not the best possible is at any rate as good as that of an[y] other institution &

should not be cast aside without better reasons than have been brought forward thus far." These words would appear again as Scott defended his department; his opinion on the subject was quite fixed (FNSP).

In referring to the phrase "effecting a closer association between the two departments," Little suggested that the committee should consider the question of amalgamation of "all the agencies" concerned in the teaching of English in the University, including the Department of Public Speaking as well as English in the Engineering and Architecture Colleges. Little mentions additionally a suggestion that Campbell later, as chairman of the College Section, considered at the 1931 meeting of NCTE—that "formal classroom work in English in the freshman year be wholly abandoned and the instruction given . . . in connection with the written work of all the subjects of a student's study" (CLSA). (This was not the only time Campbell attacked the existence of writing programs. In 1939 he published in the *English Journal* an article titled "The Failure of Freshman English.") These expressed attitudes raise some question about the agent behind the move for amalgamation—Little, Campbell, the regents?

On November 26, 1926, J. M. Thomas responded to a letter from Scott in which Scott had apparently asked Thomas to succeed him upon his retirement. He cannot understand why Scott had not assumed the chair of both English and Rhetoric upon Demmon's retirement. "If you were unwilling at that time to see the department of Rhetoric lose its separate entity, I can well understand how keenly you resent such a proposal now" (FNSP). But the whole matter was parochial. Thomas affirmed that at the University of Minnesota, the Departments of English, Public Speaking, and Rhetoric were one. The same was true at the University of Illinois. And over the summer, 1927, while Campbell was at the University of Oregon, he wrote to Strauss: "Everyone here is superciliously amused at the folly of the divided and separate departments" (DEP). From all available evidence, Scott's scheme was strictly self-preservation; in his recalcitrance, he was marching to the beat of an obsolete drummer.

The slow shift of interest from the teaching of composition to the teaching of literature had begun, with a corresponding heightening of status for those teaching literature. The professional journals of the time reveal this trend—even if one examines them only cursorily—with articles devoted to literature and literary pedagogy far exceeding in numbers—and excitement—similar articles on composition.

In 1927, health problems forced Scott to leave the University of Michigan for the third spring in a row. In January, from the comfort of sunny Florida, he confided to his loyal friend, Shirley Smith, that he had no plans to return to Michigan, for he could not tolerate another winter. "It would have been a hard struggle and would have left me open to the attack of any wandering germ that was looking for what the bacteriologists call a host" (SSP). By now, Scott had decided on retirement and had resigned himself to the merger. It no longer mattered what course the university took.

In April, Effinger wrote Scott seeking some definitive indication as to whether he would or would not return to Michigan in the fall. Scott responded that he would be sailing for New York on April 25 and expected to be in Ann Arbor the first week in May. This letter, additionally, served as his notification to Effinger of his plan to retire on July 1 (CLSA). The official letter to President Little was written on May 4 from New York City. When Scott resigned, he referred to himself as head of the Department of Rhetoric and Journalism, but when asked to designate a choice of title, he selected Professor Emeritus of Rhetoric. The inconsistency suggests two things: first, that he recognized that he really had no claim to the journalism title, not having actively participated in either the teaching of journalism or in the activities of the AATJ for a number of years; second, that he considered his work in rhetoric to have been paramount in his academic life.

Upon his retirement, the search for a successor began. Denney wrote Scott: "Sir there is *no* fitting successor to yourself. You will leave a great void behind you, in which smaller men will lose themselves" (FNSP). In mid-August 1927, a candidate surfaced who would prove to be acceptable to the decision makers. President Little had gone to Aberdeen, Scotland, where he met Peter Monro Jack.[1] Jack was young, was about to receive his Ph.D. from Cambridge, and had experience in rhetoric from his work at Aberdeen. Little offered him the job for three years, specifying that at the end of that time, he would be evaluated by the staff and the decision as to whether he would be retained would be made. Clinching the appointment was a recommendation given by T. S. Eliot.

But retirement did not mean life was over. It was with great jubilation that Scott wrote, on May 4, to Dean Effinger that he had been named a delegate to the International Conference for English to be held in London in June 1927 (CLSA). Initially, when he had been asked by G. C. Hoag, who had originated the International English Council in 1920, he had urged that Louise Pound of Nebraska or Kemp Malone replace him. The situation had changed, however, and now Scott was eager to participate.

A report in *American Speech,* taken from the *Worchester Guardian Weekly* of June 24, characterized the meeting as concerning itself with the question of how to speak and write English, the delegates consisting of American and British poets, writers, and scholars. The aim of the group is to serve as an "investigating body which will determine the facts as to disputed usages and give the results of its investigations the widest publicity" ("Notes and Quotes" 157). Representatives from the Royal Society of Literature, the British Academy, the English Association, the BBC Committee, and the Society for Pure English attended the meeting.[2]

Scott stayed in Europe over the summer of 1927. On July 5, while still in London, he gave a speech, which was well received, at the Lyceum Club. From Dinan, France, on July 25, he wrote to Shirley Smith, who had expressed surprise at Scott's early retirement: "It is only fair that I should tell you my chief reason for giving up my work so abruptly and, as it seemed, so early in my career. It is that I have been for some time subject to a growing deafness, which toward the middle of the year made it difficult for me to keep up in the classroom the rapid and incessant interchange of ideas which was about the only asset that I could boast as a teacher" (SSP). There is good reason to question why this particular disability had not been mentioned in any other communiques, and why it was so late in being relayed to Shirley Smith, one of Scott's oldest and closest friends.

Not much was made of his retirement at the time primarily because Scott was not around. But Charles Mills Gayley did write to Rankin a tribute that he instructed Rankin to file away for use on the occasion of Scott's retirement. Gayley had been ill since 1924 and knew it was unlikely he could return to Michigan. In his letter, he provides this impression of Scott: "As a teacher—lucid, effective, and inspirational, as scholar and author, as begetter of ideas and deviser of scientific methods for testing their vitality and ensuring their adoption as currency of research—especially in the field of aesthetics, poetics, and rhetorical studies, there is, in my opinion, none now living more eminent than Fred Newton Scott. Such is the recognition accorded him by his colleagues, not only in America but in Europe" (FNSP).

When he returned to Ann Arbor in November, Scott sorted out for donation to the university library his collection of books on rhetoric and literary criticism, some 761 bound volumes plus a group of pamphlets—a very generous gift. By the end of 1927, the Scotts had completed their move to Tucson, Arizona. In March 1928, Scott wrote to Harold P. Scott of his routine. Jokingly, he says it is like that of the small boy who recorded in his diary: "Got up, washed, went to bed" (FNSP). Mostly, he says, he and Mrs. Scott lie in the sun "as long as we can stand it, and then come in for tea." Scott had met the University of Arizona librarian who offered him the freedom of the library, and, though never on the faculty of the university, he had been provided a desk in the English Department. At the invitation of other professors, he lectured to classes.

In 1928, friends of Scott's organized to produce *The Fred Newton Scott Anniversary Papers*. The book, published in July 1929, contains essays by Scott's former students and colleagues: Ernest Sutherland Bates, Lawrence Conrad, George Denton, Edward Everett, Harris Fletcher, Charles C. Fries, Oakley Johnson, Helen Mahin, Herbert Mallory, Thomas Rankin, Harold Scott, Ada Snell, and Melvin Solve, as well as by the editors, Clarence D. Thorpe and Charles Whitmore.

Gayley, whose health was now seriously impaired, composed a letter to Scott in lieu of an essay. "You need no monument other than your life—your works, your pupils and your friends. Your "Anniversary Papers" will, however, be a testimony while you still live—a testimony bringing in congratulations from scholars all over the world, but also a Monument existing so long as there are Libraries and scholars in the world" (FNSP).

In the preface to the book, T. E. Rankin pays homage to the enormous gift Scott gave to each of his students. Ray Stannard Baker wrote to Thorpe that Scott probably doesn't know it, but he gave him more than any other teacher. "I took his courses at a time when I was confused in my own mind as to my own capacities, as to what I could best devote myself to. I found in the two courses with Professor Scott, which I deserted the Law School to take, the liberation which I was seeking. He seemed to have an extraordinary gift of setting men to thinking and then, by deft touches of advice, not too much of it, indicating the reading which would best enlarge the vista" (FNSP).[3]

In 1929 Scott returned to Ann Arbor to a celebration where his former students and colleagues presented the book to him. He spent "the summer," staying at the home of Albert Lockwood. According to Carlton Wells, about a dozen people gathered for a banquet in Scott's honor at the Barton Hills Country Club; Shirley Smith served as toastmaster, and the main speaker was the ex-regent and former Michigan governor, Chase S. Osborn. T. E. Rankin made the presentation.

When Scott accepted the book, he gave what would be the last speech of his life. "I wish I could feel sure that the honor is deserved. It seems too good to be true. It used to be said of Lord Haldane that no living person could possibly be so wise as Lord Haldane looked. For my part, I know that I shall never be so wise nor so scholarly nor yet so intellectual as this volume would make out. But then, fortunately, I do not have to be. I am long past the years when it is necessary to make pretense about anything. . . . In the words of Charles Lamb, "I have done all that I came into this world to do. I have worked taskwork, and have the rest of the day to myself" (FNSP).

From Ann Arbor, where he was attending to business affairs, Scott wrote in September 1929 to the bursar of the University of Arizona about arranging funds for a prize in the Fred Newton Scott Prose Competition to be given annually to students at the University of Arizona.[4] The original fund consisted of two $1,000 building bonds which were not convertible to cash at the time. By 1932, the bonds went into default, and a mere $420 was available in 1937. By 1961, there was a balance of only $578. As a consequence, the award lay dormant for many years. A number of colleagues, former students, and friends, among them Judge Richard H. Chambers, circuit judge of the U.S. Court of Appeals, added to the original bequest. Awards were reinstated in 1980–1981 and have been granted in amounts varying from $100 to $650. In 1991, Judge Chambers petitioned the University of Arizona on behalf of the awards, now memorializing Professor Scott and Howard O. Welty, the first recipient. The fund now grants one $400 award per year; it is designated for an outstanding composition by a member of each year's sophomore class as determined by the faculty of the Department of English, subject to approval by the dean of the Faculty of Humanities and the Office of Student Financial Aid.

Scott indicated that he would be leaving Ann Arbor on September 20 and provided Battle Creek Sanitarium as his forwarding address. After September 27, he intended to travel until his return to Tucson in early October. However, a letter written by John Harvey Kellogg from Battle Creek to Mrs. Scott at St. Joseph's Hospital in Joliet, Illinois, on October 2 suggests that those plans did not work out. In it, Kellogg says: "I am delighted to know that Dr. Scott is improving so rapidly. I

hope he will soon be on his feet again so that you can get to your pleasant winter home. Plenty of outdoor life and a careful diet I trust will
soon restore him" (FNSP). It is anybody's guess as to what ailment struck
him or what occurred between September 20 and October 2, 1929.

In 1928, Rankin departed Michigan, going to Carleton College
where he was asked to head the department for 1929–1930. Others who
left were William O. Raymond, Lawrence Conrad, and H. P. Scott, the
latter being replaced by Norman E. Nelson, another Harvard Ph.D.
More and more, it was obvious that, as Rankin had predicted, the University of Michigan's Department of English was being Harvardized.
The prophetic apprehensions had been fulfilled: the rhetoric faculty were
put in a less prestigious position than those in literature.

On April 11, 1928, Peter Jack, who had not been privileged to meet
Scott, wrote to him in his retirement. He says that Scott's shoes are very
hard to fill, mentioning specifically Scott's efficiency and tact. Curiously,
the seminary class which Scott taught so masterfully because of his interchange with the students and which he felt he could no longer treat
meaningfully because of his loss of hearing, was a problem for Jack, who
admits that the inclusion of literature, criticism, philosophy, psychology,
and linguistics forces him to teach by lecture. Jack is very open with
Scott, writing to him that he is aware that his own position is "not very
strong." "I do not think the department is functioning very happily as a
unit. . . . There is still a feeling of strain" (FNSP). In May 1928, Campbell wrote to Strauss from Florence: "Please get Jack fired; make the
union of the two departments one in fact" (DEP). Jack left the Department at the end of his three years.

In January 1930, Effinger signed the petition requesting that the
Department of Rhetoric "be merged into a single department to be
known as English Language and Literature." As to the Department of
Rhetoric, Scott had been the "personal inspiration [which] was responsible for its peculiar success," and with his retirement, there was no longer
any need for the separate entity (UMBR).

In the *Michigan Alumnus*, Strauss wrote an account of the merger. He
credits Scott with having created a respected department that attracted
students from all over the country and proclaims him "the ideal teacher
of the science and art of literary expression." "His seminary in the History of Rhetoric was as fundamental and vital in the equipment of a
teacher of English as any graduate course I have ever known. His course
in Interpretations of Literature and Art constituted the greatest intellec-

tual experience of many generations of students" (332). Overall, Strauss writes, "Dr. Scott's conception of rhetoric was catholic in the extreme; it was limited only by the range of his own personal interests, which really means that it was not limited at all. Under the spell of his magnetic and stimulating personality his students developed to their utmost capacity" (332).

But Strauss's view of the merger is that it was the inevitable consequence of Scott's success, for when a department is too successful, it tends to grow to "academic elephantiasis." Administrators then tire of their responsibilities: "Professor Scott was not a born executive. . . . As the department grew, he naturally fell into a *laissez aller* attitude and became ever more engrossed in the more alluring tasks of his teaching and research" (332).

For Strauss, composition has "no content of its own." "It is true that a few members of any English staff prefer and love to teach composition because of the intimate knowledge it brings to them of the student's inner life and the opportunity it affords them to influence his growth of mind, taste, and character" (332). It is amazing that Strauss could not see *why* Scott had been so lauded by his colleagues and won such a remarkable reputation. It is as if Scott were an anomaly. This article reflects accurately the attitudes that have been part and parcel of rhetoric/composition from the very beginning. The field has never been able to shake them, despite the invaluable contributions of numerous men and women equally as talented and notable as Scott.

In examining the departmental merger, it is essential to consider the prizes donated to the Rhetoric Department through the beneficence of Avery Hopwood. Hopwood had died on July 1, 1928, with his mother's death a few months later. His will, written on December 30, 1921, directed that six-thirtieths of the estate go to the regents of the University of Michigan, the accrued interest to be used "in perpetuity, as prizes to be known as 'The Avery Hopwood and Jule Hopwood Prizes.'" The awards were to be distributed annually "to students in the Department of Rhetoric of the University of Michigan, who perform the best creative work in the fields of dramatic writing, fiction, poetry and the essay. . . . In this connection, it is especially desired that the students competing for the prizes shall not be confined to academic subjects, but shall be allowed the widest possible latitude, and that the new, the unusual and the radical shall be especially encouraged" (UMBR).

The amount of the bequest is not clear, the figures differing in the various reports. In the section on bequests in *The University of Michigan*

Encyclopedia, it was $321,762.29 (Shaw, *Survey* 1:191); in the section on the prizes, the number is $351,069.78 (Shaw, *Survey* 2:563); and in a brochure prepared for the fiftieth anniversary of the prizes, it is given as $313,836.10 ("Avery Hopwood and the Hopwood Awards"), the same number given in Roy Cowden's article, "Creative Writing and the Hopwood Awards." At any rate, it was a sizeable amount (comparable to about $1.5 million today).

According to the brochure, "In the fall of 1930, a reorganization of the writing program ended the old Department of Rhetoric named in the will and brought into being a new Department of English Language and Literature and a new Department of Journalism. It was these *new* departments which were to share in the handsome bequest" ("Avery Hopwood and the Hopwood Awards" n.p.; italics mine).

At the February 7, 1930, meeting of the regents (one month after the merger) Shirley Smith wrote: "The executor of the estate of the late Avery Hopwood desires the passage of a formal resolution of acceptance of the bequest under Mr. Hopwood's will. *This acceptance has already taken place, meeting of September 1928,* page 689, but it is desired to have the acceptance embodied in a formal resolution" (UMBR; italics mine).

Roy Cowden wrote in the *Michigan Alumnus Quarterly Review* in 1942: "In the spring of 1930 at a meeting of all the members of the Department of English, Professor O. J. Campbell announced the bequest. He introduced his remarks by saying that in joining forces with the Rhetoric Department in the preceding January, the English Department had evidently married an heiress" (245). That the Hopwood prizes were first officially activated by the university only one month after the amalgamation of the Departments of English and Rhetoric raises the question of whether that large gift, originally bequeathed to the Department of Rhetoric, in any way figured in the consummation of that union.

What had originally prompted Hopwood to arrange this bequest? When Hopwood had entered the University of Michigan in 1901, he had joined the Quadrangle Club. He also worked on the *Inlander,* the student literary magazine, serving as its editor in his senior year. According to the brochure: "Of particular value were his composition and rhetoric courses under Professor F. N. Scott, who remained a link with the University in later years. . . . It is thought that the memory of his work with Professor Fred N. Scott, from whom he had taken five writing courses, influenced him in framing the terms of his will and naming the *Department of Rhetoric* to carry out his intent" ("Avery Hopwood and the Hopwood Awards"; italics mine). What occurred in the gap between

Hopwood's death in 1928, the acceptance by the University of Michigan of the bequest in September 1928 and the first of the contests held two years later, in 1930–1931? It is a question that can only be raised, not answered, for even among those whose memories might still be activated, the response would be hearsay more than fact.

Creative writing attained its exalted position at the University of Michigan only after the 1930 bequest of the Hopwood prizes, for under its stimulus young writers were attracted to the department. In the ten years prior to 1940, over $90,000 was awarded from the Hopwood fund. By 1950, the prizes represented the largest prizes in writing offered by any university in the world. As of 1948, the annual prize money averaged $8,000, and by 1979–1980 amounted to $32,425. In 1934, when Roy Cowden became director of the Hopwood Award Program, he created the Hopwood Room in Room 3227 of Angell Hall and brought in Scott's large round table, around which had clustered so many of Scott's students over the years. Among the winners of the award were such writers as Betty Smith, Arthur Miller, John Ciardi, Mildred Walker, and Max Apple. If, indeed, this legacy is traceable to Scott's friendship and encouragement of Hopwood, it is without question Scott's greatest contribution to the University of Michigan, and the lack of acknowledgment, the greatest injustice to Scott.

Early in 1930, Georgia Scott wrote to Shirley Smith from their home in Arizona: "Fred is doing pretty well, and as the spring is coming on, I have great hopes for him" (SSP). But Georgia's optimism was misplaced. Later that year, in a November letter to Shirley Smith, she writes most poignantly of Scott, whose true state of health has now rendered him a pathetic figure: "Fred was very much pleased to hear from you. Your letter came one morning when we were sitting on the porch. I read it to him, and he seemed to understand it all. 'A very nice letter,' he said. He took it and read it to himself and kept it on his lap until lunch time" (SSP).

She tells of medical treatment that had taken them to California for the summer. "You have perhaps heard that the trouble is arteriosclerosis beginning in the arteries of the brain. He looks very nice, and has no pain. He goes for a ride almost every day, but cannot walk much. He is as gentle and kindly as ever. He cannot read any more, really to understand." Her last line is most heartrending, considering the picture of the formerly vital man: "I asked him what I should say to you, but he cannot form any message except that he sends you his affectionate regards" (SSP).

In March 1930, the North Central Association of Colleges and Secondary Schools had belatedly made Scott an honorary member "in recognition of invaluable service to the Cause of Education" (FNSP). In October 1930, President Alexander Ruthven proposed awarding Scott an honorary degree: "I have, personally, felt that the University did not do quite enough for Mr. Scott when he retired" (DEP). Unfortunately, by January 1931, when he wrote to Scott announcing his intentions and inviting Scott to attend, it fell to Georgia to respond. "It is with the keenest regret that I am obliged to tell you that Mr. Scott is unable to accept your invitation of January 26 to receive an honorary degree from the university. I doubt if he could take the long journey, and I also doubt if he would understand much of the honor done him" (FNSP). Even later, on April 29, 1931, one month before his death, the American Association of University Professors extended honorary membership "in recognition of distinguished achievements in teaching or research" (FNSP). But with the one final return to California, ending on May 29, 1931, Scott had completed his travels.

But Scott's legacy was firmly grounded. In 1932, when James F. Hosic wrote a brief historical account of the twenty years of NCTE, he noted: "When it is possible to do it, it will be interesting to compare the accomplishments of the Council with aims and purposes of the founders. . . . Much light will be thrown upon them when the life story of Fred Newton Scott is told—a liberal professor of English in the Middle West, leader in a regional society of English teachers, and active in national groups as well, whose loss we mourn" (Hosic, "National Council" 107). Hosic notes that the Council came into existence to meet the needs of the great majority of teachers in the public schools which had grown in size and number in the late nineteenth and early twentieth centuries.

The last known piece that Scott published appeared in the April–June 1930 issue of the *Sewanee Review*. Titled "Art and War," it is one of the finest pieces of intellectual argument on the value of aesthetics to be found among his works. Cast as a Platonic dialogue, it reveals an amazing acumen. A professor of prehistoric embryology at the University of Philistia, an obviously esoteric sort who makes his home in the ivory tower of intellectualism that Scott has scorned so frequently in his work, is set against a visitor from Utopia. This being 1929, with the uprisings in Europe beginning just as they had in 1914, Scott prophesies the ominous rumblings of World War II and uses that for his setting. Two clever fictional aspects are established early. One is that a Public Conservator has assumed control of mental activities, so that each day has been set aside for a particular abstention. On this, a Wednesday, they observe an artless day, with "aesthetic ratiocination from nine to eleven-thirty" (218). The second aspect is the skillful exchange of insights between the two characters.

In the discussion, most of the defenses manifest Scott's intellectual depth and his adroitness in probing the very essence of artistic necessity. Although he waits until the middle of the piece to define art, such definition being crucial to his "discussion," he challenges traditional ideas about what art is and what it can generate. The Visitor, who represents Scott's views, states that "for me art is as common as the air we breathe. . . . If you will permit me to be technical for a moment, I will say that art is for me the mode of distributing intelligence. It is the sum total of all the movements of the body, of all the sounds made by the vocal organs, of all the shaping of material substances, by which thought or feeling is conveyed from one man to other men" (229).

In the battles of the world, the important factor has been the dissemination of ideas. The Visitor traces the pattern: "Someone, let us say, conceives the thought that the people among whom he lives should be free,—spiritually or politically. The idea is somehow thrown out and somehow passed around. . . . Presently common feeling leads somehow to concerted action and the idea is embodied in militant form" (225–26). As to communication as an art, Scott depicts a lone courier, carrying the heartening news that the war is over while men are still killing each other. Ultimately, he exclaims, "How much more real and valuable were the few lines hastily scrawled on the paper in his pouch than the killing of these last few hundred or thousands?" (228).

Throughout, Scott proffers his views, not only of the necessity and importance of art (in the traditional sense) and its corollary, the art of communication, but of the futility of war. Examined closely, the essay reveals all the qualities for which Scott's students and colleagues praised him, particularly his ability to penetrate to the heart of a topic by casting it in a context that enhanced its message.

15

In Memoriam

I N T H E Y E A R S after Scott formally retired, the decline in his activity, both physical and professional, was rapid. Being such a vigorous man all his life, it shocked a number of his friends and colleagues that he had but a scant four years after his retirement to
relax and enjoy himself. Although his affliction was known to his
friends, his death came as a surprise and grievous blow nonetheless.
Edwin Miller wrote to Mrs. Scott that "in view of the disabilities of age
which had crept upon him, I believe that it is best that he should be at
rest" (PMFNS). And Albert Lockwood, whose mother had died of the
same disease wrote: "I knew that he was ill and from the name of the
trouble I knew that he could not recover, but I didnt [*sic*] realize that the
end wouod [*sic*] come so soon" (FNSP). Scott's last days were spent in the
hospital in San Diego where he was admitted on May 19; on June 2, his
body was cremated, and Georgia returned to Arizona with the ashes
until she would travel to Ann Arbor to bury them in the cemetery next
to Isadore.

At the time of his death, the University of Michigan flag was flown
at half-mast in his memory, and the regents at their May 29 meeting included a long tribute. They noted Scott's national and international reputation and his achievements in the fields of "literature, rhetoric, criticism, and the history of language." They also refer to his popularity
among the students and record that he was to have received an honorary
degree at the June commencement (PMFNS).

On June 6, 1931, Georgia wrote to Shirley Smith: "The one thing
that touched and pleased me most was to know about the flag." She re-

lates that at the funeral there were a number of his relatives, including his daughter, Marion Scott Goodrich, his grandson, Fred Newton Scott II (who stayed with her), and Isadore's sister, Mrs. Molendo. (Strangely, Georgia refers to Isadore as Mrs. Scott.) She writes that Mrs. Molendo "has always been a staunch friend to me" (SSP). By November, Georgia wrote to Shirley Smith that she had rented her house and was living in a cottage overlooking the desert to the mountains. She has arranged to ship Scott's books to Mr. Bishop, the University of Michigan librarian. The portrait of Scott painted by Orlando Rouland she considers too fragile to risk shipping and indicates she will bring it herself (SSP).[1]

A letter from Mrs. Bradley L. Thompson (Isadore was the aunt of Mrs. Thompson's husband) explains that her mother-in-law, Alice Beckwith Thompson, and Mrs. Thompson's sister, Elizabeth Beckwith, took care of the cemetery plot at Forest Hill in Ann Arbor. After her mother-in-law died in 1928 and Miss Beckwith in 1934, Mrs. Thompson took over the duties of caring for the plot, and to her surprise discovered that Mr. Scott was buried there, although no one had asked permission nor told them of his death (letters from Mrs. Bradley L. Thompson to Donald Stewart, January 12, 21, 1982). Scott's ashes had been buried on August 4, 1935.

At the November meeting of NCTE in 1931, a memorial was offered to Scott at the Saturday luncheon, and a brief acknowledgment of his death appeared in the *English Journal*.[2] The tribute was accurate and fair to Scott. "The older Council members will remember him as a quiet, kindly personality, full of sense and, on occasion, of spice. His presidential address, "The Undefended Gate," and his later paper on "Poetry in a Commercial Age" were high points in the early years of the *Journal*. His clear, sparkling presentation of ideas made him a welcome contributor to the general magazines of the highest class, and his thorough scholarship was respected by the most academic. His last book, *The Standard of American Speech,* was one of the early calls to the liberalism in usage which the National Council is now advocating so strongly. Many have pointed to him as an example of sane humanism" ("News and Notes" [1931] 684).

Less publicity was provided by the other organizations, but then Scott's participation was nonexistent after the mid-twenties. His death was reported to the MLA membership, but no notice was made by AATJ, the journalism organization, nor by *American Speech,* the organ of the Society for Pure English. *Language,* the journal of the Linguistic Society of America of which Scott was a foundation member, provided a minimal obituary ("Notes and Personalia" 222).

On June 27, John Brumm wrote "In Memoriam" for the *Michigan Alumnus,* a full account of Scott's personal and academic life. He accords Scott the distinction of having made the University of Michigan the "center of graduate study in the English language" when he was made head of the Rhetoric Department. He credits Scott with having a command of aesthetics, English literature, the sciences, and as being, "a distinguished linguist, an indefatigable bibliographer, a poet, and a lover of the fine arts." Brumm describes Scott personally as "modest and reticent in the extreme," and hints that he perhaps seemed formidable to students until they became acquainted with him because "he awaited the advances of others" in forming friendships. His friendships, however, were lasting and unreserved. Brumm comments also upon Scott's sense of humor, saying: "His mentality had its whimsical cast, a delight in playful wit and subtle humor." But he also describes Scott as "morose," a characteristic that Scott had himself identified in his diary entry upon the death of Isadore (655).

Most significantly, Brumm accurately characterizes the intellectual powers of Scott. "As a scholar it was his nature to check all literary extravagance by the authority of controlled judgment . . . to weigh and refine, to guard against betrayal by the tumult and freedom of creative misadventures. . . . As a scholar he was severe in his insistence upon intellectual integrity, counting it a moral fault to be merely credulous" (655).

Others of his friends and colleagues recalled characteristics fondly. Lawrence Conrad, who had contributed to *The Anniversary Papers* and who had served in the Rhetoric Department, wrote: "How much I, personally, owe to him I cannot even estimate. The fact of his greatness gave my whole life a stir. Through his kindness to me, I started a certain march which shall never end" (PMFNS). He dedicated his book, *Descriptive and Narrative Writing,* "To Fred Newton Scott, Dean of American Teachers of Rhetoric."

Edwin Miller, who had been Scott's classmate as an undergraduate at the University of Michigan, refers to Scott's talent in creative writing. "I believe that, if he had chosen to devote himself to what our scholastic friends call 'creative writing,' he would have stood high among the poets and essayists of our country." Miller, himself one of the original founders of NCTE, rates Scott high "as a leader of educational thought and as a scholar in the field of original research" (PMFNS). Albert Lockwood cited Scott's sense of humor and his congeniality: "I remember with so much pleasure crossing the Atlantic once when he was on the same steamer and I recall what he said when I got off at Gibraltar in order to go over to Tangiers—'Kill and eat a Tangerine for me please'—such a light and merry touch he always had" (FNSP).

In December 1932, Shirley Smith wrote to Georgia about his memorial piece, "Fred Newton Scott as a Teacher," which he had been circulating in manuscript form.[3] Reminiscences for it came from Richard R. Kirk of Tulane; Karl Young of Yale; Lyman Bryson of the California Association for Adult Education; S. Emory Thomason, publisher of the *Chicago Daily Times;* Lee White, *Detroit News;* and Arthur Pound, writer. Smith writes that Scott deeply touched the lives of the students in his classes, indicating that letters from them—business men, teachers and scholars—agree on the same sense "of something still vital and pulsing in their lives that goes back to Scott" (Smith, "Fred Newton Scott as a Teacher" n.p.).

Smith describes Scott's classroom manner as "effortless . . . (he did everything as he polished his eyeglasses, gently)" and conjectured that it "had been consciously cultivated to save nervous energy, to avoid the distraction of noise or motion." He characterized Scott's teaching method as Socratic and noted that he was a master of it. Looking back, his students had difficulty saying just what Scott was an authority on or what he had said to them specifically. He exerted tremendous energy—probing, cross-examining, and interrogating members of his classes, leading them to the critical insights he wished them to discover (Smith n.p.).

According to his students, Scott paid little attention to the technical side of writing. Words were tools; the product was what interested him. Smith writes: "It was astonishing until we got used to these discussions how heated even a football guard or a prospective chemist who had elected the course wrathfully, because it was required work, could get over such questions as whether an ice-coated branch glittered or glistened or glowed in the winter sunshine." In contrast to the typical instructor of his era, Scott's concern was "with living ideals and emotions and how they might be formulated and how they might be transferred from mind to mind or soul to soul with least loss of power" (Smith n.p.).

Smith summarizes the perception of the group as to Scott's greatest contribution: "'He was a remarkable pioneer. He was at his best at a time when English was emerging from the domination of Greek and Latin and was surging toward a facile independence and popularity. It was an advantage that this period of change could have Scott's influence as it took its course'" (Smith n.p.).

Joseph V. Denney wrote the tribute to Scott for the *English Journal* in its April 1932 issue. He sees Scott primarily as a visionary who somehow recognized earlier than others the need for uniting and unifying the teachers and the work of teaching English from the public schools into the colleges. "The greatest waste in education was due, he thought, to the spirit of separation and to indifference of the colleges to the purposes and achievements of the secondary and the elementary schools" (271).

In Denney's mind, Scott through all of his activity never lost sight of the overall educational venture; he never got caught up in the fad of the moment, the wave of enthusiasm for a short-lived theory or technique that deflected so many from the central purpose of education. "To the smallest details he invariably lent a larger importance and significance by relating them to an underlying principle, or by examining their social effect. . . . Always dissatisfied with the shallow, facile, and often misleading rules of the rhetoric books, he devoted a large share of his active life to a rehabilitation of the whole subject by bringing to bear upon one topic after another pertinent data and principles drawn from the sciences" (272).

One important statement presents what Denney saw as the essential problem Scott faced in his professional life: he was ahead of his time. "For several years at the beginning of his teaching experience he was almost alone in his chosen researches but later found allies in the neighboring fields of linguistics, psychology, and aesthetics" (272). But Scott worked for a long time against the fabric of his academic environment; and the allies who eventually found him were not forceful enough to alter the tide that engulfed them.

As Scott's longtime colleague, W. W. Bishop, wrote: "Everyone agrees that he was not only an original thinker but had the power to develop thought in young people to an amazing extent" (346). Much later, Albert Kitzhaber, in assessing Scott's contribution, noted as well that Scott was "an original thinker." But he explained further Scott's lack of influence in the field of rhetoric and composition: "Most of his ideas were too new, his recommendations for change too fundamental to be generally accepted. . . . His ideas often seemed strikingly unconventional to many people" (*Rhetoric* 69–70).

Would that Scott's influence had carried further beyond his "western" university and that in merit it had not been choked by the prejudiced elitist attitudes of the scholars of the more prestigious eastern schools in a rivalry that was perceived rather than real, but which became real as it fed upon its own historical perspective. Perhaps, ultimately, Michigan was where Scott belonged, a place that offered him broad arenas and favored—indeed nourished—his growth and productivity.

The Rouland portrait of Fred Newton Scott was shipped to Roy Cowden in October 1939, later than Georgia had promised because she had been "reluctant to let it go" (PMFNS). (In their home, Scott would not have it hung in the dining room, saying "'It looks as if I had only one ancestor.'") When it arrived, Cowden thanked Georgia for the contribution and placed it in the Hopwood Room where it still hangs. He assured her that the portrait would be located "where Professor Scott can always look down upon the large round table, still in black, that used to be in his office and where he may observe generations of students so concerned with the art of writing that they would be a joy for him to know" (PMFNS).

NOTES

1. INTRODUCTION

1. For a better understanding of this matter, see Allen.

2. THE FORMATIVE YEARS

1. After his death, Georgia Jackson Scott, in a letter to Dorothy Greenwald, assistant editor to the *Dictionary of American Biography,* dated January 1935, clarified that Scott's given name was Fred, not Frederick (PMFNS).

2. There are some ambiguities and inaccuracies in Dewey's portrait (misspelling of the name of the German tutor who influenced Scott, Boisen, and the mistaken information that Boisen later taught at Boston University) which Scott did not take the trouble to correct.

3. There are some who believed that in his mature years Scott had knowledge of and considerable command of fourteen different languages, a point we have not been able to verify.

4. Scott's attitudes toward usage are discussed in more detail in Stewart, "NCTE's First President."

5. Neither James Berlin, in *Writing Instruction,* nor DeWitt H. Parker and Charles B. Vibbert (Shaw, *Survey* 2:674) question the fact that Dewey was a strong influence on Scott, but Scott's biographical sketch of Dewey, written for the *Castalian* in 1891, suggests that our assessment of the relationship is more nearly accurate. Scott notes that Dewey was drawn, early in his career, to the philosophical works of Kant, Leibniz, Hume, and, very likely, Hegel. And he was encouraged in his early efforts in this work by William Torrey Harris, editor of the *Journal of Speculative Philosophy.* Scott received his introduction to psychology and, we may presume, to philosophy from Harris's disciple, William A. Jones of the Indiana Normal School. Certainly, two brilliant young men, of comparable age, who had been exposed to the same school of philosophic thought, would find much in common intellectually. Dewey's request that Scott teach the aesthetics classes suggests a rapport that could not be characterized very well as "influence."

6. This point could be argued. See Sutton.

7. We are indebted to Professor Patrick Gormely of Kansas State University's Department of Economics for this information.

8. Not a lot has changed since Scott wrote these words in 1890. See Stewart, "Composition Textbooks"; Kitzhaber, "Death"; and Welch.

9. One must keep in mind that departmentalization was not as rigid then as it is

now. Scott was thus free to engage in the full range of language studies even though his duties were in rhetoric.

3. DISCOVERING A CAREER

1. The average college teacher at this time had 105 students in freshman classes, requiring thirty-one hours a week for manuscript reading exclusive of other duties (Wozniak 170).

2. This information appears in a letter Scott wrote to a former student, Frank Addison Manny, March 16, 1898 (PFM).

3. Maude Caldwell Perry attended classes at Michigan from 1889 to 1892 and 1894 to 1895. Over the course of her life, she published articles in *The Atlantic Monthly, Century Magazine,* and *Scribner's Magazine,* and wrote the novel *Tide House* (New York: Harcourt, Brace, and Co., 1930).

4. For a full analysis of Seager's, and Mencken's, misrepresentations and distortions of Scott's career and influence see Stewart, "Reputation Lost."

5. We would like to express our gratitude here to Marilyn Guenther, granddaughter of Scott, for sharing with us a considerable mass of correspondence between Scott and his wife.

6. Study in Germany and advanced degrees from Europe generally were common because of the lack of graduate programs in U.S. colleges before 1876 when Johns Hopkins opened its program. As late as 1907 (the numbers cannot be verified) some five hundred graduate degree candidates were still abroad [Emerson, *PMLA,* 24 (1909), lxxviii].

7. A reference to Scott's "Boccaccio's 'De genealogia deorum'" and Sidney's 'Apologie,'" (1891).

8. Hempl's name first appears in the membership rolls in 1884 where his university affiliation is listed as Johns Hopkins. He may even have been present at the first meeting of the association in 1883.

9. One of the curiosities of MLA's early history is the absence from its membership roles of people one would have expected to be there. For example, there is no indication that Francis Child of Harvard, possibly the preeminent literary scholar in America at that time, was ever a member of the organization. Kittredge did not join until the organization was in its tenth year. Isaac Demmon's name never appears; nor does that of Charles Gayley.

10. In 1892, the NEA formed the Committee of Ten to make recommendations regarding the curriculum of the secondary schools in all subjects. Serving on the English subcommittee were such notables as President Eliot of Harvard and George Lyman Kittredge. Those chosen were of disparate background so as to represent all geographical areas, a range of scholarship, and of experience. Their primary recommendations amounted to unifying the work of the schools from the primary grades through college, providing sequential writing courses, and limiting grammar study until age thirteen. The committee served to define what we now call "English" courses; they emphasized the importance of competence in writing and an appreciation of good literature. The latter led to the creation of "lists" of books as required reading for admission to college (Hook 10–11).

1. It was not universally popular, however. In 1968 Allan Seager called it a "dull, bad book" (*The Glass-House* 51). And Carlton Wells, director of the Composition Program at Michigan in the 1930s, although he admired Scott, cared little for it. "*Paragraph Writing* was a dud—as I can vouch for in the early 1920's" (personal correspondence with Donald C. Stewart, December 25, 1989).

2. The Michigan Schoolmaster's Club was founded in 1886 at Ann Arbor by educators who sought greater productive articulation between high schools and colleges. Eventually, the impetus to form the North Central Association of Colleges and Secondary Schools came from this group (Shaw, *Survey* 1:321–22).

5. Reorganization, Recognition, and Reality

1. The Department of English in the College of Engineering had its inception in 1895 not long after the Department of Engineering had been established. Engineering English enjoyed a long and distinguished history, graduating from the Department of English to the Department of Humanities in the College of Engineering at Scott's instigation. Engineering English was not dissolved until the 1980s.

2. In "Half-Lights," Helen Mahin recalls "a personal gift . . . the calm reassurance with which he kept me talking for the half-hour before my particular final ordeal [her dissertation oral], until when the formidable men gathered I was hardly aware that anything was going on more than a discussion of an absorbing subject" (2, 3).

3. Charles Freer of Detroit made possible a number of exhibits through his generosity in loaning out his art collections to the university (Shaw, *Survey* 4:1484).

4. A detailed discussion of this report and of two more which followed, in 1901 and 1902, are available in Stewart, "The Status of Composition."

5. According to the constitution, revised at the 1903 meeting, the Executive Council could authorize members to form a division and hold separate annual meetings. But it also stipulated that as often as once every five years there would be a union meeting in the interior area of the country. This arrangement did not separate the members, but merely allowed them an opportunity to meet without the hardship of travel to the East Coast; they were, in turn, accommodated every fifth year with the union meeting [Grandgent x–xii].

6. The location, at this time, of a golf course near the present football stadium would explain Scott's ability to go out, play nine holes, and return to his work.

6. Some Major Publications

1. An account of the battle over Webster's III can be found in Sledd and Ebbit.

2. If Scott's characterization of the feudal attitude, and by implication the attitude of the Harvard and Yale faculties to their students, seems too callous, one should remember that Francis Child, the father of Harvard's English Department and one of a select few American scholars of international reputation in the last half of the nineteenth century, was reported to have said "with a disarming twinkle that the university would never be perfect until we got rid of all the students." See Hart 64. For a developed comparison between Child and the attitudes he represented and Scott and his view of a university, see Stewart, "Two Model Teachers."

3. The report to which Scott refers is the eminent French educator Victor Cousin's *Rapport sur l'état de l'instruction publique dans quelques pays de l'Allemagne et particulièrement en Prusse,* 1833. A British translation was published in 1834 and an American in 1836. An excellent brief summary of the effect of this report on the founders of the University of Michigan and of the development of the organic conception at that university can be found in Kitzhaber, *Rhetoric* 26–30.

4. Cesare Lombroso (1836–1909), Italian criminologist, was a keen student of the relationships between mental and physical disorders.

5. Gabriel Tarde, a French sociologist who espoused the belief that only one person in a hundred is inventive but that progress is dependent on invention.

7. A REPUTATION ESTABLISHED

1. For more on Harvard's influence, see Stewart, "Harvard's Influence on English Studies."

2. The English Association was a prestigious organization of British and American scholars founded in 1906 "to promote the teaching and advanced study of the English language and of English literature, and to unite all those who are interested in these subjects" *(Oxford Companion to English Literature).*

3. This unpublished speech was given frequently. It dealt with the distinction between those books which are likely to be read only once and those enduring ones which can be read over and over.

4. Spingarn reported on his Committee on the Scope of Publications, the committee of five, including Scott, appointed in 1908. He said the committee had decided to defer action with the hope of amending the constitution at the union meeting of 1911. But that was not to be. Hardly had Spingarn finished speaking when Professor Benjamin Bourland suggested the committee be discharged, and the motion was carried unanimously. So, the two years of effort were wasted.

5. See Stewart, "Rhetoric Rediviva."

6. This action resulted from the 1907 resolution by E. C. Roedder.

8. SPEAKING WITH AUTHORITY

1. The 1925 edition of *Lend a Hand,* a reader produced for grade school children in 1913, which was apparently successful, identifies her as "Sometime Head of Department of Applied Psychology, Oswego State Normal School." Her coauthor was Andrew W. Edson, late associate superintendent of schools, New York City.

2. Hook credits Scott with establishing a department for Trueblood at Michigan.

3. The speech teachers "kept the classical rhetorical tradition alive almost single-handed until English departments rediscovered it a few decades ago." (Kitzhaber, Letter).

4. Martin Tupper (1810–1889), an English versifier, was the author of an immensely popular but much denigrated book called *Proverbial Philosophy.*

5. We wish to thank Emeritus Professor Walt Eitner of Kansas State's Department of English, for providing information on the amount, nature, and quality of Whitman scholarship in the early 1900s.

6. Scott has been citing Giddings's *Principles of Sociology;* Titchener's *Primer of*

Psychology; Darwin's *Descent of Man;* Borgquist's "Crying" in the *American Journal of Psychology;* Furness's *Home-Life of the Borneo Head-Hunters;* Czermak's *Sitzungsberichte d. K. Akademie d. Wiss;* Scipture's *Experimental Phonetics;* and Jespersen's *Progress in Language.*

9. OLD AND NEW VENTURES

1. According to a more recent study by Robert G. Caldwell, there was no substance to this rumor. Caldwell cites as evidence Garfield's letters to his wife and the reminiscences of his contemporaries (183).

2. Although most of Scott's papers on journalism are unavailable, this one exists in manuscript (FNSP). It focuses on word usages, listing telescoped phrases, and words Scott thinks demean the profession of journalism.

3. Scott had, on a number of other occasions, simply gone to the source to resolve issues, as with the questionnaires sent to MLA members when he chaired the Pedagogical Section; when he intended to verify his impressions on grammatical nomenclature; and when he took the *Last Supper* to grade school children to discover their spontaneous responses.

4. At this NCTE conference, delegates were selected to attend the meeting of the English Association of Great Britain. It was an organization with which Scott began a long-term affiliation. In later years, he was much involved with the coordination of British and American scholarship in rhetoric and philology through a number of British-American organizations.

5. After lengthy examination of that issue of the paper, we can find no ad that would be offensive to moderns.

10. PUBLICATIONS OF CONSEQUENCE

1. Scott reviewed Jespersen's "Origin of Linguistic Species" in 1910, and Jespersen wrote to him requesting a reprint because he did not have access to it.

2. Scott's study of Russian began in the early 1890s.

12. A SHIFT IN INTEREST

1. The April 1916 issue was devoted entirely to a symposium of some fourteen persons "who give interesting and helpful statements of their special knowledge and experience on different phases of the problems related to speech, voice, and hygiene of the vocal tract" (Rapeer 519).

2. Scott had begun affiliations with a number of British scholarly groups in these years. In 1918, he had joined the English-based Modern Language Research Association. Other memberships came later.

3. His next major use of it was as an address before the Missouri chapter of Phi Beta Kappa in June 1915, at which time it was published in the *University of Missouri Bulletin,* but it was relegated to obscurity until it was reprinted in 1917 as "Kultur by the Millimeter" in *Literary Digest.*

4. Kahn was a highly respected architect who had come to America from Germany in 1880, settling in Detroit. He designed a number of important buildings in Detroit, among them the General Motors building. He was also the chief architect for most of the buildings on the University of Michigan campus.

13. Change, Loss, and Recovery

1. Brumm had, in fact, instituted the University Press Club of Michigan in 1918, an organization that included the Associated Press, the League of Small Dailies, and the Michigan Press Association, with a membership approximating three hundred editors and publishers. In 1921 Brumm also organized the Michigan Interscholastic Press Association for high school editors and their teachers.

2. This same paper was delivered at the Conference of British and American Professors of English in New York City in June 1923, when Scott presided at the opening session.

3. When Bridges came to America in 1924, he spent three months at the University of Michigan as a lecturer. He expressly wished also to meet with the American members of the society.

4. In February 1922, Scott had received a letter of appreciation from E. Allison Peers for "all you are doing with regard to the Review. . . . We are very anxious to make the Review our Journal in fact as well as in name and I hope you will continue to do what you can for us in America."

5. This warning seems overexaggerated, yet an equally frightening caution was sounded in later years by George Orwell, who, like Scott (and Milton before them), saw the essential link between language and power and the consequences of rhetorical negligence.

6. He read this paper at MLA in March 1920; before the Philological Section of the British Association for the Advancement of Science in 1923; and at NCTE in November 1924.

14. Retirement

1. For the connection with the Scottish schools, see Horner.

2. The organization was shortlived because of the difficulty in securing funding. For a time, funds were sought from Henry Ford; later, the Commonwealth Fund of England provided money, at least for 1927.

3. An account, virtually the same as that given here, is part of Baker's autobiography *Native American*.

4. This act may reflect his immense disappointment with the handling of policy at the University of Michigan, for it does seem odd that he would endow a prize at a school where he had no affiliation rather than at one where he had spent all his active years.

15. In Memoriam

1. In 1941, Georgia Scott sent Scott's collection of personal correspondence and papers to the Bentley Historical Library in Ann Arbor; in 1957, after her death, additional materials were sent by her niece, Mrs. James Barr.

2. Scott's loss was eclipsed by the death of his former student, Sterling Leonard, only thirteen days earlier. Leonard drowned in a boating accident at age forty-three while he was still active in NCTE (president in 1926).

3. It was not published until 1935.

WORKS BY
FRED NEWTON SCOTT

"Biography of Miss Harriet M. Scott." Typed manuscript. FNSP.

"The Missing Pronoun." *The Current* 3, no. 57 (January 17, 1885): 43–44.

Songs of the Yellow and Blue. With Charles Mills Gayley and Albert A. Stanley. Ann Arbor: Sheehan & Co., 1889.

Aesthetics: Its Problems and Literature. Brochure. Ann Arbor: Inland Press, 1890.

"Albert A. Stanley." *Palladium* (1890): 70–74.

"Simple, Sensuous, and Passionate." *Modern Language Notes* 5 (December 1890): 459–62.

A Guide to the Literature of Aesthetics. With Charles Mills Gayley. Brochure. Berkeley: University of California, 1890.

The Principles of Style: Topics and References. Brochure. Ann Arbor: Inland Press, 1890.

"Materiam superabat opus." *Modern Language Notes* 6 (January 1891): 54–55.

"Boccaccio's 'De genealogia deorum' and Sidney's 'Apologie.'" *Modern Language Notes* 6 (April 1891): 193–202.

"Dante Interpretation." *Modern Language Notes* 6 (December 1891): 505.

"John Dewey." *Castalian* (1891): 23–29.

Edition of Samuel Johnson's *Rasselas*. Boston: Leach, Shewell & Sanborn, 1891.

Edition of G. H. Lewes's *The Principles of Success in Literature*. Boston: Allyn & Bacon, 1891.

Edition of Herbert Spencer's *The Philosophy of Style*. Boston: Allyn & Bacon, 1891.

"Deutsche Kunst auf der Weltausstellung zu Chicago." *Münchner Neueste Nachrichten,* no. 430, September 21, 1892.

"The Russian Verb and Its Accent." *Modern Language Notes* 7 (January 1892): 14–17.

Christianity and the Newspaper. Brochure. Ann Arbor: Inland Press, 1892.

Edition of Thomas DeQuincey's *Essays on Style, Rhetoric and Language*. Boston: Allyn & Bacon, 1893.

Paragraph Writing. With Joseph V. Denney. Boston: Allyn and Bacon, 1893.

"English at the University of Michigan." In *English in American Universities,* ed. William Morton Payne. Boston: D. C. Heath, 1895.

"The Misplacement of 'Only.'" *Modern Language Notes* 10 (November 1895): 196–201.

Edition of Daniel Webster's *First Bunker Hill Oration Together with Other Essays Relating to the Revolution*. New York: Longmans, Green, 1895.

Figures of Rhetoric: A Psychological Study. By Gertrude Buck. Vol. 1 of Contributions to Rhetorical Theory, ed. F. N. Scott. 1895?

Student Slang. By Willard Gore. Vol. 2 of Contributions to Rhetorical Theory, ed. F. N. Scott. 1895?

Works by
Fred Newton
Scott

"Diseases of English Prose: A Study in Rhetorical Pathology." Unpublished manuscript, FNSP.

"President Angell As Seen in His Writings." *Castalian* (1896): 9–23.

Composition-Rhetoric. With Joseph V. Denney. Boston: Allyn & Bacon, 1897.

Two Problems of Composition Teaching. By Joseph V. Denney. Vol. 3 of Contributions to Rhetorical Theory, ed. F. N. Scott. Ann Arbor: Inland Press, 1897?

References on the Teaching of Rhetoric and Composition. Vol. 4 of Contributions to Rhetorical Theory, ed. F. N. Scott. 1897?

The Metaphor. By Gertrude Buck. Vol. 5 of Contributions to Rhetorical Theory, ed. F. N. Scott. Ann Arbor: Inland Press, 1899.

Introduction to the Methods and Materials of Literary Criticism: The Bases in Aesthetics. With Charles Mills Gayley. New York: Ginn & Co., 1899.

"The Report on College Entrance Requirements in English." *Educational Review* 20 (October 1900): 289–94.

Elementary English Composition. With Joseph V. Denney. Boston: Allyn & Bacon, 1900.

"College Entrance Requirements in English." *School Review* 9 (June 1901): 365–78.

Review of Reuben Post Halleck's *English Literature. School Review* 9 (January 1901): 56.

Composition-Literature. With Joseph V. Denney. Boston: Allyn & Bacon, 1902.

"Carlyle's Dante." *New York Nation,* December 24, 1903: 502; rpt. *New York Evening Post,* January 4, 1904.

Review of *Essays on the Study and Use of Poetry by Plutarch and Basil the Great. JEGP* 5 (September 1903): 120.

"Rhetoric" and "Figures of Rhetoric." *New International Encyclopedia, 1902–1904.* New York: Dodd, Mead, 1903.

The Teaching of English in the Elementary and Secondary Schools. With George R. Carpenter and F. T. Baker. New York: Longmans, Green, 1903.

"The Most Fundamental Differentia of Poetry and Prose." *PMLA* 19 (1904): 250.

Review of George Edward Woodberry's *America in Literature. New York Nation,* January 7, 1904: 18.

Review of Greenough and Kittredge's *Words and Their Ways. Educational Review* 27 (January 1904): 96.

Review of Ferris Greenslet's *Walter Pater. New York Nation,* October 20, 1904: 318.

Review of Gustavus Holzer's *Elementary English Grammar. School Review* 12 (December 1904): 823–25.

Aphorisms for Teachers of English Composition. With Joseph V. Denney. Brochure. Boston: Allyn & Bacon, 1905.

Brief English Grammar. With Gertrude Buck. Chicago: Scott Foresman, 1905.

"The Figurative Element in Grammatical Terminology." New England Association of Teachers of English, leaflet 26 (December 1905).

Memorable Passages from the Bible. New York: Macmillan, 1905.

"The Scansion of Prose Rhythm." *PMLA* 20 (1905): 707.

"A Primitive Short Story." *Modern Language Notes* 21 (November 1906): 208.

The Value of English to the Practicing Engineer. By Harold Breitenbach. Vol. 7 of Contributions to Rhetorical Theory, ed. F. N. Scott. Ann Arbor: Library Printing Plant, 1906.

On the Limits of Descriptive Writing Apropos of Lessing's Laocoön. By Frank Bryant. Vol. 6 of

Contributions to Rhetorical Theory, ed. F. N. Scott. Ann Arbor: Ann Arbor Press, 1906.

Lessons in English. Books I–II. With G. A. Southworth. Boston: Sanborn, 1906.

"The Genesis of Speech." December 1907 speech. *The Standard of American Speech and Other Papers.* Boston: Allyn & Bacon, 1926.

"A Substitute for the Classics." *School Review* 16 (June 1908): 360.

A Question of Textbooks. By Justin Frolich, pseud. New England Association of Teachers of English, leaflet 57 (January 1, 1908).

Inertia and Stimulus. New England Association of Teachers of English, leaflet 62–63 (June 1, 1908).

"Longfellow's Bedeutung für Amerika." *Deutsche Revue* (January 1909): 58.

"What the West Wants in Preparatory English." *School Review* 17 (January 1909): 10.

"A Brief Catechism on Textbooks in English." *Educational Review* 37 (April 1909): 359.

"Rhetoric Rediviva." 1909 speech. Ed. Donald C. Stewart. *CCC* 31 (December 1980): 413.

"A Note on Walt Whitman's Prosody." *JEGP* 7 (1910): 134.

Review of C. Täuber's *Die Ursprache Und Ihre Entwicklung* and Otto Jespersen's *Origin of Linguistic Species. JEGP* 10 (1910): 576.

Selections from the Old Testament. New York: Macmillan, 1910.

"The Art of Dictation." *Mill Supplies,* January 1911.

"Advertisement Writing as an Art." *Mill Supplies,* February 1911.

"As to Tone in Advertising." *Mill Supplies,* March 1911.

"Simplified Spelling for Business Men." *Mill Supplies,* May 1911.

"Keats's 'Missal.'" *New York Nation,* May 1911: 470; rpt. *New York Evening Post,* May 3, 1911; rpt. *John Keats* by Amy Lowell, II (New York: Houghton Mifflin, 1925), 173.

"Questions of Good English." *Mill Supplies,* June 1911.

"How to Read the Newspaper." *Mill Supplies,* July 1911.

"The Use of Superfluous Words." *Mill Supplies,* August 1911.

"The Father-Tongue." *Atlantic Monthly,* August 1911: 283.

Review of *Columbia Lectures on Literature. Educational Review* 62 (September 1911): 196.

"English as Sometimes Distorted." *Mill Supplies,* October 1911.

"Brain-Borrowing." *Mill Supplies,* November 1911.

"The Problem from the Standpoint in English." *School Review* 19 (November 1911): 620.

"Two Ideals of Composition Teaching." *Proceedings of Indiana Association of Teachers of English* (November 1911): 6.

"A Cry from Macedonia." *Mill Supplies,* December 1911.

Edition of Thomas Hill Green's *Value and Influence of Works of Fiction.* Ann Arbor: George Wahr, 1911.

"A Fable of Bidpai." *English Journal* 1 (January 1912): 122.

"Simplified Spelling and Simplified Pronunciation." *Mill Supplies,* February 1912.

"Verbal Taboos." *School Review* 20 (June 1912): 361.

"Beauties of Our Pronunciation." *Mill Supplies,* July 1912.

"Slang and Its Perils." *Mill Supplies,* August 1912.

"Hatred of Inoffensive Words." *Mill Supplies,* November 1912.

"The Adjustment of School to College." *New York Sun,* October 5, 1912; rpt. *Michigan Alumnus* as "The Relation of School and College," November 1912.

"Our Problems." *English Journal* 2 (January 1913): 1.

"Training and Mistraining." Editorial. *English Journal* 2 (September 1913): 456.

Review of William Brewster's *English Composition and Style. Educational Review* 46 (October 1913): 308.

"Mene, Mene, Tekel, Upharsin." Editorial. *English Journal* 2 (October 1913): 524.

"The Order of Words in Certain Rhythm-Groups." *Modern Language Notes* 28 (December 1913): 237.

"The Undefended Gate." *English Journal* 3 (January 1914): 1.

"Efficiency for Efficiency's Sake." *Publications of the North Central Association* (1914); rpt. *School Review* 23 (January 1915).

"Through Oriental Eyes." *The Quadrangle Book* (Ann Arbor: 1914).

"The Congress of Letters." *University of Missouri Bulletin* 18 (June 1915): 15; rpt. as "Kultur by the Millimeter," *Literary Digest* 55 (August 11, 1917): 11.

"Vowel Alliteration in Modern Poetry." *Modern Language Notes* 30 (December 1915): 233.

Plays by Leonid Andreyeff. Trans. with Clarence L. Meader. New York: Charles Scribner's Sons, 1915.

"An Anchor to Windward." *The Inlander,* April 1916: 11.

"Speech and the Community." *Journal of Ophthalmology, Otology and Laryngology* 22 (April 1916): 327–28.

"Evading the Prospect." By Justin Frolich, pseud. *Mill Supplies,* November 1916: 23.

"The Standard of American Speech." *English Journal* 6 (1917): 1.

"Three Poems by N. A. Nekrasov." Trans. *Russian Review* 3 (July 1917): 86.

"Accentual Structure of Isolable English Phrases." *PMLA* 33 (March 1918): 73.

"An Experiment in Aesthetics." *The Inlander,* April 1918; rpt. as "When Leonardo's Message Failed," *Literary Digest* 57 (April 20, 1918): 36.

Pause. By Ada L. F. Snell Vol. 8 of Contributions to Rhetorical Theory, ed. F. N. Scott. Ann Arbor: Ann Arbor Press, 1918.

The Critical Principle of the Reconciliation of Opposites as Employed by Coleridge. By Alice Snyder. Vol. 9 of Contributions to Rhetorical Theory, ed. F. N. Scott. Ann Arbor: Ann Arbor Press, 1918.

Review of Louis Untermeyer's *The New Era in American Poetry* and John Livingston Lowes' *Convention and Revolt in Poetry. Detroit Sunday News,* April 20, 1919: 18.

Review of John W. Cunliffe's *English Literature During the Past Half Century. Detroit Sunday News,* June 1, 1919: 14.

Review of W. N. P. Barbellion's *Diary of a Disappointed Man. Detroit Sunday News,* September 7, 1919: 14.

Review of H. L. Mencken's *The American Language* and George P. Krapp's *Pronunciation of Standard English in America. Educational Review* 58 (September 1919): 170.

"Familiar Quotations." *Classical Journal* 15 (November 1919): 109.

"Inscriptions" for *Detroit News* building. In *American Patriotism in Prose and Verse, 1775–1918,* ed. J. Madison Gathany. New York: Macmillan, 1919.

Review of Wilfrid Shaw's *The University of Michigan. Michigan Alumnus,* February 1921: 323.

Review of Oliver Elton's *Survey of English Literature, 1780–1880. Detroit Sunday News,* March 6, 1921: 465.

"Poetry in a Commercial Age." *English Journal* 10 (December 1921): 549; rpt. *The Way of Composition,* ed. Morris, Johnson, Wells, and Rankin. New York: Harcourt Brace, 1925.

"English Composition as a Mode of Behavior." *English Journal* 11 (October 1922): 463.

"The Colloquial Nasals for Yes and No." *Journal of Education* 55 (November 1923): 717.

"Tribute to Gertrude Buck." *Vassar Miscellany Monthly* 9 (February 1923): 3.

"Improving the English of America." *English Journal* 14 (January 1925): 48.

Review of John o'London's *Is It Good English? Saturday Review of Literature* 1 (May 9, 1925): 747.

"English and American Vernacular." *McNaught's Monthly* 3 (May 1925): 144; rpt. *Further Adventures in Essay Reading,* ed. Rankin, Morris, Solve, and Wells. New York: Harcourt Brace, 1928.

"American Slang." *Society for Pure English Tract* 24 (1926): 118.

The Standard of American Speech and Other Papers. Boston: Allyn & Bacon, 1926.

Review of Will Durant's *The Story of Philosophy. Michigan Alumnus* (January 1927): 329.

"Art and War." *Sewanee Review* 38 (April–June 1930): 217.

"Mr. Dooley Among the Professors." *Michigan Alumnus,* July 1934: 150.

WORKS CITED

"Acts of the Executiv Council." *PMLA* 33 (1918): cxxi–cxxii.

Alden, Raymond. "Preparation for College English Training." *English Journal* 2 (June 1913): 344–56.

Allen, Don Cameron. *The Ph.D. in English and American Literature.* New York: Holt, Rinehart and Winston, 1968.

"Avery Hopwood and the Hopwood Awards, 1931–1981." Brochure. University of Michigan.

Baker, Ray Stannard. *Native American.* New York: Charles Scribner's Sons, 1941.

Berlin, James. *Writing Instruction in Nineteenth-Century American Colleges.* Carbondale: Southern Illinois University Press, 1984.

"Bibliographical Department." *American Speech* 3 (October 1927): 73–80.

Bishop, W. W. "College Days—1889–93." *Michigan Alumnus Quarterly Review* 54 (1947–48): 346–47.

Blanshard, Frances. *Frank Aydelotte of Swarthmore.* Middletown, Conn.: Wesleyan University Press, 1970.

Brereton, John. "Sterling Andrus Leonard." *Traditions of Inquiry.* Ed. John Brereton. New York: Oxford University Press, 1985.

Brumm, John. "In Memoriam." *Michigan Alumnus* 37 (1930–31): 655.

Buck, Gertrude. "Another Phase of the New Education." *The Forum* 22 (November 1896): 376–84.

———. "What Does 'Rhetoric' Mean?" *Educational Review* 22 (1901): 197–200.

Caldwell, Robert G. *James A. Garfield.* Hamden, Conn.: Archon Books, 1965.

Cooper, Lane. "On the Teaching of Written Composition." *Education* 30 (March 1910): 421–30.

Cowden, Roy W. "Creative Writing and the Hopwood Awards." *Michigan Alumnus Quarterly Review* 48 (1942): 243–51.

Cross, Arthur L. "The University of Michigan and the Training of Her Students for the War." *Michigan History Magazine* 4 (1920): 115–20.

Curwood, James Oliver. "Sons of the Forests." *McCall's Magazine* (May 1930: 33–34, 178–80, 182.

Day, J. Christian, and Aksel G. S. Josephson. "Report of the Bibliographical Society of America." *PMLA* 26 (1911): x–xi.

Denney, Joseph V. "Fred Newton Scott." *English Journal* 21 (April 1932): 271–74.

Dewey, John. "Fred Newton Scott." *The Early Works, 1882–1898*. Ed. Jo Ann Boydston. 4 vols. Carbondale: Southern Illinois University Press, 1971.

Dimorier, W. E. "Newspaper Week." *English Journal* 6 (March 1917): 170–74.

Dunkel, Harold B. *Herbart and Education*. New York: Random House, 1969.

Dykuizen, George. *The Life and Mind of John Dewey*. Carbondale: Southern Illinois University Press, 1973.

"Editorial." *English Journal* 3 (February 1914): 124.

"Editorial." *English Journal* 7 (June 1918): 397.

"Editorial." *English Journal* 8 (February 1919): 126–28.

"Editorial." *English Journal* 8 (September 1919): 436–37.

"Editorial." *English Journal* 8 (October 1919): 507.

Emerson, Oliver F. "The American Scholar and the Modern Languages." *PMLA* 24 (1909): lxxiii–cii.

"Fifteenth Annual Meeting of the National Council of Teachers of English." *English Journal* 15 (January 1926): 45–76.

"The Founding Years: AATJ, AASDJ (1912–1938)." *Journalism Monographs* 104 (November 1987): 9–30.

"Fourteenth Annual Meeting of National Council of Teachers of English." *English Journal* 14 (January 1925): 47–76.

Fries, C. C. "Report of Present-Day English Section." *PMLA* 40 (1925): xxvii–xxviii.

Gathany, J. Madison, ed. *American Patriotism in Prose and Verse, 1775–1918*. New York: Macmillan, 1919.

Grandgent, Charles H. "Constitution of the Modern Language Association of America." *PMLA* 19 (1904): iii–xxx.

Hart, Albert Bushnell. "Ten Years of Harvard." *Harvard Graduates' Magazine* 11 (September 1902): 58–69.

Hook, J. N. *A Long Way Together*. Urbana, Ill.: NCTE, 1979.

Horner, Winifred Bryan. *Nineteenth-Century Scottish Rhetoric: The American Connection*. Carbondale: Southern Illinois University Press, 1993.

Hosic, James Fleming. "The National Coucil After Twenty Years." *English Journal* 21 (February 1932): 107–13.

———. "The National Council of Teachers of English." *English Journal* 10 (January 1921): 1–10.

———. "Report of the Committee on the Preparation of College Teachers of English." *English Journal* 5 (January 1916): 20–23.

Jameson, John. Letter to "The Alumni Forum." *Michigan Alumnus* 37 (1930–31): 536.

Kellogg, John Harvey. *The Battle Creek Sanitarium System*. Battle Creek, Mich.: Gage Printing Co., 1908.

Kenyon, John S. "Present-Day English Section Report." *PMLA* 37 (1922): xxvi–xxvii.

Kitzhaber, Albert R. "Death—or Transfiguration?" *College English* 21 (April 1960): 367–73.

———. Letter to Patricia L. Stewart. February 7, 1994.

———. *Rhetoric in American Colleges: 1850–1900*. Dallas, Tex.: Southern Methodist University Press, 1990.

Lewis, Edwin H. *The History of the English Paragraph*. Chicago: University of Chicago Press, 1894.

Lounsbury, Thomas R. "Compulsory Composition in Colleges." *Harper's Monthly Magazine* (November 1911): 866–80.

Lynch, William O. *A History of Indiana State Teachers College*. Terre Haute: Indiana State Teachers College, 1946.

Mahin, Helen. "Half-Lights." *Fred Newton Scott Anniversary Papers*. Ed. Clarence D. Thorpe and Charles Whitmore. Chicago: University of Chicago Press, 1929.

Mead, William E. "Report of the Pedagogical Section of MLA." *PMLA* 16 (1901): xix–xxxii.

———. "Report of the Pedagogical Section of MLA." *PMLA* 17 (1902): x–xxiv.

———. "Report of the Pedagogical Section of MLA." *PMLA* 18 (1903): viii–xxiii.

Mencken, H. L. *The American Language*. 3rd ed. New York: Knopf, 1923.

Mott, Frank L. *American Journalism*. Rev. ed. New York: Macmillan, 1950.

Murphy, James J., ed. *A Short History of Writing Instruction*. Davis, Calif.: Hermagoras Press, 1990.

"The National Council at Chattanooga." *English Journal* 12 (January 1923): 39–71.

"The National Council of Teachers of English." *English Journal* 1 (January 1912): 30–45.

"The National Council of Teachers of English." *English Journal* 4 (January 1915): 47–74.

"The National Council of Teachers of English." *English Journal* 5 (January 1916): 33–78.

"The National Council of Teachers of English." *English Journal* 6 (January 1917): 40–68.

"The National Council of Teachers of English." *English Journal* 7 (January 1918): 39–75.

"National Council of Teachers of English." *English Journal* 8 (April 1919): 254–78.

"National Council of Teachers of English." *English Journal* 10 (January 1921): 39–60.

"News and Notes." *English Journal* 2 (January 1913): 61–68.

"News and Notes." *English Journal* 3 (December 1914): 663–70.

"News and Notes." *English Journal* 4 (November 1915): 605–14.

"News and Notes." *English Journal* 7 (November 1918): 608–11.

"News and Notes." *English Journal* 9 (October 1920): 478–88.

"News and Notes." *English Journal* 10 (September 1921): 407–22.

"News and Notes." *English Journal* 11 (May 1922): 305–16.

"News and Notes." *English Journal* 20 (October 1931): 679–92.

"Notes and Personalia." *Language* 7 (September 1931): 222–25.

"Notes and Quotes." *American Speech* 3 (December 1927): 157–58.

Payne, William Morton, ed. *English in American Universities*. Boston: D. C. Heath, 1895.

Peckham, Howard H. *The Making of the University of Michigan, 1817–1967*. Ann Arbor: University of Michigan Press, 1967.

Pope, Virginia. "Poet Laureate Argues Here for Pure English." *New York Times*, April 13, 1924: 8.

Potter, David. Foreword to *Selected Essays on Rhetoric by Thomas DeQuincey*. Ed. Frederick Burwick. Carbondale: Southern Illinois University Press, 1967.

"Proceedings of the Eleventh Annual Meeting of the National Council of Teachers of English." *English Journal* 11 (January 1922): 38–63.

Rapeer, Louis W. "Reviews." *English Journal* 5 (September 1916): 519–20.

"Report of Committee on Place and Function of English in American Life." *English Journal* 15 (February 1926): 110–34.

Russell, David R. "Romantics on Writing: Liberal Culture and the Abolition of Composition Courses." *Rhetoric Review* 6 (Spring 1988): 132–48.

Seager, Allan. *The Glass-House: The Life of Theodore Roethke*. New York: McGraw-Hill, 1968.

Shaw, Wilfred B., ed. *The University of Michigan: An Encyclopedic Survey*. 4 vols. Ann Arbor: University of Michigan Press, 1951.

———. *The University of Michigan*. New York: Harcourt, Brace and Howe, 1920.

Sledd, James and Wilma Ebbit. *Dictionaries and That Dictionary*. New York: Scott, Foresman, 1962.

Smith, Shirley. "Fred Newton Scott as a Teacher." *University of Michigan Senate Collection*. Ann Arbor: University of Michigan, 1935.

Stewart, Donald C. "Composition Textbooks and the Assault on Tradition." *CCC* 29 (May 1978): 171–80.

———. "Harvard's Influence on English Studies: Perceptions from Three Universities in the Early Twentieth Century." *CCC* 43 (December 1992): 455–71.

———. "NCTE's First President and the Movement for Language Reform." *College English* 48 (September 1986): 444–56.

———. "Rediscovering Fred Newton Scott." *College English* 40 (January 1979): 539–47.

———. "Reputation Lost: A Brief Note in the History of American Letters." *Menckeniana* 85 (Spring 1983): 1–8.

———, ed. "Rhetoric Rediviva." *CCC* 31 (December 1980): 413–19.

———. "The Status of Composition and Rhetoric in American Colleges, 1880–1902: An MLA Perspective." *College English* 47 (November 1985): 734–46.

———. "Two Model Teachers and the Harvardization of English Departments." *The Rhetorical Tradition and Modern Writing*. Ed. James J. Murphy. New York: MLA, 1982.

Strauss, Louis. "Regents Merge Two Departments." *Michigan Alumnus* 36 (1929–1930): 331–32, 336.

Sutton, Albert A. *Education for Journalism in the United States from Its Beginning*. Evanston, Ill.: Northwestern University, 1945.

Thorpe, Clarence D., and Charles Whitmore, eds. *The Fred Newton Scott Anniversary Papers*. Chicago: University of Chicago Press, 1929.

"The University at War." *Michigan Alumnus* 24 (April 1918): 405–17.

Van Deusen, Marshall. *J. E. Spingarn*. New York: Twayne Publishers, 1971.

Welch, Kathleen. "Ideology and Freshman Textbook Production: The Place of Theory in Writing Pedagogy." *CCC* 38 (October 1987): 269–82.

Wells, Carlton. Letter to Donald C. Stewart. December 25, 1989.

Williams, Sara Lockwood. *Twenty Years of Education for Journalism: A History of the School of Journalism of the University of Missouri*. Columbia, Mo.: E. W. Stephens, 1929.

Williams, Talcott. "The Teaching of Journalism." *College Teaching*. Ed. Paul Klapper. New York: World Book Co., 1920.

Williams, Walter, ed. *The Press Congress of the World in Hawaii*. Columbia, Mo.: E. W. Stephens, 1922.

Woodburn, James A. *History of Indiana University*. Bloomington: Indiana University, 1940.

Wozniak, John M. *English Composition in Eastern Colleges 1850–1940*. Washington, D.C.: University Press of America, 1978.

INDEX

Entries for titles of works in quotation marks or italics are for works authored or co-authored by Fred Newton Scott.